D1055400

FIFTY FABULOUS YEARS

Also by H. V. Kaltenborn

WE LOOK AT THE WORLD

KALTENBORN EDITS THE NEWS

I BROADCAST THE CRISIS

KALTENBORN EDITS THE WAR NEWS

EUROPE NOW

Fifty Fabulous Years

1900 – 1950

A PERSONAL REVIEW BY

H. V. KALTENBORN

G. P. Putnam's Sons New York

Published on the same day in the Dominion of Canada by Thomas Allen, Ltd., Toronto.

Third Impression

Manufactured in the United States of America

To Olga, who has made forty of the fifty years truly fabulous.

A section of illustrations will be found following page 152. An index will be found starting on page 303.

Foreword

LAST YEAR, SHORTLY AFTER MY SEVENTY-FIRST BIRTHDAY, it occurred to me that if I ever intended to do what I had so often been urged to do—to write the story of my life and times—I'd better do it. Perhaps I am already too old. In this accelerated century few persons wait to achieve the Biblical age of three score and ten before they look back to what has gone before.

To record all that happened in seventy-two years seemed too much of a task. So I decided to make it a little easier for myself and the reader by skipping my first rather uneventful twenty and concentrate on the last fifty. When one half century ends and another begins should be an appropriate time to review the record of the last fifty years. Of course, it might be even better to wait until a full century has passed, but who could expect to live that long?

To make it still easier for myself, I decided to talk this book instead of writing it, for talking has always come much more easily to me than writing. Among the many wonders of this twentieth century, there is a recording machine which preserves on thin wire the sounds picked up by a small unobtrusive microphone. My son Rolf agreed to stimulate my reminiscent talking by going over my vast store of clippings, notebooks, articles, books, speeches, and radio broadcasts and then asking me pertinent questions. The result was a deluge of recorded material, which we later transcribed, edited, and revised. I thoroughly enjoyed doing this book, for who does not like to talk and write about himself? My son Rolf did most of the hard work.

This book is not intended to be a comprehensive history of these past fifty years. That I leave to historians, who are far better qualified than I for that task. This book is not purely autobiographical. It is, rather, a summary and interpretation of what one man has written about, talked about, and experienced in Fifty Fabulous Years. Since 1898 my work has consisted almost altogether in observing and commenting on current affairs, which explains why this book had to be a compound of personal history, American history, and world history.

H. V. Kaltenborn

FIFTY FABULOUS YEARS

1

As THE TWENTIETH CENTURY OPENED, BOTH THE United States and "Spiderlegs Kalty," as my Wisconsin friends called me, were coming of age. The Spanish-American War had just ended. My service in that brief but "splendid little war," as John Hay called it, had carried me out of the small-town environment of my youth into a larger world. I was twenty years old when I enlisted, young and inexperienced. I was twenty-one when discharged, only a little older in years but much older in experience. Army life has a way of speeding the growing-up process. Young men who have seen army service are completely convinced that they have at last "become men." And I was no exception.

The United States had also done a bit of growing up during the war period. A few weeks of scattered fighting and a few crucial naval engagements against a hopelessly weak opponent projected the United States beyond its own frontiers and gave it the beginnings of an overseas empire. The United States became a world power almost overnight. But there was no realization of the great role America was to play on the world stage. Scarcely anyone dreamed in 1900 that 1950 would find the United States the world's mightiest industrial and military nation. The so-called imperialists against whom William Jennings Bryan campaigned so vigorously may have had long-range, far-sighted plans for a vast American empire. That is what some present-day historians now claim with the wisdom of hindsight. Certainly most of us had no such notions at the time. There was much talk of "great destiny" and it sounded fine, but no one took it very seriously. Only a few recalled that decades earlier Walt Whitman, with a poet's vision, had predicted world leadership for these United States. "Have the elder races halted? . . . wearied over there beyond the seas? We take up the task eternal . . . Pioneers! O pioneers!"

My own feelings were rather typical. When I volunteered for military service, I felt I was doing something to free "poor little Cuba" and to avenge the "Maine." I was also happy that, for once, I was doing something that everyone applauded. More concretely, I saw the war as a chance for adventure, an opportunity to travel, to break dull routine, to become a man.

There was little talk of the horrors of war in those days. The grim realities of the Civil War were dim memories from another age. A few old men living on pensions and little flags on the graves on Memorial Day were about the only reminders I encountered. The stories told by the Civil War veterans concerned happy and exciting adventures. Pacifist propaganda was virtually unknown. When I asked an old veteran how to be a good soldier, all he had to say was, "Eat plenty of prunes. Nothing like prunes to keep your innards happy. Eat prunes, my boy, and you'll make a good soldier."

The entire course of world history might have been different had the United States encountered a first-class efficient military power in 1898 instead of an enfeebled Spain. Two years before, Teddy Roosevelt had written, "I do not think a war with Spain would be serious enough to cause much strain on the country, or much interruption to the revival of prosperity."

From T. R.'s perspective, things may have looked rosy but from my vantage point first as private and later as top sergeant, there was little I saw to inspire confidence in the military strength of the United States. The regular Army consisted of a tiny force of only twenty-eight thousand. The effort to build a sizable civilian army was a continuous comedy of errors. In the camps where the disorganized but eager Fourth Wisconsin Volunteers were stationed there was much confusion. For the first weeks we were soldiers without uniforms. We slept, ate, drilled, and marched in civilian clothes. Occasionally some regulation gear arrived for us—piecemeal. Much later we got our rifles, the old Springfield type, while the expeditionary and occupation forces got the more modern Krags. Ammunition was only issued on the rare occasions when we had target practice.

In addition to serving as a soldier, I was also acting as a self-styled war correspondent. Every week I mailed back to my home town weekly, the *Merrill* (Wisconsin) *Advocate,* reports of the progress of the war as I saw it in camp. Actually I was sending back two reports, one in English to the *Merrill Advocate* and the other in German to the Lincoln County *Anzeiger,* a German language weekly also printed in Merrill. But my greatest source of pride was that the *Milwaukee Journal* had designated me as its special correspondent with the Fourth Wisconsin Volunteer Infantry. One of my letters to the *Advocate* concerned the impending visit to camp of some of the girls and relatives from our home town. My story expressed the concern we all felt:

> It is very doubtful if we will have our uniforms by that time, and also whether we will be drilled enough to make a good showing on parade. Now all the boys take great pride in our company and we'd very much hate to have our Merrill girls come down and find us in the same duds we were wearing when we left. These, by the way, are much the worse for wear as sleeping in one's clothes does not have a tendency to improve them.

The United States has always been slow in getting its military machine into operation. In both World Wars conditions in the training camps during the early phases paralleled my experiences in the Spanish War. Supplies were weeks late and inadequate. When we had our first target practice with the old Springfields, the defects of this heavy, obsolete weapon were painfully apparent. If and when they did go off, they left many an unsuspecting rookie painfully surprised as the result of their powerful kickback.

Some of the Spanish War's military leaders were Civil War heroes. Stories about "Fighting Joe" Hooker, the Southern General of Civil War fame, were constantly in circulation. The best of these concerned the General's excited cry during a charge against the Spaniards in Cuba, "Come on boys—let's get those damn Yankees!"

I took life in the Army pretty much as it came until I learned that a sergeant's pay and position were much to be preferred to a private's. Then I became ambitious for promotion. After a bit, I managed to become top sergeant despite the handicaps of being the youngest and the lightest man in the company. I had been rejected as underweight, but a week of heavy eating plus the consumption of a quart of milk and a dozen bananas before getting on the scale enabled me to pass. With promotion went new responsibilities and innumerable headaches. As top sergeant, I was on the receiving end of all the justifiable and unjustifiable gripes from the men in my company. Finally in self-defense I posted the following sign outside my tent:

> We have no matches, no tobacco, no gun oil, no stamps, no paper, no envelopes, no shoe blacking, no brush, no brush-broom, no pens, no pencils, no lantern, no underwear, no leggings, no candles, no money, no time—and the mail is not yet in.

Health conditions in most training camps were bad. The official statistics now reveal that during the entire war only seven hundred army men were killed in action or died from wounds, while 5,772 died of disease. Many of these deaths were preventable. Typhoid fever was rampant. Bad food was another prime cause of sickness. Sometimes whole companies of men were incapacitated after partaking of army chow. There were food scandals in many camps. In my camp the quartermaster had been sold on one occasion a trainload of rotten beef. This laid up large numbers of the men and finally provoked a visit from a Congressional investigating committee. While the congressmen were looking over the camp, a group of us decided to look over the congressmen, who had arrived by special train equipped with a fancy private dining car. A luscious apple pie donated by the amiable chef of that Pullman diner did more to lift my morale than anything else the visiting congressmen accomplished. I never eat an apple pie today without remembering the cheerful face of the Pullman cook as he passed out that unforgotten treat.

Political pressures were commonplace throughout the militia and volunteer companies of which my regiment was composed. Initially there had been keen competition between the states to establish volunteer regiments. One measure of a congressman's abilities was whether he could secure permission from the Army for the creation of a volunteer regiment. If successful he became the regiment's personal godfather and devoted his best efforts to looking after his boys. In Merrill, we were mighty proud of the efforts of our congressman which enabled us to organize Company F of Merrill as part of the Fourth Wisconsin Volunteers. Even furloughs were a matter of politics. Our congressman on a visit to Camp Douglas, Wisconsin, our first training camp, learned that some of us had not yet been on furlough. He instantly went into action. A few words with the Colonel and he came back to tell us it was all arranged. This was my first personal experience of the power of political pull.

On another occasion when the local farmers complained that numerous watermelons had mysteriously disappeared from their fields near camp, the congressman of the district secured more than generous compensation for the farmers from the federal government. Once we readjusted the plush seats in a railway coach for better sleeping purposes during our transfer from Camp Douglas to Camp Shipp at Anniston, Alabama. On the basis of my examination, the alleged damage claimed by the railway could have been repaired by one man in a few hours' time. I was amazed to learn later that the railway company had succeeded in getting about half the value of the cars we occupied. Uncle Sam paid the bill. The Spanish War launched an open season on the public treasury setting a precedent for the wars that followed.

Most of the Spanish American War training camps were located in the South. As a result, thousands of Northerners and Westerners crossed the Mason and Dixon's line for the first time. This travel opportunity made an important contribution toward promoting better understanding between North and South. Being united in a common national patriotic enterprise also helped blur the lines of demarkation that had remained ever since the Civil War. The songs we sang stressed the Blue *and* the Gray. Those of us who came from the North entered a different world when we arrived in the South where the humiliations of the postwar reconstruction period had not been forgotten. For the South remained proud and poor.

In these days of easy, rapid travel, it is hard to imagine the time when a rail trip to the South was a big adventure, almost like going to a foreign country. The first thing we saw as we piled out of the troop train that had taken us down to Alabama was a crowd of smiling Negro children, the first I had ever seen. I had a small box camera and took endless pictures of my fellow soldiers standing with the Negro boys and girls. These photos excited much comment and interest among the home folks in far-off Wisconsin.

Our Southern stay taught us that Southern hospitality was no myth. The treatment we received from the Anniston townsfolk and merchants was uniformly pleasant. We were a source of profit but also a good deal of a nuisance. A large encampment of soldiers near a small city is always a worry and a problem for the locality. My first personal experience with North-South relations was when I unthinkingly rejected a shot of corn "likker" offered as a gesture of friendly hospitality by a fellow soldier from Georgia. Noting the frown that greeted my rejection of his well-meant generosity,

I quickly changed my mind. In the interest of better relations between the Blue and the Gray, I took my first swallow of whisky. It was evidently raw corn and tasted like liquid fire. That was the nearest I came to being a war casualty.

The Southerners received us with kindness but always with a certain amount of reservation. Memories of the carpetbaggers lingered and they were not sure just how we would behave. I witnessed the complete failure of a military exercise due to the survival of anti-Union prejudice among southern farmers. The soldiers in the mock war maneuver were divided into the Blue and the Gray forces. The maneuvers were virtually ruined because the local population helped the Gray uniformed soldiers in every possible way. They did all they could to confuse and misdirect the Blue forces.

After I was mustered out of Spanish War service, I decided to learn more about the South. The war had whetted my appetite for travel. I resolved not to return to Merrill with the other members of my company but to travel instead. The only hitch in my travel plans was lack of cash. Most of my fellow soldiers didn't care what Southern railroad they used to get home. As a favor to me, they agreed to travel via the Louisville and Nashville. The competition in those days between the different lines was keen and for my services in routing Company F, I was rewarded by a free pass to travel over any part of the Louisville and Nashville system.

So off I went to New Orleans. What impressed me most there, believe it or not, were the old buildings. The oldest building I remembered in northern Wisconsin dated back to the eighties. But here were lovely, old iron grillwork houses more than a hundred years old! New Orleans was the first big ocean port I had ever explored. The mystery of boats from far-off lands had a strange fascination. I spent many hours on the docks, watched the unloading of bananas, and talked to the sailors who told me long yarns of their trips. The fever for foreign travel got into my blood and I have never recovered. I determined then and there to see the rest of the world. My horizon had expanded far beyond the limits of Merrill, Wisconsin.

I was tempted to sign up as a sailor on one of those boats in the port of New Orleans and work my way around the world. But I was homesick, and after all my adventures I was anxious to see my father again.

My father had come to America and settled in Milwaukee, Wisconsin, in 1867. After the Prussian-Austrian War of 1866, Hesse, which had been a small independent German state, was absorbed by the increasingly powerful Prussia. My father thought that he would prefer the freer atmosphere of the United States than to remain in Hesse under Prussian rule. His family for centuries had served in the Hessian Army and he himself had served as a page at court before entering a Guards regiment. But rather than serve under Prussian officers, he resigned his commission and emigrated to America. Later he returned to Germany to lead his company in the Franco-Prussian War and entered Paris with the victorious German Army. On the steamer en route again to the United States, he met and fell in love with a young girl, Betty Wessels of Bremen, who was going to the United States to become a teacher of German. They were married soon afterward. Accompanied by his bride, Baron Rudolph von Kaltenborn-Stachau, ex-lieutenant of the Hessian Guards, arrived in Milwaukee, Wisconsin, in the fall of 1872 to resume his new life in the New World. He began working as a teacher, later became a bookkeeper and secretary in a wholesale drug business in Milwaukee, and still later bought a building supply business in Merrill. I was the second child, born in 1878, three years after my sister Bertha. My mother died when I was born.

Once back in Merrill, I confided my desire for travel to my father, who sympathized and encouraged me. To get a little nest egg together I worked for a while for the *Merrill Advocate* and later in a lumber camp in northern Wisconsin. During the long, dark winter evenings in camp I had ample opportunity to read. I alternated between old copies of the *New York Sun* and the plays of Shakespeare. This rather odd combination was dictated primarily by availability, but both had considerable impact on my life. Shakespeare, whom I read slowly and digested as thoroughly as a twenty-one-year-old can, opened my mind and gave me some understanding of humanity. I dearly loved to read passages aloud which I did to the amazement of my fellow lumberjacks, who didn't quite know what to make of me. The senior member of the lumber firm for which I worked was particularly unimpressed by my addiction to reading. "You should be scouting around camp salvaging empty potato bags," he said. "You read too much. You'll never amount to anything." Many years later, I had occasion to meet him again. Patting me on the back he said, "I always knew you would amount to something. You were always such a great reader."

The copies of the *New York Sun* I perused those long winter evenings fed my restlessness. Stories about the rest of the country, stories about Europe, stories about New York—all added to my wanderlust. One day there appeared in the *Sun* an account of the forthcoming World's Fair to be held in Paris in the summer of 1900. I read and reread the glowing lyrical account of all the beauties and marvels that were to be displayed. My restless longing for more travel, and especially travel abroad, now had a specific goal—Paris for the World's Fair of 1900!

I gathered together my savings, got an agreement from the *Merrill Advocate* to print my forthcoming travel dispatches at a dollar a piece plus a railroad pass to New York, got my father's blessing, and loaded myself and my bicycle on the train. I was on my way.

2

New York City was my port of embarkation for Europe. It was also to become my new home. Perhaps I realized that this city about which I had often dreamed as I read the *New York Sun* would give me my chance to make good. I got off the train in Jersey City with my bicycle and my hopes, a bit overwhelmed by my first glimpse of the already developing skyline. This was where I wanted to live. I, too, had read the Horatio Alger stories. I felt sure that in the future when I presented myself as the "experienced, widely traveled foreign and war correspondent" of the *Merrill Advocate,* fresh from a sojourn in Europe, the doors of the newspaper world would open.

The New York of 1900 I first wondered at has undergone the vast physical transformations so well pictured in the then-and-now photograph albums. There is something else about New York which cannot be photographed but can only be experienced—the elusive, restless, exciting, stimulating feeling of this city. Sometimes when strolling on Fifth Avenue at dusk, I can still recapture the old thrill which the city first gave me half a century ago. Euripides says that the first requisite of happiness is to be born in a famous city. The Greeks loved city life, none of your country life for them. Since I was not born in New York City, I did what I consider the next best thing. I adopted New York City as my own preferred home. Once New York has seized you, it never lets you go. New York got me in 1900. Since then I have seen all the world's great cities and have lived in many—but New York still has my heart.

Like most newcomers, I had not been in New York more than a few hours before I realized things were going to cost more than I had supposed. Of necessity I began to search out ways to live cheaply to conserve my meager savings for travel in Europe. I slept for ten cents a night in the Mills Hotel on Bleecker Street. I paid fifteen cents for a good egg breakfast and twenty-five cents for a substantial lunch or dinner. There were all sorts of things that a penny could buy on the streets of downtown New York—daily newspapers, old dime novels, big pieces of candy, pieces of watermelon, small dabs of ice cream known as penny licks, and, my greatest joy, ripe bananas (sometimes there were two or three for a cent, depending on the degree of ripeness). The bananas helped still the gnawings of an empty stomach on days when I economized by skipping lunch.

These prices made a vivid impression. To my regret, they still stay in my mind and I have an involuntary and, what my family regards as unfortunate, habit of comparing them with the prices of today. It seems that the prices and values one learns when young remain embedded as a sort of norm. Because when I first bought newspapers they cost a penny, I have a wholly unjustified feeling that I'm being overcharged when I have to buy them for a nickel. Milk and a loaf of bread used to cost me twelve cents and provided a satisfactory meal. Those days are gone forever, but I still think kindly of them and of the saloon free lunch counters in old New York that provided the better part of a free meal with a five-cent glass of beer. I became skilled in the art of patronizing the free lunch without patronizing the bar. My entrance through the swinging doors had to be carefully timed to coincide with occasions when the saloon was well filled and the proprietor busy filling up the schooners of beer. I soon learned that this was a dangerous practice down on the Bowery where every kind of chiseling was practiced by experts.

I spent ten cents to ride up Fifth Avenue seated beside the driver of the horse-drawn Fifth Avenue bus. The genial coachman pointed out the sights and called my attention to the cracked front window in the house of millionaire Russell Sage. "That old skinflint," he said, "hasn't repaired that window in the twenty years I've been driving up this avenue."

Elevated trains, the aquarium, the Palisades, and Coney Island were some of the wonders of New York I described in the letters I sent back to the *Merrill Advocate*.

> The study of the various costumes, or perhaps one should say the lack of them, worn by the thousands of bathers, should also afford considerable amusement. Throughout the afternoon the sands along the beach are lined with scantily attired men and women who lounge about in various unconventional attitudes and get tanned OTHER PLACES besides their faces. But they all seem to enjoy it, both the see-ers and the do-ers, and there are always any number of the former who are obliged to pay ten cents for the privilege.

Once again the *Sun* exerted an influence on my life. I had been casting about for the best and cheapest way to get to Europe when I read in the *Sun* a brief account of how one could get to Europe by working on a cattle boat. There weren't many details about the nature of the job. Maybe it was just as well. So I hung around the docks and made inquiries about the next cattle boat sailing for Europe. It was not long before I was signed as nursemaid to five hundred young steers on the White Star freighter "Georgic" sailing for Liverpool.

The realities of that crossing had nothing to do with the glamorous account I had read about the romance of working your way to Europe. The amateur cattle hands, of whom

I was one, were assigned to so-called bosses—regular members of the crew whose task it was to get the most work possible out of us.

The more we did, the less they had to do. So the hardest and dirtiest part of the work such as crawling around in the lowest hold to pull out the bales of hay for the steers, fell to us. Watering the animals was also difficult. They were always thirsty and would knock over the pail in their eagerness to get at the water unless we managed to kick them away. I held on to a stanchion with one hand to balance against the rolling of the ship, tried to hold the hose over the pail with the other, and with my two feet pushed away those steers trying to drink when it was not their turn.

We soon found it necessary to organize to keep individual bosses from abusing any one of us. It was my first experience of the value of a labor union. We put ourselves under the leadership of a six-foot Irishman who was completing a trip around the world on which he had worked his way. He refused to take any kind of abuse without resistance, and throughout the journey was in a constant battle with the minor bosses of the ship. His vigorous leadership helped us get a few meager privileges. We were allowed to send an emissary to the ship's galley to pick up our food with the result that we got more of it and were able to keep it hot.

That experience taught me something about the war between the classes, the bosses and the bossed. I also learned that even in common misery, men of different races are not necessarily drawn together. The Irish leader of our group made a great point of drawing a chalk line across the center of our quarters. He then told a dozen rather dirty Arabs who were working with us, that they would cross that line at their peril. As a result, the Americans and Europeans had twice as much bunk space per man as the representatives of the ancient and glorious sons of Allah who paid their obeisance to Mecca each morning and evening.

The best part of the journey was that it was comparatively smooth. Had it been a rough and stormy trip, I would have had to take some of the cuffs and kicks that came to those who couldn't work because they were seasick. I often wonder whether my great fondness for sea food as opposed to meat has not sprung from my close contact with those five hundred young steers during the twelve days it took the good ship "Georgic" to cross the Atlantic.

At Liverpool I disembarked, practically a vegetarian, and began a week's bicycle trip to London. I remember visiting the cathedral town of Chester a few miles outside of Liverpool and the thrill I felt as I circled the town on the old walls.

Bicycling through the English countryside was an altogether new and delightful experience. The well-kept roads, the carefully trimmed hedges, the huge trees, the charming country villages and the picturesque taverns made familiar by the Cruikshank drawings in my old copy of Charles Dickens, were an unending source of pleasure. The only thing to mar my joy were the thorns from the roadside hedges that gave me a series of flat tires all the way to London.

I stopped, awed and respectful, at Oxford. The scholarly atmosphere around the Bodleian Library, the first large library I had ever seen, made an unforgettable impression. Here was the world of learning so alien to my untutored mind. For the first time I realized how much there was to know and for the first time I felt ashamed of my own ignorance. It was this visit to Oxford as much as anything else that determined me to get a college education. But I was destined to wait five more years until at the ripe age of twenty-seven I stood before one of the great memorial gates leading into the Harvard Yard in Cambridge, and there in chiseled stone read the legend I wanted to realize, "Enter here to grow in wisdom."

Stratford upon Avon was a beautifully romantic experience. Ann Hathaway's cottage, the Shakespeare house, the church, the river—established a whole series of indelible impressions. Shakespeare had become my favorite author after I graduated from the dime novel and boy's book stage.

The exciting climax of my bicycle trip across England was my evening entry into the great city of London. The dull glow in the sky told me where it was long before I reached the outskirts. It was late when I finally landed on London Bridge. It was raining and there was a great snarl of traffic.

I wore my Spanish War rubber poncho to keep the rain off. My army felt hat was pulled down over my ears. My small telescope bag was strapped to the handle bars. It was an effective entrance to London for the sophisticated Londoners stopped to stare in amazement as I wheeled my bicycle across the bridge.

With the help of a guidebook I made the rounds of all the famous sights of London. It rained most of the time. This coupled with a gloomy Sunday night sermon in St. Paul's Cathedral entitled "The miserable conditions under which the poor people of White Chapel are compelled to live" made me eager to get to Paris.

I left for France the next morning. The crossing was rough but my trans-Atlantic experience on the cattle boat had developed my sealegs and I made the four-hour trip with little discomfort. Alas, the few French lessons I had taken with a kindly Catholic priest in Merrill, Wisconsin, were of little avail even in dealing with French porters.

My first Sunday in Paris provided a most striking contrast to my last Sunday in London. Under a bright sun, I walked first through the famous Place de la Concorde, up the Champs Élysées, and then climbed the Arc de Triomphe. From the top of the Arc, the historic landmarks of the world's most beautiful city were spread out before me in the brilliant afternoon sunshine—the golden dome of the Invalides, the great white mass of uncompleted Sacré Cœur, the beautiful bridges of the Seine and the great Eiffel Tower. Before me stretching along the banks of the Seine were the shining exposition palaces of the World's Fair of 1900.

Here was the chief objective of my long journey and I resolved to see the Fair the very next day. After climbing down from the Arc, I walked along the Bois de Boulogne Boulevard where an unending stream of handsome carriages was moving to and from the Bois. I strolled the length of the avenue to where the park begins and sat down at a sidewalk café to sip an inexpensive drink and rest myself for the walk back. I did a prodigious amount of walking in Paris just because it seemed more simple to walk than to enter into a long and difficult conversation concerning which particular bus would carry me back to my lodging. The waiter gave me my grenadine and placed a whole tray of cakes in front of me that I assumed went with the drink. I was hungry and ate half a dozen only to discover later to my great chagrin that they cost ten cents each. My budget provided only fifty cents a day for food so this mistake was serious. Sorrowfully I paid and resolved to be more careful. For the next few days I ordered only the cheapest dishes on the menu. Several days passed before I learned that I was eating horse meat more often than any other kind.

Paris was full of visitors and the French people were most friendly and helpful. The World's Fair had apparently attracted an enormous number of "ladies of the evening." I had many occasions to improve my French explaining that I was not a rich American, and therefore hardly worthy of their solicitations.

As a spectacle the World's Fair was up to my expectations. I had never seen anything more than the Lincoln County Fair in Wisconsin so the Paris Exposition was indeed an experience. I was amazed at the elaborateness of the great buildings that had been built just for this occasion. The extravagant lighting at night made everything even more beautiful than it was by day. A moving sidewalk carried weary visitors over a good part of the Fair grounds. For me, the most impressive single exhibit was the great Eiffel Tower itself, which, for Parisians, was already an old story. I took the elevator to the top and gazed out on the great city at night with its myriad lights spreading in all directions and the colorful firework displays from the Fair grounds far below.

Lacking money, I had to confine myself to the free exhibits at the Fair. These were mostly of an educational nature. But I did part with a bit of my money to see one special performance. La Loie Fuller and Her Sensational Fire Dance were well worth the price of admission. So from the point of view of both education and entertainment the Fair was a great success.

3

I LEFT PARIS DETERMINED TO RETURN SOON. I WAS, OF course, curious about Germany, the land of my ancestors. My father had often spoken to me about the country of his birth. At home in Wisconsin, we spoke more German than English. My father supervised my early education and saw to it that I was thoroughly grounded in German language and literature. Many of the first books and magazines which I read as a child were German. As a result, I still speak German with practically no American accent. Through kindergarten and up through the fourth grade, I went to the German-English Academy in Milwaukee, which helped increase my interest in everything German. We subscribed to what was called a *Mappe,* a circulating library of German magazines which included the humorous weekly *Fliegende Blaetter* and *Jugenfreund* (Friend of Youth). I read these eagerly coming as they did from a world beyond the Atlantic. All this German reading did much to broaden my horizon and left me grateful to my father for insisting not only that I learn German but that I learn it well.

My first impression of Germany in 1900 was the prevalence of that characteristic German word *verboten*. There were signs ordering you to keep off the grass, to keep away from certain buildings, not to cross the streets except at designated places, not to smoke, not to wear your hat, and a host of other petty prohibitions. I became *verboten*-conscious in a very short time. What amazed me more than the number of *verboten* signs was the conscientious way in which all Germans obeyed them. This unquestioning acceptance of authority was something I had never encountered except in the relation with my father who was a stern, albeit kindly, parent. The Germans lined up to get on streetcars and obeyed to the letter all the traffic signs and regulations. On public occasions, they never crowded or pushed. They seemed to have a unique sense for order and discipline.

Berlin was the first large German city I visited. In both London and Paris I had been a tourist, necessarily catching only superficial impressions. In Germany because of my relatives and my knowledge of the language, I was able to delve deeper into the life and attitudes. Most Germans conceived the America of 1900 as still rather wild, crude, and undeveloped. They asked me endless questions about cowboys and Indians for their favorite boyhood novels featured our wild West. They had no sense of the extent to which the United States was slowly developing its role as a world power. As a veteran of the Spanish-American War, I was chagrined to find they had little respect for our military achievements during that war. They did not even consider it a war nor did they feel that Spain was an enemy worth talking about. They gave us no credit for winning.

The feeling toward France was one of superiority. There was much talk of another Franco-German war. The Germans were sure that they were better fighters than the French and superior in every aspect of warfare. They could not understand why the French did not recognize what they called "their natural limitations" and try to get along with Germany on a basis of friendship and co-operation instead of heaping mourning wreaths on the Strasbourg statue in the Place de la Concorde and dreaming of *la revanche*. Although I did meet some Germans who spoke highly of French civilization, there was, on the whole, a definite feeling of hostility. My uncle who served in the Franco-Prussian War would not have gone to France even as a tourist. France, to him, was enemy territory. There was, and I sensed it even then, a growing antagonism between the two countries. No one seemed to doubt that eventually there would be another war. I have often wondered to what extent the thought and feeling that war is inevitable helps to make war inevitable.

My father's brother, with whom I stayed in Berlin, and his sons, three of whom had chosen a military career, were weaned in the atmosphere and traditions of Prussian militarism. My uncle, a lieutenant general, was head of the Kaiser's highest military court, the *Reichsmilitaergericht*. While the family was not well off, the privileged position of a high military rank and belonging to the *Uradel,* the most ancient aristocracy, gave them a keen sense of *noblesse oblige*. It was crucially important to keep up a good appearance, to do everything *standesgemaess,* as required by position. The entire family scrimped and saved so that the eldest son could belong to one of the fashionable Guards regiments. One of my cousins had just been made a Guards lieutenant. During my entire stay in Berlin, I was a great trial to this young popinjay. His immaculate military dress—he always stood in public conveyances to preserve the crease in his trousers—contrasted sharply with my well-worn, well-wrinkled American suit. He always introduced me as an American cousin from Wisconsin to explain my wild West appearance. In Germany I was always addressed as Baron von Kaltenborn, but long ago my father had explained to me that my belonging to the *Uradel* was far more important than this title. On one occasion I caused my lieutenant-cousin no end of anguish by buying and eating a hot dog while we were walking along the *Sieges Allee,* the Kaiser's famous Avenue of Victory. Finally, he could stand this indignity no longer and insisted I walk at least ten feet behind him. I often followed the American custom of running for a streetcar. He would never follow suit. Instead he signaled the conductor and, to my amazement, the car would wait until he caught up.

My cousin showed me the traditional sights of Berlin in response to his father's request but he refused to accompany me on a visit to the *Reichstag*. The military had nothing but contempt for parliamentary government and resented even the mild and relatively weak checks on the Emperor's authority imposed by the *Reichstag*. The aristocratic upper house, the *Bundesrat,* dominated by Prussia was still the more important law-making body. The *Reichstag* was slowly developing restraining powers over the budget and its often bitter debates were assuming larger importance. Most of the real authority lay with the Imperial Chancellor who was appointed by the Kaiser.

My uncle refused to intervene to have me admitted and I stood in line three times before I got to the *Reichstag* building early enough to be admitted to the public gallery. The debate I heard concerned the military budget. It produced a dramatic clash between the rather stiff and stodgy Chancellor von Bülow and August Bebel, the fiery leader of the Social Democratic party. Bebel was much more than a match in debate for von Bülow. The Chancellor wielded much power in the Germany of that day but free speech in the *Reichstag* had already become a real weapon in the hands of an able leader of the opposition.

The Kaiser himself was still an autocrat surrounded by the pomp and panoply of power, his dignity protected by special laws. This was forcefully impressed upon me one afternoon as I watched Kaiser William II dedicate another statue along the *Sieges Allee*. This avenue was the Kaiser's pet project. There was to be a statue to every elector, grand duke, king, and emperor of the Hohenzollern line and it was nearing completion. Here is what I wrote in one of my letters to the *Merrill Advocate:*

> On a public occasion of this kind there is no such thing as getting close to royalty and a respectful distance of at least forty yards must be kept. The attempt to get near the great may bring much more serious consequences than with us in the States. Daring individuals have been known to feel the

prick of the sword belonging to the guardian of the law on the slightest provocation.

My cousin and I were keeping at the "respectful distance" and I remarked to him that the Emperor's helmet looked to me a good bit like the fire helmets worn by our Wisconsin volunteer firemen. That quiet but disrespectful remark was overheard. Threatening glances and the red-faced glowering of my cousin told me I had nearly committed *lèse-majesté,* an insult to the Emperor which I was informed entailed at least a six-month jail sentence. Free speech as I had known it in America was unknown in Germany.

After a month or so in Berlin, I was happy to leave for Bremen, my mother's native city, where I found the atmosphere more congenial. I liked the *gemütlichkeit,* the friendly informality of the people of Bremen, so different from the stiff Prussian military atmosphere which surrounded me in Berlin. In Bremen I lived in the comfortable house of my uncle who was a wealthy merchant and one of Bremen's sixteen senators—one-sixteenth of a king, as he loved to call himself. Here in Bremen I met my mother's friends and relatives. For the first time I began to create a picture of what she must have been like when I was told about her love of people and her optimistic attitude toward life. My father had been reluctant to talk much about her. He never got over her death, yet felt a strong sense of loyalty to his second wife, the only mother I had ever known.

The young people I met in Bremen were genuinely interested in America and anxious to hear all about the New World. One of the things nearly everyone asked about was the Niagara Falls. On my way from Milwaukee to New York, my train had a two-hour stopover in Buffalo. I was determined to get a glimpse of Niagara Falls within that time if possible. I was lucky in catching a Buffalo trolley car that went directly to the Falls in fifty minutes, stayed there for ten minutes and then returned. It was a quarter of a mile from the trolley station at the Falls to the best point of vantage on the American side. I sprinted as hard as I could go, and my so-called spider legs carried me along at a good pace, spent three breathless minutes in fervid contemplation of one of the wonders of the world, then raced back and caught the trolley just as it was leaving. As a result of this brief visit, I was able to give my German friends a vivid firsthand description of the wondrous Falls.

The Germans I met in Bremen were very much like the Germans I had known in Milwaukee. They were prosperous middle-class businessmen who did not put on airs and who loved good food, good drink, and good times. There was a succession of parties and excursions. One of the things I loved best was that at every party we all joined in singing German folksongs. In Bremen there were many Germans who spoke English and knew a good bit about America. Many of them had traveled to and from New York on the ships of the North German Lloyd Line which had its headquarters in Bremen.

A popular book in Germany at that time was called *America—The Land of Unlimited Possibilities.* Many young Germans dreamed of going to the United States to make their fortunes. Some were rather surprised to learn that I was not on my way to being a millionaire—"with all those wonderful opportunities in America." The desire to travel was strong in the young men of the merchant middle class. In 1900 America was still welcoming emigrants from foreign countries with open arms. Until 1910 we had few restrictions against entering the country. The North German Lloyd carried on a big promotion campaign urging Germans to take advantage of the special twenty-five dollar steerage rate from Bremen to New York.

In Berlin I sensed that Germany was a great military power. In Bremen I became aware that Germany was working hard to become a great naval power. I recalled the inscription over the entrance to the German pavilion at the Paris World's Fair: *Unsere Zukunft liegt auf dem Wasser*—"Our future lies on the water." The two cities, Berlin and Bremen, symbolized the rapidly growing military and commercial power of Germany. There was no single military power in Europe that could match the strength of Germany, and Britain was her only naval rival. In 1898 the Kaiser had already launched his big naval building program. The two large merchant shipping lines, the North German Lloyd, and the Hamburg-American Line were working closely with the German Navy. I saw the giant tanks where different types of hulls were being tested for speed and seaworthiness. Every officer of the North German Lloyd was also an officer in the German Naval Reserve. Those I talked with were proud of being part of the German Navy. The Kaiser's birthday was the great day on which they displayed their uniforms. This close relationship between the Merchant Marine and the Navy proved most effective during World War I when the German merchant ships became naval vessels. Some of the great liners were converted into successful commerce raiders. The Germany I saw in 1900 was fundamentally a military nation. All of her resources were so developed and organized that they could be used for military ends. Even the railroad network was constructed with mobilization and military transport needs in mind. Strategic lines could rush troops either to the Polish or the French frontiers.

Aware of my wanderlust, my uncle in Bremen offered to help me get a job on a North-German Lloyd steamer headed for the Orient. It was tempting but I had not forgotten my determination to return to Paris and stay there until I had conquered the French language. The trip to the Orient was postponed.

4

I ARRIVED BACK IN PARIS IN A SERIOUS MOOD AND with a sense of trepidation. My money was about used up and I would soon have to find a job to sustain myself. I had no letters of introduction, no friends or relations in France to whom I could turn for help. I was too proud to borrow from my German relatives or to call for help from home. The only English paper, the Paris *Herald,* had a few "Help Wanted" notices which I studied hopefully. One offered a position as secretary for a club in the Bavarian Alps. A young man was wanted who could speak German, English, and French. Since I was fluent in two of the three languages and had great expectations for fluency in the third, I applied for the position. A most imposing gentleman, living in what seemed to me like a palace near the Arc de Triomphe, interviewed me for the position. The duties were light enough as he explained them. They consisted mainly in carrying on correspondence and supervising accounts. My potential employer seemed satisfied with my qualifications and it looked as though I had found a job. Then came the catch. Just as we were coming to terms he told me that, of course, every officer of the club, including the secretary, was expected to make a cash investment of five thousand dollars in the organization. Rather aghast, I protested that I had nothing like five thousand to invest. "But you are an American!" he expostulated. "Certainly you must have wealthy friends who will lend you the money so that you can take this interesting job?" I told him I was sorry but such was not the case. He rose and said coldly, "I am sorry, sir, the position then is not open."

There was one other job possibility I had seen advertised in the *Herald* that morning: "Seeking young American for sales position. Apply 44 Rue de Rivoli." I applied. After climbing three flights of stairs of the Hotel du Toison D'or, I entered a small room crowded with young men. I explained to the man in charge that I was the answer to his sales problems. "What is it you want me to sell?" I asked. "Foote," he called, "show the young man the little American invention."

The little invention turned out to be an old-fashioned stereoscope which gave life to a double picture by adding perspective—one of the type that was already an old story in the United States. "This is what we are selling to the Frenchies," he said, "and they certainly go for them." He explained the method of demonstration and outlined the type of sales talk they found most successful. "We call it 'la petite invention Americaine,' " he said. "The French are wild about anything American. They are convinced we're a nation of mechanical geniuses." He told me that the inexperienced salesman only needed to get a signature for an order for the eighty-five-cent stereoscope. It was the second visit when the machine was delivered and the pictures were sold that was the crucial one. You had to sell the largest possible number of pictures at seventeen cents each and collect the money for both pictures and stereoscope. Selling lots of pictures was the real trick. "If you're a good salesman," the genial Mr. Foote told me, "you can make your fortune in this business."

I was impressed but not so sure of my ability as a salesman, particularly since my knowledge of French was so meager. "It looks like a fine business," I said, "but how do you sell stereoscopes to Frenchmen when you can't speak French?"

"Don't worry about that," he said. "We've had others like you. We just write out a little speech in French which you paste in your order book. You can memorize it if you want but if you forget it, just show it to the French customer. Don't worry—you'll make out all right."

Taking a deep breath I agreed to sell stereoscopes. I was down to my last twenty francs and I had to do something. To take out a sample case for demonstration purposes, I had to leave my old camera as a deposit.

It took me a little time to get up enough courage to make my first call. In selecting a prospective customer, I chose badly. He was a busy little Frenchman behind the counter of a tobacco shop. Ignoring the cold light in his eye, I launched into my memorized sales talk about "la petite invention Americaine." He soon made it clear to me even with my limited knowledge of French that he definitely was not interested in "la petite invention." Nevertheless I persisted. But, when he said something about *gendarmes* and came out from behind the counter, I left!

After this false start, it took a bit of talking to myself to try again. The next prospective customer only laughed at me but didn't buy. But at the end of the first day, I returned to the office and proudly displayed three orders. The sales staff was pleased. "If you can do that without talking French, you should be a whiz when you've learned the language."

I never made a fortune during the fifteen months I sold stereoscopes, but I certainly learned French! The kindly French have a good sense of humor. They enjoyed the spectacle of a young American trying to sell something to Frenchmen without knowing their language. Each encounter was an adventure for them as well as for me and there was usually much mutual laughter. And each day my knowledge of the language was expanding.

One of the most effective pictures in my sample set was a telescopic photograph of the moon which showed the mountains and the craters. Another picture showed the footwalk over Brooklyn Bridge with a receding perspective of the huge suspension cables. The New York skyline and a lower Broadway canyon view were equally popular. The thirty-one story

Park Row Building was then the tallest skyscraper in New York and amazed the Frenchmen. My only racy picture showed a woman garbed in corset and pantaloons which carried the title: "Biddy serving the salad undressed." One other picture in this category was of a man with his foot in the small of a girl's back, tugging away at her corset strings. That, too, was popular. There was a heavy demand for what the Frenchmen called "something special" but I always replied with a smile that "naughty pictures" were taboo because American censors were extremely puritanical—that always got a laugh.

Most of my encounters with the French people were pleasant and friendly. Selling door-to-door in Paris, Cannes, Boulogne, and in Corsica gave me a real insight into French life and customs.

There were many sharp contrasts between France and Germany. While the position of the French army was important, I was not impressed by French soldiers as compared with those I had seen in Germany. The uniformed Frenchman was not as neat nor did he carry himself with that stiff erect posture which characterized the Prussian soldier. The military formations did not seem well disciplined. To the outward eye the French army seemed no match for the German. In some ways the French army resembled the American army of which I had been a part. But my own experience had taught me that outward appearance does not necessarily reflect the fighting ability of a soldier or an army.

The feeling in France for revenge against Germany was strong. The defeat of 1871 had been a bitter humiliation. In the Place de la Concorde, there are stone monuments representing the principal French cities. The one for the city of Strasbourg which had been lost to Germany with Alsace-Lorraine in 1871 was always draped in black. There was an inscription to the effect that Strasbourg would always remain a daughter of France and never be forgotten even though in alien hands. The Strasbourg monument served as a perpetual reminder of French determination to recover Alsace-Lorraine.

The French Chamber of Deputies presented a sharp contrast to what I had seen in the German *Reichstag*. I was struck by the undisciplined character of French parliamentary meetings. There was much shouting and back talk, expressing the differences among the many party factions. I was present on one occasion when the Assembly had to be adjourned to prevent an open riot. This lack of decorum shocked me but in time I came to realize that underneath there was a stable, hard core of real democracy.

When I was not busy selling stereoscopes, I visited the sights of Paris and spent much time in the glorious art galleries of the Louvre and the Luxembourg. I heard my first orchestral concerts in Paris and also attended the opera for the first time. I was present when the great Adelina Patti sang a farewell concert to a packed house. I attended the opera as a "super"—a nonsinging member of the chorus. For the magnificent salary of one franc, I donned a musty old costume and carried the traditional spear. They had tested my voice for the chorus and gave me strict instructions never to open my mouth.

At the Comédie Française I practiced my French from the back row of the balcony. As the actors spoke their lines, I repeated them in a quiet whisper in an effort to copy their diction and pronunciation. I followed the plays with a text which I studied carefully in advance. This, with a regular reading of the French newspapers and night classes at the French Y.M.C.A. broadened my knowledge of French. Gone were the days when I had to depend on the memorized sales speech pasted in the front of my order book.

The people of Paris will always retain my affection. The friendly reception they gave an alien itinerant salesman testified to their courtesy and good nature. Those were gay, happy days in France. They came to a close in the spring of 1902 when a cablegram arrived from my stepmother asking me to return home as my father was seriously ill. He died before I got back to the United States.

I returned to Merrill, but with my father gone there was little to hold me there. After two months studying shorthand and typewriting I left for New York determined to become a big city journalist.

5

From early youth there had been no doubt in my mind about my vocation. I wanted to work on a newspaper. Nothing else would do. After my return from France I realized that I needed experience on a big city newspaper. Once back in New York in the fall of 1902 I started the rounds of the newspaper offices looking for work. It was not easy even for the "war correspondent of the *Merrill Advocate* with foreign experience." The *World* and the *Times* had no openings. The *Sun* where I applied first might have taken me on if my shorthand had been better. The city editor needed a secretary but when I failed to reproduce correctly a technical paragraph which he read to me from the financial page, he said I wouldn't do.

You might not expect the thoughts of a man without a job in a big city to turn toward poetry—but mine did. The spectacle of the workers hurrying home at night across Brooklyn Bridge inspired me to write a paraphrase of Southey's poem "The Cataract of Lodore" which I took to the *Brooklyn Daily Eagle*. That did the trick. Managing Editor Gilbert

Evans called me in and told me the *Eagle* would break a precedent by paying me five dollars for the poem. Better still he offered me a job. It was to work on the stock tables during the day for eight dollars a week and cover night assignments without extra pay. The job was largely clerical. It consisted in keeping track of the high, low, and final prices of New York Stock Exchange transactions. The tables had to be ready ten minutes after the market closed.

It was not uncommon in those days for newspapermen to work regularly from twelve to fourteen hours a day. In an effort to improve my status I did occasional stories on my own. Newspaper reporters in those days were allowed much more freedom than they are today. The articles were not always signed, but could be written in a personal fashion on your own time. The signed articles were usually done for the Sunday issue on your own time. There was no extra financial reward for neophytes like myself—the privilege of signing an occasional article was considered sufficient reward. The *Eagle* of that day kept its reporters working both day and night. Covering night assignments often meant working until well past midnight since the stories had to be written before you turned in.

The *Brooklyn Daily Eagle* at the turn of the century was a nationally known newspaper. It owed its continuing reputation in great part to Dr. St. Clair McKelway, its editor in chief, whose powerful editorials were quoted all over the country. McKelway, like his contemporaries Henry Watterson of the *Louisville Courier-Journal,* Samuel Bowles of the *Springfield Republican,* and Charles Dana of the *New York Sun,* was among the last of the great American newspaper editors to continue the tradition of personal journalism. His full-column leading editorials, which he dictated to his secretary as he stomped up and down his office, reveled in the mighty line and the balanced sentence. Today, we would call them ponderous, but like the Macaulay essays whose style they resembled, they had solid content and always drove home a vigorous, outspoken message.

The *Brooklyn Eagle* was primarily a provincial newspaper and took an active interest in everything that concerned

Brooklyn affairs or people. Brooklyn had been incorporated into Greater New York City for only a few years and continued to pride itself on local identity and past history. The *Eagle* was really a big city newspaper run in some respects on small-town lines. It had been owned by the Van Anden-Hester family since its foundation in 1841. It retained an intimacy with Brooklyn problems and Brooklyn personalities which gained for it a strong local following. The problem faced by its editors was to achieve a satisfactory balance between Brooklyn news, New York City news, national news, and international news. Foreign news received the least space of all. This was characteristic of most American papers of those days. The front pages of the New York newspapers of 1900 when contrasted with those of today, reveal to what a tremendous extent we have become aware of and are concerned with world affairs.

In those days foreign news in the *Eagle* consisted chiefly of brief, daily Associated Press dispatches and the more leisurely long foreign letters written from abroad and printed in the Sunday edition. Most of these came from the Paris bureau which the *Eagle* maintained for many years. This bureau was established for the purpose of welcoming Brooklyn people visiting abroad. The visitors' names were duly noted and cabled to the *Eagle*. Longer stories about their doings in foreign parts were sent by mail. Foreign travel in those days was a big experience and Brooklyn visitors to Paris were grateful for the travel assistance and suggestions the *Eagle* bureau was able to provide. The travelers were naturally proud of their trip and happy to have their adventures reported. The head of the bureau also sent regular letters dealing with European affairs. In many ways these European letters had a more distinctive quality and greater value than the shorter, more hurried cable stories of later years. The letters were less concerned with immediate spot news and more apt to deal with long-range trends. They gave much solid, thoughtful information on events and personalities.

While serving my apprenticeship on the *Eagle's* financial page, Count Montesquieu de Fezenzac, leader of a French esthetic cult, came to New York to lecture. As the only *Eagle* reporter who could speak French, I was sent to interview him. My satiric story made the front page and won me my first promotion. I became a full-fledged reporter with a fifty per cent salary increase from eight to twelve dollars a week.

As those who have seen *The Front Page* or countless other movies and plays well know, competition between the different newspapers has always been keen. The New York papers had representatives in Brooklyn and the *Eagle* reporters were competing against them as well as against the reporters from the other Brooklyn papers. Every day the City Desk checked the news that appeared in the other papers. If any rival paper ran a story from my beat which I had not reported the managing editor asked for an explanation. This practice kept us all on our toes, but it also developed more or less secret agreements among reporters to exchange news. In my day the men covering police headquarters had the best organized news pool. They took turns covering the news and unless something big was in the wind, the daily poker game was well patronized. City editors knew what was going on and accepted the practice because it reduced news expense. But in most departments the papers were in keen competition and getting exclusives was our greatest goal.

Then, as now, traffic was a New York problem. The subway was under construction during 1902-03. This was a laborious undertaking because so much of the previously laid underground pipes and connections had to be cut off and rebuilt. Progress was painfully slow and countless streets were torn up. Since I have been in New York, the city has never caught up with its traffic problem. Every improvement in transportation has been overtaxed upon completion. Every traffic improvement seems to create more traffic.

One of the early nicknames for Brooklynites was "trolley dodgers." That is how the world's most famous baseball team got its name. But there were many who could not dodge in time and every day people were injured by trolley cars. Somehow the horsecar generation just could not get used to these newfangled speedy vehicles.

In the winter of 1903-04, I became the City Hall reporter

for the *Brooklyn Eagle* and got an education in practical municipal politics. The *Brooklyn Eagle* branch office was located across Brooklyn Bridge in the *New York World* building right by New York's City Hall. This was the era when Lincoln Steffens was bringing out his muckraking stories exposing municipal corruption. His magazine series, "The Shame of the Cities," was making people conscious of the methods by which political bosses controlled elections and ran city governments for their own profit. There was considerable awareness of the need for reform and the first city managers were being installed.

In 1902, New York had just installed a new reform mayor, Seth Low, who had been President of Columbia University. As I watched him in action, I realized that it takes something more than honesty and good intentions to make a reform administration effective and keep it in office. This was particularly true in a large cosmopolitan city like New York where a great proportion of the citizens was foreign born. Mayor Low had an impeccable background. He had a superb theoretical understanding of municipal government. As mayor, he introduced many important reforms, but he lacked popular appeal and could not mobilize public support for his worthwhile projects. Seth Low lacked warmth and seemed remote. His public addresses were uninspired. It was not surprising that the Tammany machine was able to defeat Seth Low at the end of his first term and make their candidate, George McClellan, son of the Civil War general, the next mayor of New York. McClellan, a man of charm and dignity, was, of course, in the hands of Tammany but no big scandals broke during his administration.

The inevitable group of hangers-on carried the orders from the political bosses at Tammany Hall down to City Hall. Every city department was beset by pressures from the Tammany boys. Tammany had a sort of rival city government with its headquarters in Tammany Hall on Fourteenth Street. This shadow government was on the job day and night all year round. The voters in the districts learned that they could go to the Tammany boss with their problems and find someone to listen sympathetically. Often the boss intervened and helped. In return for these personal services Tammany got loyal support at the polls.

As City Hall reporter, I came to know some of the many undeniable tangible benefits that Tammany conferred upon the poorer groups in the community. There were Christmas baskets and Thanksgiving baskets stocked with food which went to the poorer groups in the community who in those days were largely left to shift for themselves.

The Tammany boys did a good job as far as they went, but a well-run city government could have done twice as much for the poor at half the cost, all of which came out of the taxpayer's pocket. But the Tammany boys have always had a warm personal touch which an impersonal official charity administrator seems unable to achieve. Until those who do not make their living out of politics learn to help people with the same degree of human warmth and sympathetic understanding that characterizes so many politicians, political machines will continue their hold upon the voters.

Another thing I learned while covering City Hall is the fine line between legitimate and illegitimate graft. The astute political leader knows where to draw that line. We go wrong when we assume that most political leaders or bosses are dishonest. Politics has its own standards and morals. After all, what is wrong about giving a city contract to one of your friends provided he does the job efficiently and at no greater expense to the city than his competitors? Men must be paid for work and politics is no exception. The man who rings doorbells in a precinct to get out the vote cannot be expected to do much of that hard and tedious work for no reward. We don't expect the man who sells goods over a counter to do it free. Professional politicians must be paid in some way for the necessary work of organizing voters in a democracy. They must either receive an adequate salary or they will seek recompense through appointments, jobs, rake-offs, and special privileges. Politics is a business, though we do not like to admit it, and most of those who enter it as a profession expect to earn a living.

6

IF THERE IS ONE THING MORE THAN ANY OTHER THAT characterizes the average American, it is his eagerness to learn about almost anything at almost any age. In that respect I was typical. I sometimes think I was born with a particularly unquenchable thirst for knowledge although Samuel Johnson said that a desire for knowledge is the natural feeling of mankind. My trip to Europe had opened vistas which I longed to explore. This yearning stayed with me and nagged at me even during my first busy years at the *Eagle*. As a working newspaperman I was, of course, piling up valuable information and having invaluable experiences, but I longed for something more—for broader, cultural knowledge. I tried organized reading at night or in the early morning, but was usually too tired to make much progress.

To quit work on the *Eagle* to go to school seemed the only way. It was a bold step, especially since I had certain financial obligations to my family in Wisconsin. But I decided to take the step. I reasoned that the immediate financial loss would be more than compensated later, for with a college education

I should be able to write better and advance further in my chosen field.

I approached the problem of a college education with great seriousness. I thought of Oxford, but decided it would be best to stay in America since I would have to work as well as study. I chose Harvard because it was the oldest and was widely renowned for its English faculty.

My plan was to go to Harvard for one year as a special student specializing in English and history and perhaps one or two other cultural subjects. After studying the Harvard catalogue I became far more ambitious. When I saw what this great university had to offer I decided to swallow all I could. I determined to take courses in philosophy, harmony, astronomy, music, art, literature, in addition to English and history. This freedom of choice in selecting courses was the result of President Charles W. Eliot's elective system. His basic idea was "Most profit grows where is most pleasure taken." This was a motto that suited me perfectly. I simply selected those courses which I thought would give me the most pleasure. It was reassuring to take the word of this famous educator that they were also to give me the most profit.

Once enrolled and registered at Harvard I soon found my reach had far exceeded my grasp. On my first day in class I opened up my elementary music book, Prout's *Harmony,* and discovered that harmony seemed to consist of abstruse mathematical problems. I could see no connection between that sort of thing and the beautiful music I had expected to hear and learn to appreciate. Puzzling out the writing of notes and making bar lines was not what I had bargained for. After one lesson in harmony, I gave it up.

Astronomy was equally bad. I had envisioned myself as a sort of Galileo gazing in wondrous meditation at the stars through Harvard's powerful telescope. After two sessions of mathematical formulas and no telescope I gave up astronomy.

I was even more bitterly disappointed by Art 1. Instead of wandering through art galleries looking at beautiful paintings, I was given a little brush and some paint and ordered to block out different shades of color on a piece of paper. This struck me as being absurd and more like kindergarten work than college level art. When the instructor told me to draw one hundred circles, I resigned from Art 1.

The only courses I continued after the first week were History 1, English Composition, English Literature and a course in debating. I was also informed by those in charge that four courses would prove a sufficiently heavy load at Harvard for anyone who expected to earn his living as well. I had been granted a scholarship, established for special students like myself, and was told that to retain it the second half year I would have to make an A and B record the first half.

My scholarship paralleled in some respects the Nieman Fellowships of today, which are granted to working newspapermen for a year of study at Harvard in any field they desire. During my freshman year I met additional living expenses by doing newspaper work on the side. I was the Harvard correspondent for the *New York Post* and the *Brooklyn Eagle* and did occasional special articles for the *Boston Transcript* and other papers. For my courses in English, I frequently wrote essays on Harvard life and my reactions to it as an older man since I was ten years older than the average Harvard freshman. These essays, improved by professorial suggestion, found a ready market. I also picked up extra money teaching German and doing some translating. The employment service at the college was most efficient and co-operative in helping students like myself to get these part-time jobs. Translating scholarly theses on abstruse subjects from German to English was in some ways the easiest occupation, but also the dullest.

During my first months at Harvard, social contacts with my fellow freshmen were few. I was separated from them by more than years. I just couldn't spare the time for the ordinary college social activities—but at the student commons in Memorial Hall it was my good fortune to sit at a table with a varied group of graduate students. Their conversation opened new worlds to my eager interest.

I found studying very difficult. For the first few weeks it was particularly hard to do the kind of concentrating required to assimilate the required reading. Although I had always been an avid reader, I had never been required to read and to remember. My English literature and history courses required the retention of names and dates. It was a type of intellectual discipline that I had never experienced. This first Harvard year required twice the effort of those that followed. I was appalled at the poor marks I got in the first examinations and only by the most vigorous efforts and intellectual discipline was I able to bring them up to scholarship standards. It dismayed me to see the young members of my classes breeze through examinations which had me stumped.

These difficulties of adjustment reduced still further my modicum of leisure time. Because I needed some exercise I did make a try for the cross-country team since I considered myself a fair runner with my "spider legs." The first five-mile race with the cross-country squad caused me to abandon that project. I found myself utterly exhausted and unable to stay awake long enough to study.

Although I had expected to spend only one year at Harvard, that one year merely served to whet my appetite for more, and once having decided to stay, I also decided to go out for a degree. That made it necessary to pass certain entrance examinations that had been waived during my first year because I was registered as a special student. To go on with my class of 1909 as a regular student I had to pass examinations in geometry, algebra, physics and Latin. This was a dismal prospect, and to get back into Harvard for a second year, I had to do some serious summer cramming which I did not relish. With algebra it was always touch and go. I just squeaked through with a bare passing mark one week before being elected to Phi Beta Kappa. Good marks were, of course, necessary to keep the scholarships that helped me during my first two years at fair Harvard, but after the first two years, tutoring my fellow students in my own courses proved an easy and doubly profitable way of earning a living.

Charles W. Eliot was president of Harvard during three of my four years. He was succeeded by A. Lawrence Lowell in my senior year. President Eliot was an outstanding personality. He left an indelible impression on all who came in contact with him. He was tall and dignified and spoke impeccable English with an impressive resonant voice. He had a curious habit of twiddling his thumbs as he spoke. I never heard him address an audience without seeing those two thumbs spin around one another. A sight to be remembered was Dr. and Mrs. Eliot, both in their seventies, riding their bicycles through the streets of Cambridge. They carried it off with the same erect dignity that a King and Queen would display riding to Ascot in the royal carriage.

On one occasion, I presided at a dinner of the Harvard Cosmopolitan Club where President Eliot was to deliver the principal address. The other honor guests were the German Ambassador to the United States, Count von Bernstorff, and the Japanese Ambassador, Baron Takahira. These men had come to present President Eliot with honorary decorations from their respective governments on the occasion of his retirement. The Japanese Ambassador had presented him with The Order of the Rising Sun that morning. The German Kaiser had sent the Order of the Crown Second Class which Count Bernstorff presented at the dinner. President Eliot made a charming speech, in the course of which he acknowledged receipt of the Japanese decoration. I expected him to turn to the German Ambassador and acknowledge the Order of the Crown Second Class, but to my surprise, he finished up his speech without saying a word about the German decoration. Then he sat down. Since this was the end of the dinner, I asked the audience to rise for the traditional singing of "Fair Harvard." Then picking up my courage, I stepped up to President Eliot and suggested that he had probably forgotten to acknowledge the German decoration. He nodded his head quietly and remarked, "So I did." "May I call on you for an added word?" I asked. "You may," he replied. So when the singing ended, President Eliot rose and resumed his speech on German scholarship just where he had left off. By a deft transition, he then added a few gracious words of thanks to the German Ambassador as if he had deliberately intended to save these remarks for the very end in order to give them particular emphasis. As for me, I felt most important, convinced I had prevented an international incident.

It is a common failing of old college graduates to look back and remember primarily those classmates who in later life gained fame and prominence. There seems to be a natural tendency to exaggerate the intimacy of acquaintanceship with those who later achieved fame. A goodly number of my classmates at Harvard have found their way into the pages of *Who's Who*. Some of these revealed in their college days the potential that was to bring them fame, others did not.

Heywood Broun and John Reed were at Harvard in my day. I remember little about Heywood Broun except his size, that he was vaguely associated with the Liberal Club, and that I used to see him in Professor Charles T. Copeland's room at some of "Copey's" famous evening sessions. I did get to know John Reed rather well. He and I were among the small group who helped Edward Sheldon form the Harvard Dramatic Club, of which Sheldon was the first president and I the first business manager.

This club was established originally to produce plays written by Harvard undergraduates who were studying playwriting with Professor George Pierce Baker. John Reed was assistant business manager and succeeded me in the post. Both he and I had dramatic aspirations but our fellow club members seemed to feel we would do better off stage than on. We worked hard and actually made money for the club, although I had to challenge author Owen Davis to a fight when he insisted on an expensive sunset backdrop for the final act.

The great issue within the Dramatic Club was whether Radcliffe girls should be permitted to act in our dramatic productions. It was argued that in the past in German and French plays produced at Harvard men had always played the female parts as they still do in the Hasty Pudding productions. Those who opposed breaking this tradition said that if we expected to achieve any social distinction at Harvard with our newly organized club, we simply could not permit the participation of Radcliffe girls. After a long and heated debate, a majority voted to break the tradition "in the interest of better drama." We made history by permitting Radcliffe girls to play the female roles in our productions.

Lee Simonson, who has since become an outstanding figure in the American theater, was one of those who argued for the Radcliffe girls. He displayed even then remarkable talent as a stage designer and was most ingenious in preparing our first stage sets on a very limited budget.

John Reed was not a fiery left-winger in those days. He was a nonconformist. He and I had planned to spend one brief vacation period together, walking through New England. This fell through when he was suspended or was rusticated," as it was then called, for a brief period because of some minor infraction of university rules. He was extremely likable, good humored, and attractive. He was possessed of great mental and physical vigor. Had he bothered to study he would have been a brilliant student. But he seemed rather bored by the intellectual discipline of college. He did a good bit of writing while at Harvard and Copey, who had an almost unerring judgment in detecting potential authors, set great store by his work. His later book, *Ten Days That Shook the World,* is still an extremely exciting and readable account of the Russian Revolution. He was sympathetic to the idealistic aspirations of the Soviets and was greatly stimulated by the exciting possibilities of the Communist experiment. He covered the opening phases of World War I for *Colliers.* When he later visited me after his first experience at the front I recognized a profound intellectual change. He had become much more mature and much more radical. He hated everything about the war and resented a governmental system that made war possible. Nevertheless, he hated authoritarianism of any kind. In view of what has happened in Russia since the Revolution, I am certain that he would not have tolerated the use of his name as a means of ensnaring idealistic American youth into the Communist party. That is what is being done at Harvard today. The John Reed Society has been little more than a cover for Communist party activities at Harvard since its inception.

Walter Lippman, another Harvard contemporary, has also achieved great prominence. I remember him as an earnest, hardworking intellectual who was known in Cambridge respectfully as one of Harvard's bright young boys. He was desperately serious about the campaign for woman's suffrage and submitted an article about the woman's suffrage at Radcliffe College to me as editor of the *Harvard Illustrated Magazine*. Although I was impressed with the logic and persuasiveness of the Lippman article, as an editor I just did not feel that an article on suffrage for our Radcliffe sisters would appeal to Harvard undergraduates. Walter Lippman told me that I was a pretty poor editor not to realize the great importance of this article.

Having been a working newspaperman before I went to Harvard, I was rather distressed at the low opinion of the press held by many Harvard professors. Their bias was understandable since then, as now, the standards of many newspapers were none too high. Professor Charles T. Copeland when asked about newspaper work advised his students, "Get in, get wise, get out." Professor Barrett Wendell loved to contrast the plebeian Charles Dickens, who was little more than a journalist, with the aristocratic Sir Walter Scott who wrote greatly about great people. And so I ventured to write him a letter pointing out that a man could be a reporter and still be a great writer. I made what I considered a glowing defense of the reporter's trade. He answered me rather tartly and compared my attitude to that of a man who openly resents not having been invited to a party and thereby makes it sure that he will never be invited. In my commencement address I defended the American press and reporting as a craft. I did not endorse commercialism or sensationalism but tried to point out that the best way to improve the standards of the press was to encourage more college-trained men to enter the profession.

Charles Townsend Copeland, one of Harvard's great teachers in my day, was the Harvard professor with whom I had the closest contact. When I arrived at Harvard in 1905, he was a well-known figure in the college. I met him on my second day in Cambridge while applying for admission to his advanced English composition class. My newspaper experience had been accepted by the authorities as proof that the elementary English course was not necessary, and I was authorized to apply for admission to more advanced courses. Copeland's famous English 12 was in advanced composition. No one could be admitted without his personal approval. When I spoke to him of my desire to enter his course, he was most forbidding and told me that I would have to pass a special examination. This consisted in the preparation of an essay explaining why I wanted to take the course. Apparently I produced the right formula for I received a postcard reading, "You are admitted!—C.T.C." This course, for its teacher, fellow students, and class discussion, proved to be one of the most interesting of my Harvard career. Among the members of the class were Maxwell Perkins, Robert E. Rogers, Herman Hagedorn, Frederick Moore, Lee Simonson, and Edward Sheldon, all men who attained later prominence.

In selecting men for his English 12, Copey sought the well-rounded man rather than the industrious grind. I once asked him why he had admitted a certain man whose intellectual virtues were not readily apparent to me. "Oh, he just looked so healthy," Copey replied. His judgment was far more perceptive than mine and that healthy individual later proved to be an exceptional student.

At one point Copey needed a secretary. I applied for the job and got it. This proved to be more than I had bargained for. Copey was not robust and nearly always was complaining of some ailment, real or apprehended. He took all sorts of precautions with his health; maybe that is why he is still alive today. Getting him to an outside lecture was always a big expedition. He liked to have someone with him to look after him and see that everything corresponded to his wishes. There were elaborate preparations in the lecture hall. The light had to be just right. The windows had to be just so. The desk and the books had to be arranged in meticulous fashion. Drafts had to be cut off.

An unvaried ceremony preceded each lecture or reading. Copey would draw up his chair and look quizzically from right to left. He would single out some unsuspecting student and say, "You haven't been to hear me read in some time!" The accusation was invariably correct and the student would blush and stammer an embarrassed apology. Then Copey would look at the desk light and shake his head in disapproval. After a few minutes of unsuccessful tampering, someone would be called to help. Then he would look up accusingly —"Has someone been smoking in this room? It is absolutely forbidden to smoke." He would look over to the window and ask, "Isn't there a draft coming from that window?" All the while he would fumble with his books, as if he did not know what he was planning to read. Actually, he had his little list all in proper order carefully prepared in advance.

When he finally began to read, all these pretensions and personal idiosyncrasies would be forgotten. He was a small man but had a magical, organlike voice. His perfect enunciation and his keen sense of dramatic timing enhanced every word and line. His readings have been recorded and each time I visit Cambridge I spend a little time in the library recording room. Like nothing else those readings carry me back over forty years to the days when I first heard Copey bring alive the Book of Ruth or a Kipling story.

Because of his weak eyes and the notoriously bad handwriting of undergraduates, Copey insisted that his students read their themes to him. I have always remembered what he said to me after I read to him what he called "the pledges of your genius"—"Very interesting, Hans von Kaltenborn-Stachau, *Hochwohlgeboren!* Now let us turn this over and write: 'If I could write as well as I can speak, I would soon become a successful author.'" My later career has vindicated his judgment of the comparative distinction of my writing and speaking. Extemporaneous speaking has always come far more easily to me than any kind of writing.

Copey once helped me abridge a short story called "Gentlemen, The King!" into a dramatic short speech for delivery in Harvard's annual Boylston Oratorical Contest. When my turn came to deliver the speech, my memory went blank after the first few lines. After what seemed to me a ghastly pause, I ad-libbed the rest of the story in my own words. Immediately after finishing I had to rush off to make a speech in Boston and felt happy to have a good excuse to leave the hall. Next morning when I picked up the *Harvard Crimson* from under my door, I was utterly stunned to read that I had been awarded the first prize. This undetected bit of extemporaneous oratory helped develop a confidence in extempore speaking which has been a great asset ever since.

Copey was truly a wonderful and generous teacher. He was crotchety to a degree and it wasn't always easy to tell when he was putting on an act, but he spared no pains to help young aspiring writers improve their work and to get it placed. He kept up a brisk correspondence with numerous editors and publishers, urging them to consider the work of this or that young student. He was always ready with constructive suggestions and encouragement.

As sometimes happens with great teachers who are not great scholars, Copey was not always well liked or respected by his colleagues. He did not have a Ph.D. Degree and he didn't want one. Nor had Copey written much for publication. A short biography of Edwin Booth and an occasional magazine article were about all. I took down in shorthand and later typed out for him some of his lectures on Johnson and his circle, but I don't know whether he carried out his intention to have them published. As a teacher, he made a lasting impact on his students. He had a rare knack for stimulating young men to read good books. Any teacher who can inspire his students to reach out for themselves into the world of literary masterpieces is assuredly a good teacher. Copey's enthusiasm for the best in good writing was contagious. Personal contact with such a man is a precious experience because the born teacher instinctively teaches in all he says and does. Copey was a master of that conversational art which is the essence of the Socratic teaching method. Unfortunately, in our overcrowded educational factories we seem to have less and less time or tolerance for such teaching. These days college youths miss a lot that we used to take for granted in what is now called Harvard's Golden Age.

Of all the Harvard professors of my time, William James seemed to me to combine the best features of the practical world and the academic world. He had a wonderfully catholic, curious, and inquiring mind. He was probably the most genuinely open-minded person I have ever met. There was no aspect of human activity that did not interest him. He was always willing to explore any new avenue of belief, to experiment with it and to test it. He was always responsive to something that might open a new door to knowledge. He appealed to me as a romantic adventurer in the realm of ideas, eagerly hospitable to new thoughts. For example, he was keenly interested in the famous spiritualist medium Eusepia Palladino. She was invited to Cambridge so that James and others might investigate her theories about the spirit world. As always, William James was open-minded about possible contacts with the spirit world. When others said flatly that she was an impostor, James said, "I don't know and I should like to find out." At a carefully controlled séance, the German psychologist, Hugo Münsterberg, then at Harvard caught her in the act of ringing a bell with her naked toes. As the result of this exposure, a current jingle in the Harvard Yard ran as follows:

Eenie, meenie, minie moe
Catch Eusepia by the toe
If she hollers, that will show
James' doctrines are not so.

Even those who laughed at the occasional credulity of William James revered him as a delightful human being, a great psychologist, a remarkable writer of clear, pregnant, expository English, and the exponent of a pragmatic doctrine that has made a real dent in the history of philosophy.

Many people have given too literal an interpretation to the Jamesian doctrine, "That is truth which works," one of those illuminating but sometimes dangerous phrases for which James is famous. Later philosophers have challenged his pragmatism as being too materialistic. James was a deeply spiritual and truly religious human being who helped me sense my relation to God and my personal responsibility to my fellow human beings. Experience should be the true test and experience comprises a wide variety of human activity. William James rightly felt that pure theoretical speculation untested in the realm of practical experience was too often worthless. He realized that much philosophical debate is merely abstract argument between two equally unrealistic theories.

I had the privilege of several visits at the home of William James while I was at Harvard and remember riding with him in an open trolley car from Boston to Cambridge. He always had the gift of striking expression. On this occasion, he told me that he thought we lived in a "megaphonic era." By this he meant that everything was exaggerated in sound, in importance, and in appearance. He pointed to the glaring headlines of the newspapers being read by our fellow travelers in the trolley. He called my attention to the exaggerated claims made by advertisers on the trolley car signs and on the giant billboards we passed. He called ours a megaphonic world even before the days of radio and loud speakers and a myriad other such mechanical devices through which we are accosted night and day by unseen sounds and voices coming from nowhere and everywhere so that silence has become one of man's most appreciated blessings.

In my senior year I was a member of the last class William James gave at Harvard. My complete stenographic notes on some of the lectures on pragmatism have been used by several students of philosophy. When James retired from teaching, we devoted an entire issue of the *Harvard Illustrated Magazine* to him. The number was filled with appreciative essays contributed by his various colleagues. Bliss Perry wrote on "James, the Master of English"; Josiah Royce wrote on "James, the Philosopher"; and George Santayana wrote on "James, the Teacher." This issue received attention not only in the United States but from readers in many countries outside the United States where James was known and loved. It became necessary to make several reprints of this particular James issue. He wrote me a very gracious letter of appreciation in which he used these memorable words: "I have tried all my life to be good, but have only succeeded in becoming great."

Professor Hugo Münsterberg, who caught Madame Palladino by the toe, had come to Harvard shortly after the turn of the century. He gave courses in philosophy and was primarily known as an experimental psychologist. He was brought from Germany to Harvard by William James. After he arrived, the two men were in constant friendly disagreement. William James once said to me, "If only that fellow Münsterberg would leave philosophy alone and concentrate on psychology which he really understands." Münsterberg, on the other hand, once said to me, "Oh, James and all his pragmatic philosophy! Why doesn't he stick to psychology about which he really knows something!"

Münsterberg was popularizing experimental psychology and stimulated a great deal of interest in the subject with his books and magazine articles. Many American businessmen applied his research to their personnel problems. He was carrying out all sorts of experiments on the speed and nature of human reactions; many had practical relevance to current problems. He devised ways of testing the reaction speed of prospective telephone operators and other workers. He proved to us how the consumption of one glass of beer reduces the accuracy of physical and mental operations. On one occasion he startled his students with a famous experiment during one of his lectures. Without warning, a couple of men burst into the lecture hall, started to shout at one another, ran up to the front of the room, fired a shot, and then ran out as fast as they had come in. Naturally this produced pandemonium. Several students started to run after the two men. Münsterberg quickly called for order and explained that it was only an experiment. He asked all the students to write down exactly what happened. The well-known result was that no two students agreed on the description of what the men wore, what they did, how they acted, or even on just what had happened. It was a perfect demonstration of Münsterberg's theory that under exciting circumstances different witnesses are bound to see things differently. There were several famous criminal cases in those days where he was called in as an expert to testify on the fallibility of witnesses. Experiments of this sort and Münsterberg's outside activities did not please some of the more conservative Harvard professors. There was a good deal of jealousy about his position and particularly about his publicity. Ever since the time of

Socrates and probably even before, teachers who have been popular with their students and successful in the nonacademic world have run into trouble with their colleagues and Professor Münsterberg was one of them.

He died in 1916. His last years were rather blighted by the anti-German sentiment that developed against him after the outbreak of the World War. He had tried so hard to develop friendly relations between Germans and Americans and was tragically disappointed to see his hopes disintegrate under the tensions of the war. It was at Münsterberg's home and at the parties of the Deutscher Verein which he attended that I first met my classmate Ernst Hanfstaengl, who later became notorious as the friend and supporter of Adolf Hitler. "Putzi," as we called him, was president of the Deutscher Verein while I was vice-president. He played the *Neffe* and I the *Onkel* in Schiller's famous play *Der Neffe als Onkel.* Putzi used to point out to me the importance of the social clubs at Harvard. He always went with the "right people" but never achieved his ambition of making one of the exclusive final clubs.

Although the academic life in those days was rather separate from the main stream of practical life, there was an increasing tendency of college professors to participate in outside affairs. Some professors were even considering running for political office in Boston and Cambridge, a new and daring thought.

There was talk of Harvard's establishing a School of Business Administration. The idea that Harvard should train men for practical affairs was also a revolutionary concept. Another issue was how much Harvard professors should write for current and popular magazines. Economic professors like Taussig had always written scholarly articles for economic journals, but popular exposition was far less common. Within the academic profession, there was considerable contemptuous criticism of those professors who expressed their findings in popular magazine or newspaper articles. These critics maintained that Harvard professors should only write what could stand the test of scholarly examination over a period of time. They opposed popularization as vulgar and unscholarly. The standards of the outside world were too low for men of Harvard. The academic and the real worlds were separate and should remain apart. But those who voiced such thoughts were rapidly becoming a minority. The Harvard of my day was beginning to feel itself in the world.

7

DURING MY JUNIOR YEAR AT HARVARD, I WAS LUCKY enough to secure a job as secretary to Professor William H. Schofield of the Comparative Literature department. He was going to spend several months during the fall and winter of 1907-08 in Germany as an exchange professor from Harvard and engaged my services as teacher of German and overseas secretary. I welcomed this break in the regular college routine and at the University of Berlin took Professor Schofield's course in comparative literature so as not to fall too far behind at Harvard.

In 1907, Berlin was a wealthy, gay capital, devoid, so far as I could see, of any outstanding problems. There was a great deal of entertaining and much to see in the world of art, music, and the theater. As before, I found the attitude toward Americans friendly but questioning. We were still regarded as rather crude, materialistic, and ignorant. Few Americans were concerned about European affairs. The cabarets that featured political satire always included a skit which lampooned the American businessman and poked fun at our cultural standards.

The Germany I saw that year was enjoying unprecedented prosperity. The military atmosphere was omnipresent but the Germans did not feel then that war was coming in the near future. Several recent crises had been overcome. While the Germans saw England as a commercial rival they did not believe that the British would side with the French in any war of revenge. The Anglo-French entente had not yet ripened into a full-fledged alliance. The Germans for their part seemed sincere in their desire to live at peace with France. After all, they had Alsace-Lorraine. There was no talk of aggression toward France. Many Germans regretted the Kaiser's belligerent gestures but seemed convinced that the Chancellor and the *Reichstag* would curb his indiscretions. The antiwar, moderately socialistic Social Democratic party was forging ahead. It had become the most powerful single political party in Germany and its influence in the *Reichstag* was steadily increasing. By 1912 the Social Democrats won more than a third of the popular vote cast in Germany. Its antiwar propaganda reached millions of German workers. It was widely believed throughout Europe that the antimilitarist Social Democrats could check the German militarists. But in 1914 the Social Democrats and the German workers forgot their antimilitary education. The call of country and popular enthusiasm swept them into supporting the Government's war policy.

Soon after our arrival in Berlin in 1907, Professor Schofield and his wife were invited to attend a reception at the Kaiser's Palace. This was an elaborately formal affair and necessitated much advance preparation. The Schofields took special lessons in court etiquette. Their teacher was a dignified elderly baroness who made a specialty of instructing those who were making their first bows at the palace. We had several rehearsals in our hotel and I assisted by playing the part of the Kaiser. Under the direction of the Baroness the professor and his wife repeatedly and with great dignity approached my august person and made proper obeisance. My histrionic talents may have helped put the professor and his charming

wife into the proper mood; anyway the court reception was a great success.

The most important thing about this trip was that I met the woman who was to become my wife. The meeting took place on the German steamer that carried me back to the United States in January, 1908. A mutual friend in Berlin had given me a letter of introduction to a Baroness von Nordenflycht, wife of the German Consul General, then stationed in New Orleans. She was returning to America with her two daughters from a visit to Constantinople. It was the twenty-year-old daughter Olga who caught my fancy. Her blond beauty, her agile mind, and her cosmopolitan background made such an immediate appeal that I resolved on the first day of our meeting to make her my wife. I had to prepare for and pass my examination in Professor Schofield's Berlin course in comparative literature on the steamer—so my heart was torn between love and books. But I managed to make a proper division of my waking hours since I passed the exam and also won a definite, though unspoken response from the blue-eyed Baroness. My father had met my mother on a similar ocean crossing and I never had the slightest doubt that I had met the woman I wished to marry. But I was still in college and had no money with which to support a wife. I also suspected that an immediate application to her mother might result in a refusal. So, having done my best to win her heart without asking for her hand, we parted rather sadly with a firm agreement to correspond.

In order to marry as soon as possible, I resolved that immediately after my graduation from Harvard I would seek a job that would enable me to save some money. Thanks to the friendly intervention of the Harvard Appointments Office, I was recommended to John Jacob Astor, the well-known New York millionaire, as just the man to prepare his son Vincent for Harvard. My job was to coach him for his entrance examinations to Harvard, some of which were still a year away, and to look after him during a trip to Europe.

It was truly a well-paid lark of a job, though I felt a little uneasy about it, like Faust who sold his soul to Mephistopheles to taste forbidden pleasures. For the first time in my life,

I learned how a few fabulously rich Americans lived in the preincome tax era. We spent a few days at Rhinebeck at the huge Astor estate on the Hudson. I dined on culinary masterpieces prepared by a French chef. I enjoyed viewing the Hudson from the deck of a quiet electric launch and riding around the large estate with Vincent in his water-cooled Franklin automobile. But I never felt altogether comfortable when awakened each morning by the impeccable English butler who intoned the phrase: "Good morning, sir, your bath is drawn."

I was placed in charge of finances for the European trip. Vincent and I had some differences on what should be spent because I found it hard to waste even the Astor money on first-class railroad tickets and luxury suites in hotels. Vincent soon taught me that we could have a compartment all to ourselves for tutoring purposes by a judicious tip to the conductor, and that there is always room in a hotel for those who know how to ask and who can afford to pay. For the first time, I saw Europe as a rich American tourist. Ritz hotels were a combination of luxurious appointments and services I knew little about. In Paris a single meal for Colonel Astor, Vincent, and myself cost more than I spent for food in a month at Memorial Hall in Cambridge—but it was good. The opera from an orchestra chair seemed quite different from what I had seen when I was backstage as a "super."

On the whole Vincent and I got along fairly well. He didn't object to a certain amount of study and I remembered President Eliot's maxim that "Most profit grows where is most pleasure taken." But I was almost frightened at the ease with which I learned to spend money as befitted an American Astor. We reached an impasse only once in Amsterdam when he wanted to buy a large dog that had caught his fancy. Only the fact that I held the purse strings enabled us to continue without the complications incident to carrying a huge animal around Europe.

At Frankfurt, Germany we saw for the first time the flight of a heavier-than-air plane. The historic flight in 1903 at Kitty Hawk had received scant notice and had escaped my attention altogether. At this German air show we saw small planes racing around a track and every now and then one got off the ground for a few seconds at a time and it was a real thrill each time they rose. Here, too, I faced a great temptation. A German engineer friend said that for fifty dollars he could get all three of us the right to participate in a balloon race. Vincent was eager and so was I, but my conscience forbade letting him take any unnecessary risks.

Once back in the States, Vincent passed several of his entrance examinations for Harvard and I was asked to continue his preparation for the others. John Jacob Astor was leaving for a cruise to the Caribbean on the Astor yacht "Nourmahal" and I was to tutor Vincent on the trip. I agreed to go if I could leave the yacht when it reached its southernmost port in the Caribbean. I was anxious to get to Rio de Janeiro where the Baron von Nordenflycht was now the German Consul General. I had managed to save a thousand dollars of my Astor income and was ready for marriage.

Olga and I had been corresponding as we promised, and we were both fully aware that ours was more than a fleeting shipboard romance. Before leaving New York I wrote my beloved a formal offer of marriage, outlining my prospects. I asked her to cable to one of the yacht's prospective ports of call a one-word reply—Yes, No, or Maybe.

We stayed briefly off Havana, the first stop, and then sailed around to the southern part of the island. For the first time I had contact with the clear, warm water, the blazing sun, and the rich fauna and flora of the tropics. It was a new kind of thrill. The yacht dropped anchor at the small town of Cienfuegos. There we spent several days and I learned something about the pressures and temptations that beset a rich American. With the appearance of the luxurious yacht, all the townspeople realized that here was a heaven-sent opportunity. All sorts of promoters sought to sell Colonel Astor this or that, or they tried to persuade him to invest his money in some particular project.

American millionaires are usually considered fair prey not only at home but particularly when they venture abroad. It seems almost impossible for people to approach them honestly in human relations. Few people can meet the wealthy without banishing from their mind the thought that somehow they can turn the meeting to their own personal advantage. The rich are lied to, cajoled, flattered, misunderstood, and abused—rarely treated as the normal human beings they are. Their possession of wealth colors every human relationship with those who are less well off.

My particular job on this cruise was to prepare Vincent Astor for the Harvard entrance examination in English literature. Among the books with which he was supposed to be familiar was Dickens's *Tale of Two Cities.* Vincent flatly refused to read the book so I sometimes followed him around the yacht vainly seeking to arouse his interest in poor old Dr. Manette. Poor young Vincent tried to escape to a hammock on the upper deck but I soon was by his side reading away. I told him that his father paid me to do a job and somewhere, somehow I was going to do it. My persistence wore Vincent down. He soon learned that the best way to get rid of me was to yield and listen to my reading.

From Cuba we went on to Jamaica where we stopped at Kingston. Along the way we fished for sharks. They were caught by baiting a large hook with a good-sized piece of pork and reeling them in by means of a winch. The Botanical Garden in Kingston was the first place where I saw tropical flowers at their luxuriant best. A small British cruiser in the harbor exchanged courtesy visits with us and Colonel Astor invited some of the officers for dinner. He warned me that it would be my duty to entertain them after dinner. They entertained themselves, largely by drinking the Colonel's liquor and singing soulful solo ballads—while the Colonel slept.

We next cruised along the south shore of Haiti and anchored off what seemed to be a deserted section of coastline. We rowed ashore for a swim on the lovely beach and to get a change from the rather cooped-up quarters on the yacht. While we were swimming and enjoying ourselves on the beach, a group of fierce-looking armed men on horseback suddenly appeared. They surrounded us brandishing their rifles. I imagined that these were some sort of pirates or bandits who had heard about the Astor yacht and planned to hold us for ransom. They spoke no English so I tried French which they understood. They explained that they assumed we were revolutionary gunrunners. They thought we were planning to smuggle rifles ashore to help promote a native uprising. Nothing I could say in my best salesman's French convinced the leader that we were on a tourist cruise so we finally sent him out to the yacht where he made a thorough investigation. This convinced him that we had no interest in Haitian politics and after a drink or two he departed in a most amiable mood.

We also stopped at the Dominican Republic where we saw the remains of the first colony established by Christopher Columbus. The local townspeople at Trujillo, then Santo Domingo, tried to persuade Colonel Astor that he should invest some of his millions in establishing a large resort hotel. But the Colonel was unimpressed with the proposition. Instead, like any other tourist, he invested in a hardwood souvenir cane which he presented to me and which I still own.

When we left Dominica, the yacht got into the midst of a tropical storm. This proved a most uncomfortable experience. The "Nourmahal" was not built for heavy weather. She rolled on her beam-ends and pitched violently. Everything was closed down tight and we suffocated in the small unventilated cabins. I spent most of my time on deck where I had myself lashed to a mast to keep from being swept overboard.

The "Nourmahal" finally reached Ponce, Puerto Rico, having put up her sails to supplement a failing coal supply. There we rode out the rest of the storm at anchor. When we finally got ashore we learned that the yacht had been reported missing. The American newspapers carried stories reporting that all on board had been lost at sea. We issued denials but not in time to prevent the papers from printing our obituaries. The *Brooklyn Eagle* carried a flattering notice about my incipient career which made me hope they would raise my pay when I resumed my job. The news of my possible death had also reached Rio de Janeiro and my beloved Olga told me later that for a week she refused to go swimming in the same body of water that might have claimed my life.

San Juan, Puerto Rico, was the farthest point south the Astor yacht planned to visit and there I boarded a German steamer headed for the Virgin Islands. I had to move to a Dutch, an English, and finally a Brazilian ship to get down to Rio de Janeiro, my ultimate destination. During this whole period, I had received no word in reply to my marriage proposal. I had sent frequent letters and cables following my original proposal but received no answer. At the island of Barbados I had just one hour between boats. The captain of the Booth liner, which was to take me to Pará at the mouth of the Amazon, wouldn't promise to wait for me, but I engaged a boat with six sturdy rowers to hurry me to shore. I raced to the American Consulate where I was sure I would have some word from my beloved. To my dismay I learned that only the day before the obliging Consul had returned a batch of letters addressed to me back to Brooklyn. Thus, I still did not know whether or not my offer of marriage had been accepted. So it was in an agonizingly uncertain state of mind that I continued my trip to Rio. When my Brazilian coastal steamer finally reached Victoria, only a short distance from Rio, I advised Olga by telegram of my impending arrival and asked her to be sure to leave word for me with the American Consul. In my imagination I pictured her aristocratic father refusing to countenance marriage with an impecunious American and began to wonder whether I could manage an elopement.

As the ship finally neared the dock in Rio I became more and more nervous. Her presence at the dock would be a definite affirmative indication. She was not there. Things looked bad but I consoled myself with the thought that I could win her in spite of her parents. My last hope for mail was at the American Consulate and that is where I went immediately after registering at a hotel. When I called for mail, I was told once more that it had been forwarded this time to the German Consulate. Just as I turned to leave, the consular clerk called out: "Why here is the German Consul General." He introduced me to Olga's father, Baron von Nordenflycht whose greeting was courteous but casual. His reserved attitude made me wonder whether his daughter had even told him about my marriage proposal and he gave me no hint on how matters stood. He said that his wife and daughter were at the German Consulate and asked me to accompany him there.

That walk over to the Consulate was a harrowing experience. The Baron gave absolutely no indication whether I would ever become his son-in-law. In turn, I was noncommittal since I had no idea how much or how little he knew about my intentions. As we walked along we discussed the beauties of Rio de Janeiro and he pointed out the various points of interest. We never deviated from this casual conversation and entered the German Consulate fifteen minutes later. There in the office were Olga and her mother. Our greetings were friendly but formal. Nobody made a decisive move. Finally Olga's mother could stand it no longer. "Aren't you going to kiss the poor girl?"

Noting my hesitation she asked in amazement, "For heaven's sake, didn't you get the cable with Olga's answer?"

I shook my head—"What did it say?"

"She said 'yes,' " they all shouted together.

For a moment I swallowed hard and caught my breath. Then I regained enough composure to give Olga a kiss and an embrace to seal my engagement. As it turned out, I had been engaged for six weeks without knowing it. Her many cables and letters had all missed me beginning with the one that said "Yes" which had reached New York after I left. Olga and her mother had met the boat, but because of confusion about the time of arrival I was already en route to the hotel.

For the next few weeks we spent a most happy time together exploring Rio and attending all kinds of parties and festivities. Her parents had given full approval to our marriage and we planned to have the wedding take place in Berlin before the end of the following summer.

With a new sense of responsibility, I returned to New York to resume my job on the *Eagle* and add enough to my savings to take my bride on a honeymoon trip and establish a home.

8

THE BROOKLYN EAGLE SHOWED ITS APPRECIATION OF my Harvard diploma by raising my salary. When I left for Harvard, I was earning twenty-five dollars a week. Now I was to earn forty dollars. I was assigned to an editorial desk and my prospects for advancement looked good.

I awaited the day of my marriage impatiently and when the time came I was off for Europe once more, this time to fetch home my bride. There were more legal formalities involved in getting married than I had imagined. All sorts of papers and licenses were necessary. In those days passports were not required for foreign travel and I had been able to cross from country to country without having to identify myself. However, when I first applied for a marriage license in Berlin I was refused because I lacked the necessary documentation. It was no easy matter for an American to marry a German girl without the proper documents. The punctilious German official at the license bureau demanded a birth certificate, a baptismal certificate, citizenship papers, and a health certificate. I had a baptismal certificate and that was all. Fortunately, my uncle on my mother's side, the senator in Bremen, came to my rescue and provided affidavits which, after much headshaking, the authorities decided to accept.

The marriage ceremony itself was most impressive. My cousin Georg von Kaltenborn as my best man was a most imposing figure in his fancy guardsman's uniform. There were quite a number of people in attendance at the handsome Kaiser Wilhelm Gedaechtnis Kirche in Berlin. I was much impressed with my own and the bride's importance when the Associated Press correspondent in Berlin considered the occasion sufficiently important to warrant sending back a cabled account of the wedding. As is the custom at German weddings, the pastor who married us made a speech at the ceremony. We had visited him a few days earlier to give him a little biographical data. He pointed out that we had met on shipboard as my father had met his wife. He dwelt dramatically on my long trip to South America to become engaged and on my long trip across the ocean to be married. We represented, he said, an international union that spoke well for the peace of the world.

On the day following the wedding, my wife and I attended a performance of Goethe's *Faust* at one of the Max Reinhardt theaters. In the lobby we met Professor Hugo Münsterberg, the psychologist with whom I had studied at Harvard and who had attended our wedding the day before. He was surprised to see us attend such a serious dramatic production on the second day of our honeymoon and told us we would lay the foundations for a happy marriage by developing joint intellectual interests.

Our honeymoon trip took us through southern Germany. From Munich we went to Switzerland and then to Italy. I will always remember the experience of coming out of the tunnel through the Swiss Alps upon the smiling plains of sunny Italy. Venice, our next stop, is to European honeymooners what Niagara Falls is to newly married Americans.

There are certain aspects of Venice that one does not hear about in the usual lyric descriptions. One of these is the omnipresence of summer mosquitoes. The first hotel we stopped at was completely infested. With my ingrained instinct for economy, which cropped out even on my honeymoon, I had chosen a small, inexpensive hotel. After one look at my bride's unhappy face, I forgot economy and took her to the bridal suite in one of the luxury hotels. This had the appropriate balcony overlooking the Grand Canal where illuminated gondolas carried singers and instrumentalists underneath our windows. Venice was the fitting climax to our honeymoon trip. From nearby Genoa we sailed back to New York.

My bride and I had scarcely settled down in Brooklyn when one of my dreams was realized. I was appointed Washington correspondent for the *Brooklyn Eagle*. Chauncey Brainerd, the *Eagle's* longtime capital reporter, had been called back to the home office to become city editor. This appointment flattered and pleased me. I have always felt that the principal Washington correspondents are the elite of the newspaper profession.

The Lame Duck Session of Congress was under way in December, 1910, when I arrived in the capital. This was the second year of the Taft administration and the initiative had shifted from the presidency to Congress. In the election of 1910, many of the Old Guard Republicans had lost. Progressive Democrats were coming to the fore. The long reign of "Uncle Joe" Cannon was at end and he yielded his power and authority in the House of Representatives to a Democrat.

In those days the Washington correspondents had little direct contact with the White House. There were no White House press conferences and few press releases. The process of news dispensation by government agencies had only begun. Some press releases were sent to the correspondents' offices but these were primarily texts of speeches or certain factual information. The modern machinery of public relations and publicity representatives was virtually nonexistent. Press conferences and publicity cocktail parties were few.

My primary job according to instructions from the *Eagle* was to cover the activities of the Brooklyn representatives and New York senators. Coverage by most papers at that time was more local and provincial than it is today. In recent years, there has been increasing emphasis on national news.

This is also due to the fact that in 1910 the individual states had a far more powerful position vis-à-vis the federal government than they have today. Now we take the vast powers of the federal government for granted. In 1910 state affairs were often considered more important than national affairs.

Many people felt that Uncle Joe Cannon, as speaker of the House of Representatives before his power was curtailed, held a position of greater importance than President Taft. He certainly had much more control over legislation than Taft. He had a direct personal relation to every legislative proposal that came before the House. President Taft's prestige was never high with Congress and there was no close liaison between the Hill and the White House. There was a more rigid insistence on the separation of powers than there has been since. The necessity of maintaining a proper balance between administration and legislation was constantly emphasized. There was less stress on collaboration.

Theodore Roosevelt, by virtue of his dominant, vital personality, had maintained a more personal relationship with Congress. He summoned to the White House those legislators whom he wished to influence. This more personal type of government provoked a reaction away from executive dominance toward legislative dominance. It was generally felt that Theodore Roosevelt had meddled too much in matters that were not his direct concern. There was considerable resentment of the vigorous but not always tactful way in which he pursued his ends. He was a president who excited almost as much violent opposition as loyal support. Throughout his presidency there was constant debate as to the respective rights of the President and Congress. This did not occur during the Taft administration. I soon became aware of the tremendous importance of the personality of the President in determining the relations among the different branches of the government. Personal vigor and aggressive action by a President could easily weight the balance of power.

As the result of my first contacts in Washington, I was not particularly impressed with the general quality of the chosen representatives of the people. Like many others who see

Congress in action for the first time, I expected too much and hence was disappointed. Senator William E. Borah was probably the most outstanding orator in Congress and one of the ablest legislators. His oratory was at once intellectual and emotional. He had a fine command of language and was a striking personality. His colorful and heavy voice possessed a ringing, penetrating quality. An important speech by Borah was an event that would attract a packed gallery. Borah was also a master of debate and repartee. In listening to him, I had the feeling that his brain dominated his heart, whereas with William Jennings Bryan, it was the other way around.

This Lame Duck Session of Congress in the winter of 1910 was not productive of many dramatic news stories. One less-than-world-shaking interview I wrote up was with a marcel hairwave expert who had his salon near the *Eagle* office on Fourteenth Street. He told fortunes by feeling the texture of his clients' hair and enjoyed a considerable vogue. He claimed that by touching the hair he could tell what part of the country a person came from. He was probably a good student of speech habits.

I also reported some of the stories told on the floor of Congress. On one occasion, senators were debating a minor Pennsylvania claim against the federal government. It dated back to 1830. One opposing senator said that it was like ox-tail soup—and "That's going pretty far back for soup." The *Congressional Record* reported "Laughter!"

9

I HAD BARELY SETTLED DOWN TO WASHINGTON LIFE when, such being the vagaries of the newspaper business, I was summoned back to Brooklyn. Chauncey Brainerd did not like his job as city editor and wanted to go back to Washington. To compensate for my disappointment, I was given a job considered by many to be a plum. I was made dramatic editor of the *Eagle*.

From 1911 through 1913 the theater was my beat. I reviewed plays regularly, although I did some extra stories, interviews, and editorials on the side. The Broadway theater was a flourishing business and I was kept busy four evenings a week covering the new plays or revivals. Acting was more demonstrative, less natural and realistic than it is today. Gestures and facial expressions were more exaggerated. David Belasco was the great realist producer. Some of his innovations now commonplace were considered rather daring in those days.

I found that I thoroughly enjoyed only about one in ten of the new plays. And so, to make my work more interesting,

I reviewed all kinds of odd performances by stock companies and amateur groups when they were doing classic plays. The German performances at the Irving Place Theater were nearly always good. Rudolph Christians, the actor-manager, provided excellent performances of German drama. I did my best to encourage organizations like the Drama League which helped support and promote the dramatic art. My regular work also had its moments and enabled me to see memorable performances by such outstanding stars as Mrs. Patrick Campbell, Billie Burke, John Drew, Minnie Maddern Fiske, John Barrymore, and the divine Sarah Bernhardt whose magical voice has, in my opinion, never been equaled, although Katherine Cornell's voice affects me even more strongly, though in a different way.

Together with Dr. St. Clair McKelway, the *Eagle* editor, I attended the gala performance that marked the reunion of Weber and Fields. These two superb comedians had been partners for years before I became dramatic critic. Then they separated and came together years later for one great revival performance with Lillian Russell. I have never seen an audience of old-timers laugh as hard or as long as on that night. Everyone seemed to be renewing a happy experience of long ago which joined audience and performers in nostalgic delight.

Very early in my career as the *Eagle's* dramatic editor, I learned that there is apparently a great difference between criticizing the merits of a play and criticizing the way in which the producer advertises his play. Along with several other New York critics, I had panned Klaw and Erlanger's production of the play *Trail of the Lonesome Pine* which starred June Walker. To my surprise, the producers inserted an advertisement in all the papers which lifted one favorable line from each unfavorable review. From my review in the *Eagle,* they took the two words "good scenery." Thus, by a process of selection, they gave the impression that the play had been well received by the critics. In my next Sunday column I took occasion to select the most condemnatory phrases used by the critics and printed them in a parallel column with those in the advertisement. On Monday, I received an imperious summons from the business office. Klaw and Erlanger who operated many New York theaters had canceled all their *Brooklyn Eagle* advertising. This was a hard blow since the *Eagle* had spent years of effort in fighting for it. The business office suggested that I go to the producer's office and try to set things right. At first I refused—but relented when the business manager agreed to set up an appointment to enable me to explain my position. Mr. Erlanger proved to be both amiable and reasonable. He argued that selecting phrases from reviews was his business and telling the public what I thought about his plays was mine. We discussed this distinction in amiable fashion, and we parted good friends. The advertising was restored. It was a critical situation because Colonel Hester, the owner of the paper, always believed new plays should be merely reported and not criticized and he used the Klaw and Erlanger episode to reassert his point of view. However, I was allowed to keep on with real dramatic criticism.

One night because of a special disaster all *Eagle* staff members were pressed into service. This was when the great ship "Titanic" struck an iceberg and went down with such an appalling loss of life. There was a good boyhood friend of mine from Merrill, Wisconsin, on board. He was Dan Cochran, or, as he was better known, "Dan, Dan, the Popcorn Man." He was a lame cockney Englishman who had somehow drifted to Merrill where he operated a popcorn stand. He was one of the best-known characters of Merrill, full of stories, good-natured, and generous. Thanks to Dan, I developed a lifelong passion for buttered popcorn.

Dan had written me early in 1912 that he was coming through New York on his way to visit relatives in England. He arrived clad in his heavy bearskin coat, which was a necessary part of a Wisconsin winter wardrobe. I put him up at my home in Brooklyn and made arrangements for his round-trip steerage passage. He was on his way back on the "Titanic."

In first class was another man I knew well, Colonel John Jacob Astor, Vincent's father. Both Dan, the popcorn man, and Colonel Astor, the millionaire, were swallowed by the Atlantic. It was a sad business for those of us whose lot it was to report the disaster and compile the names of the dead and missing. We reporters were often the first to notify those whose loved ones were lost. This was the first disaster where the miracle of radio was responsible for saving many lives. Radio gave the time and location of the ship and enabled rescue boats to get to the scene. It was the loss of the "Titanic" that prompted legislation making it mandatory for all ships to be equipped with radio.

Like many young New Yorkers, I, too, had my Greenwich Village period. Then as now intellectuals, artists, writers, poets, and radicals made Greenwich Village their headquarters. There was a Poetry Society where at regular intervals known and unknown poets would read their work or have it read. My wife and I traveled over from Brooklyn to attend these meetings at the National Arts Club in Gramercy Park. When they were over we would adjourn to a Greenwich Village studio or restaurant to continue our discussion. Some poems were sent in anonymously by fellow members. Following the reading, there was much good critical debate. I recall that works of Margaret Widdemer, Robert Haven Schauffler, Conrad Aiken, George Sylvester Viereck, Brian Donn Byrne, Amy Lowell, Carl and Mark Van Doren, and Joyce Kilmer were read. The poems of Joyce Kilmer were just becoming known. His writing was moving and simple. He had a great deal of personal charm, was extremely likable, and sometimes irresponsible. For several summers his family lived near ours on Martha's Vineyard. He had a wonderful imagination and could discuss any topic amusingly and with insight. I will never forget one session at which corpulent Amy Lowell read a poetic and altogether delightful description of herself sitting in a bathtub, watching the water ripple in the sunlight.

Don Marquis and I became good friends during my early days on the *Eagle*. He was an able reporter and was then only beginning to develop his great talent as a humorous writer, which flowered when he began writing his daily column for the *New York Sun.* I will always remember a swim we had together one summer on Long Island. I had lent him a pair of trunks which were too large even for his portly frame. While he was swimming the trunks slipped down and tangled around his legs. He began thrashing about calling for help. I first thought he was joking but soon realized he was in serious trouble. By the time I got him ashore, he had swallowed a good deal of water. When he had recovered from his fright, he delivered a side-splitting commentary on the humiliation of being drowned by a pair of ill-fitting swimming trunks. His sober disquisition on this experience was the most amusing monologue to which I have ever listened.

I like to remember that I helped Donn Byrne, the Irish short story writer, get a reporter's job on the *Brooklyn Eagle.* Donn objected to any kind of routine and sometimes ignored his regular assignment and wrote whatever he pleased. Only a very tolerant and understanding city editor would have kept him on his staff and he and the *Eagle* soon parted company. This was just as well since it forced him to concentrate on fiction, a field in which he achieved immediate success. He began with the pulp magazines but soon his imagination and poetic style won him a more sophisticated audience and lasting fame.

The anarchist Carlo Tresca, whose murder is one of New York's unsolved mysteries, was another colorful personality I remember from this period. He lived in an apartment which abutted on the backyard of our Garden Place house. He was a most charming and attractive person who loved good food, good drink, and good conversation.

Before World War I, anarchism, communism, and socialism were little more than parlor conversation topics. No one took them too seriously. After the war had unleashed the forces of hate, terror, and oppression, discussion of these theories was never the same as in that Age of Innocence.

By 1912 the progressive quality with which Theodore Roosevelt had endowed the Republican party had all but disappeared. The Republicans were following policies out of line with the real needs of the country. They had been in power too long. They had fostered trusts and "money barons" and had often helped the privileged few instead of the needy many. They had fostered the high protective tariff which I always felt had outlived its usefulness. I was a Democrat because I felt that the Republican party represented the wealthier classes and the Democrats represented the workers and that segment of the middle class to which I belonged. Even though President Taft had actually carried out more trust prosecutions than his more voluble predecessor, he could not overcome the stigma of being the leader of the party controlled by big business.

I attended several meetings of the Progressive party during the 1912 campaign and was much impressed by their militant crusading spirit. This was the year of the split within the Republican party between the Taft and Roosevelt forces. "Onward Christian Soldiers" was the theme song of the Progressives and Teddy Roosevelt's famous phrase. "We stand at Armageddon to battle for the Lord" was the party's slogan.

Although I had high respect for Teddy Roosevelt and the men around him, I was even more attracted by Woodrow Wilson and the Democratic party. I had studied Wilson's textbook on American Government while at Harvard and after seeing and hearing him at a Harvard commencement felt that he was a man who combined a superb academic and theoretical background with practical experience as an administrator and politician. He was one of our great authorities on government and had displayed considerable practical ability as an administrator during his term as governor of New Jersey and as president of Princeton. This combination of practical and theoretical knowledge, not often found in those seeking public office, has always seemed to me to be ideal.

While the 1912 campaign was in progress, I joined the Woodrow Wilson Speakers Bureau and made a dozen or so speeches for Wilson. The Democrats hired empty stores in various parts of the city and I delivered vigorous campaign speeches to small and large crowds during the noon luncheon hour.

There was much interest in 1912's three-sided campaign. The many exposures by the muckrakers who emphasized the seamier sides of American political and business life had stirred up the public. The writings of Upton Sinclair, Ida Tarbell, and Lincoln Steffens had shaken complacency. The American public felt that the Republican party had somehow tied itself up too much with the ultraconservative and sometimes venal financial interests. This restless stirring and political ferment contributed to Wilson's victory. But it was the split in the Republican party that seemed to contribute most to the Democratic triumph. In thinking back over the general mood and spirit of the times, I believe that many, perhaps most of those who decided to support Teddy Roosevelt would have supported Wilson if there had been a straight choice between Taft and Wilson. Those who supported Roosevelt supported him because of his progressive ideas and not because of his Republican background.

Foreign affairs played the same minor role in this campaign as in most previous presidential campaigns. There had been war crises in 1905, 1906, and 1907 in the course of the rivalry among the great powers over North Africa and the Balkans, but they seemed of little immediate interest to the United States. Theodore Roosevelt enjoyed playing at intervention but his action aroused little popular interest or support. Everyone expected that sooner or later there would be a war in Europe but no one seemed to worry much about it. We Americans get stirred up when something seems imminent; then, if it does not happen right away, we forget all about it and give the continuing situation far less attention than it deserves. Not until the assassination of the Archduke Ferdinand at Sarajevo in 1914 did our headlines really suggest the imminence of war in Europe.

In January 1914 the *Brooklyn Eagle* took me off the drama desk and sent me on an interim assignment to run the *Eagle's* Paris office. Emma Bullett, the *Eagle's* longtime Paris correspondent, was on her deathbed and someone was needed to look after the office until the *Eagle* was ready to make a permanent appointment.

I had spent many enjoyable evenings at the theater but I was happy to get back to what I felt was my real vocation—dealing with current affairs as reporter and editor. And, of course, I was also happy at the prospect of returning to Paris.

10

In January, 1914, I sailed for Paris with my wife and three-year-old daughter, Anaïs. War was close—you could feel it in the air. Everyone assumed that if war came, it would be a short war. Everyone agreed that no nation could pay for a long war because of the great expense involved in modern armed conflict. We were told by financial experts that a war of more than a few months would bankrupt all of the participants. The fact that wars could be carried on by printing paper money or bonds and letting future generations pay through inflation or repudiation did not seem to occur to anyone. Yet it had been done before.

The press of most European countries did much to inflame nationalistic sentiments. Every diplomatic incident was blown up into "a war crisis." Because the press often exaggerated the importance of the incidents the diplomats found retreat or compromise difficult. This did not facilitate negotiations. Give and take became more difficult politically. Prestige assumed tremendous importance and every nation feared "to lose face" if it failed to insist on having its way.

The sometimes irresponsible and irrepressible public utterances of the Kaiser also did much to fan the flames of latent anti-German sentiment, particularly in France. Every one of the Kaiser's phrases that could be given a bellicose twist, and there were many, was lifted from context and played up in the nationalistic and partly jingoistic French press. Having seen the Kaiser publicly parade in his fancy uniforms, I was not surprised that his strutting lent itself to easy exaggeration. He loved to pose as a military man, perhaps Freudians would explain this as compensation for his crippled arm. This posturing may well have been a species of psychological compensation. I remember how surprised I was when I first saw him and discovered that he was nowhere near as tall or impressive as he had appeared in pictures.

In April of 1914 I paid a brief visit to Germany and was astonished at the extent and thoroughness of the German war preparations. On a visit to the barracks of my cousin's regiment, I found his unit in total readiness for instant action. Every mobilization detail was planned and prepared. The German Army was even then beginning to be motorized and I was amazed to hear my cousin explain that every German unit had its own gasoline depots lined up all the way from Berlin to the French frontier.

In the port cities of Bremen and Hamburg, I found much less enthusiasm for war. The merchants of those Hansa cities realized that war would kill Germany's foreign trade which was the source of their livelihood. Germany had become an integral part of the European economic system and was gaining ground with every passing year. An extensive or long European war, even if Germany won, would dislocate and injure her trade and commerce. Ever since the Napoleonic wars the true interests of international finance and international trade have been on the side of peace. This was expected to militate against the outbreak of any European conflict involving the major European powers. The entire development of capitalist enterprise during the nineteenth century actually contributed to the maintenance of the unprecedentedly long peace between the Great Powers. Such wars as did occur were brief in duration and limited in extent. From 1815 to 1914 the major powers of Europe were at war for a total of only eighteen months. Here, if ever, was a chance for the forces of peace to gain the ascendancy.

By the spring of 1914, the French were beginning to boycott German goods. I mentioned this in a brief dispatch to the *Brooklyn Eagle* but the stories I sent from Paris which dealt with the latest fashions and the doings of various visiting Brooklynites received far greater attention and more space. At home in America, the general feeling was that if France and Germany should gravitate into war it would be strictly a local affair. The Atlantic Ocean still separated us in fact and thought from the serious problems of Europe. There was even an American slogan in those days: "Europe's war, our opportunities." We could and would sell goods and munitions to whatever country was willing and able to pay.

But in those months before the outbreak of war, Paris was still a gay and lighthearted city. The Comédie Française was playing to capacity houses and my wife and I enjoyed happy evenings there. Claude Debussy was playing his new compositions in the concert halls. After one of his piano concerts, I was privileged to exchange a few words with him. He was a charming, shy, and awkward individual, huge in frame, with dark, shining eyes. He conveyed in a strange fashion a certain sense of tragedy. Only a few years later he died, saddened by the futility of the war.

The most thrilling event I witnessed in Paris in early 1914 was the state visit of King George and Queen Mary to President Poincaré of France. It was intended to develop the Anglo-French Entente and accomplished its purpose. The highlight was a gala performance in the famed Paris Opera House, outlined in myriad lights for the occasion. I was privileged to witness the ceremonial entrance of the crown-wearing King and Queen. Preceded by uniformed attendants bearing silver candelabras with lighted candles, they slowly walked up the grand staircase between two rows of officers of the Garde Républicaine who raised their glittering sabers in salute. Paris seemed to need royalty to stimulate her best efforts at pomp and parade.

Aligned against the powerful coalition of the Triple Entente were the Central Powers, Germany, Austria-Hungary, and Italy. Germany was fighting for what she called a "place in the sun" commensurate with her growing industrial and military power. Austria-Hungary feared the Russian challenge in the Balkans and turned to Germany for support. Italy wanted an empire. She was a formal member of the Triple Alliance but maintained an ambiguous one-foot-in-each-camp policy.

Of the two combinations, Germany's Triple Alliance was the weaker. The flexible, shifting balance of power system, which for a hundred years had helped preserve peace, had broken down. A much more powerful and expanding Germany was being surrounded and her imperial ambitions curbed by a superior combination of powers.

I came back to America in June, 1914, two months before the war began. My first Sunday magazine article for the *Brooklyn Eagle* was headlined "Big Powers of Europe Stand Ready for War." The outbreak of hostilities in Europe naturally aroused great interest in the United States. Newspapers began to readjust their staffs and send correspondents abroad. I was made war editor of the *Eagle* with the job of selecting and editing the war news. At that time, the *Eagle* decided to sponsor a series of current events talks in the *Eagle* auditorium which occupied a large part of one floor of the *Eagle* Building. Proof of the growing interest of the American public in war news was the fact that the hall was regularly filled to capacity. Different members of the staff reviewed different aspects of the news and answered questions from the audience. My assignment was to report and comment on the progress of the war. Thus began my career as a regular speaking commentator on world affairs. It was not long before I was offered more speaking engagements than I could accept.

There was a good deal of apprehension during the first months of the European war, particularly in financial and business circles. The stock market dropped until the exchange was closed. The value of sterling fell off and there was a scramble for loans by all belligerents. Part of the huge British investments in the United States were dumped on the market for conversion into sorely needed dollars and this further depressed the stock market. There was immediate fear that large scale foreign loans would commit us to one side or the other. J. P. Morgan and Company, with their natural British affiliations and sympathies arranged for Allied loans in this country. These were viewed as private loans and outside the direct jurisdiction or responsibility of the American Government. It was frequently stated that if Germany wanted to give the same security as Britain, she would also be entitled to loans. But I doubt that any of our major banking houses would have tried to float a sizable German loan. A few German war bonds were sold privately.

In the early months of the war, almost everyone believed that America could and should stay out. From August, 1914 until April, 1917 when we finally entered the war, the continuing debate was over how we could best remain neutral. While the bulk of American loans and sales of goods were to Great Britain, a fair amount in the beginning was also sold to Germany. The amount would have been larger had not the British Navy ruled the seas. I recall the excitement when a German cargo submarine arrived in Baltimore loaded with dyestuffs and other precious German goods which were to be exchanged for nickel and other metals Germany lacked. Our markets were still open to those who could call for the goods and pay "cash on the barrel head." Whoever controlled the seas had access to American markets. We insisted on freedom of the seas for ourselves and demanded the right to travel on the oceans wherever we wanted to go.

One of the outstanding differences between World War I and World War II was the 1914 emphasis on international law. The newspapers were filled with legalistic discussions and interpretations of such international law agreements as the Declaration of London on freedom of the seas. Virtually every college professor who was familiar with international law was making speeches or writing articles and letters to the newspapers. In theory, the laws of war were very specific and relatively humane. Food was supposedly exempt from blockade. To starve out the citizens of another country was considered a violation of international law. The laws of sea warfare provided that when a ship was sunk by an enemy raider, the raiding ship had an obligation to provide for the safety of the passengers and crew.

My war clipping book is filled with articles by editors, lawyers, and judges dealing with legalistic aspects of blockade, freedom of the seas, and contraband. At the time I thought these were significant and important discussions. Today as I flip through these yellowed clippings, I realize what little impact they had on the march of events. In wartime each belligerent makes his own interpretation of international law. Until there is a supranational force to act as referee and to enforce punishment, the law of nations will be violated in the heat of conflict.

The greatest debates in this country naturally centered around the submarine. As a new naval weapon, it was not considered in the previously written provisions of international law. A submarine could not accommodate the crews of the ships it sank nor could it without danger rise to the surface to lend assistance to the victims of its torpedoes. The unexpected power of the submarine was dramatically demonstrated early in the war when three British warships were torpedoed in the English Channel. The German submarines could always elude the naval blockade and from the first they roamed the seas. The submarine nearly became the decisive weapon. It crippled British shipping to the point where the population of the British Isles was within a few weeks of starvation.

Another new weapon that did not fit into the older categories of international law was the mine. Freedom of the seas was a basic tenet and the mine interfered with freedom of the seas. The question arose whether you could lay mines in a harbor for self-protection, and to what extent was it permissible to sow mines in the open seas? The high seas were an open highway on which all ships had a right of way.

Both the submarine and the mine seriously interfered with American interests. We were beginning to develop our foreign trade and were building up a merchant marine. The

German submarine was a definite threat to this development. It was frequently charged that America was on the Allied side merely because it was good business. This did influence our opinion but it must also be remembered that Americans had an instinctive sympathy for the underdog. Germany, in the war's opening phase, was the victorious and the occupying power. It was Germany that had overrun would-be neutral Belgium and northern France. The stories that emanate from an occupied country are never favorable to the occupying power.

For two years after the outbreak of the war, every belligerent country produced books which justified its course of action. There were White books, Blue books, Yellow books, and Orange books that explained each country's entrance into a defensive war and which featured its pacific intentions and actions before the war began. All this propaganda disclaimed responsibility for starting the war and justified whatever had been done during the war. This debate on the war's origins continued for many years. Every month saw new documents and arguments presented by both sides. There were long historical analyses which purported to show the imperialistic and belligerent designs of all the great powers. The Germans discussed at great length the Boer War in South Africa and recalled every atrocity story associated with British imperialism. The British in turn constantly stressed the three wars launched by Bismarck and the brutalities of the Huns. History was rewritten for propaganda purposes.

Because of severed cables and the British blockade it took the Germans much longer than the British to get their propaganda machine operating in the United States. The language barrier created many difficulties and delays. But even after German propaganda was organized it made little headway. The Germans sought to overcome the bad effect on American public opinion of the Belgian invasion by charging that Belgium had made secret military agreements with France and Britain long before the outbreak of war. A special book was published containing photostatic copies of documents found in the Belgian archives. The treaty of neutrality between Germany and Belgium was more than one hundred years old. Bethmann Hollweg, the German Chancellor, was injudicious enough in his final prewar conference with the British Ambassador to call it a "mere scrap of paper." The British exploitation of this treaty violation was most effective.

When Dr. Charles W. Eliot, ex-president of Harvard and an early pro-Allied sympathizer, sought to prove that Germany had a long and infamous record of treaty-breaking by citing past history, Dr. Bernhard von Dernburg, a German publicist, instantly drew up an equally impressive list of treaties that England had violated.

Dr. Dernburg, though a skillful propagandist, could not overcome pro-Allied sentiment. Most of the newspapers that tried to be neutral gave Dernburg space to reply to British charges, but he could not beat back the tide. Since German communications lines had been cut, the bulk of war news and articles came from the Allied side. Later the erection of a powerful radio receiving station on Long Island made it possible to pick up news and military communiqués directly from Germany. The United States government co-operated in the establishment of this station in a genuine effort to maintain neutrality. Most of our leading newspapers printed military communiqués from both the Central and Allied Powers but it was the explanatory and supplementary material written by Americans that affected public opinion. The atrocity stories, most of which were later disproved, had a strong impact on American public opinion. These tales of crucifixions, bayoneted babies, and cut-off hands helped crystallize American sympathy on the side of the Allies. They supplemented the real horrors of submarine warfare. The sinking of the "Lusitania" in May, 1915 was probably the decisive turning point for American public opinion. After that tragedy few voices were raised to defend Germany's conduct of the war.

The presence of Czarist Russia on the Allied side accentuated the original desire of the Americans to remain neutral. Throughout history the Russian and American governments have never been at war but neither have they had warm and friendly relations. We did not enter World War I until Russia had virtually been eliminated as an Allied Power. There always was considerable American antagonism to the Czarist dictatorship. There was strong resentment against the anti-Semitic pogroms which frequently occurred in Czarist Russia. Russia's presence gave the Allied cause a moral handicap in this country. Russia's intrigues in the Balkans were regarded as one of the basic causes for the war.

The Irish Easter Rebellion of 1916 against British rule was another factor that militated against complete sympathy with the Allied cause. The anti-British feeling among our Irish population further stimulated the neutrality arguments. The American Irish were anti-British throughout the war and the stern methods used by the British in putting down the Irish rebellion alienated many Americans from supporting the British cause.

My chief complaint against our wartime newspapers was the practice of featuring relatively unimportant news stories issued by the belligerents for propaganda purposes. Both sides exaggerated their military advances and minimized their retreats. To check on their claims, I kept close track of the progress of the war by pins on a map. When a communiqué spoke of a magnificent advance, I frequently discovered that this so-called magnificent advance was unimportant except as propaganda. In the deadlock of trench warfare, neither side made decisive gains, yet almost every day each side claimed important advantages. It was no easy task to reconcile the conflicting military communiqués. The Germans charged that the Allied communiqués were all lies. The Allies made similar claims. As a matter of clear fact, both sides lied by suppressing essential parts of the truth and there was little to choose between them. Both sides were most truthful when they were winning and did the most lying when they were losing.

During the 1916 Charles Evans Hughes-Woodrow Wilson presidential election I was in charge of the city desk on election night. It was my job to send down brief election bulletins which were then chalked up on the *Eagle's* street bulletin board. The early returns favored Hughes. But to these reports I added a comment, "The election is still undecided" —since neither side had a clearcut majority in the electoral college vote. I also sent down the comment that the votes of several doubtful states could tip the victory to either candidate.

I was about the only person in the *Eagle* office who refused to concede the election to Hughes. The Republican candidate himself had gone to bed that night confident that he would be the next president. Finally late at night after I had sent down one of those bulletins saying the election was still undecided, a group of angry Hughes supporters charged into the newsroom. They demanded I send down "truthful reports." I told them my comments were based on the Associated Press dispatches and that I would stand by them. Fortunately it turned out that my hunch was right and the *Brooklyn Eagle* was one of the few papers on the streets that morning that did not announce the election of Hughes. California, the deciding state, went to Wilson and tipped the scales for a Democratic victory.

It is an interesting sidelight that the Republican candidate was caricatured by the opposition as wearing a German helmet. I remember a talk I had with the German Ambassador, Count von Bernstorff when he told me of his suspicions concerning Wilson's neutrality. I had the definite impression that he favored the election of Hughes. Generally speaking, the pro-Germans did favor Hughes as against Wilson. The Wilson administration was steadily drifting toward war, although it won the election on the slogan: "He kept us out of war." The idea that there would be a sharp change in American foreign policy with a change of administration showed a frequent foreign misconception about American politics. In general, there is no sharp difference between our two major political parties in regard to the main lines of foreign policy. There are differences in emphasis, in degree, and in personalities but few major cleavages.

Until the sinking of the "Lusitania," we were sending almost as many notes of protest to Britain as to Germany, and they were just about as ineffective. The notes we sent to Britain protesting interference with our shipping were more politic and not quite so harsh in terminology. We protested the way in which British ships used neutral flags and especially the flag of the U.S. to escape the Germans. There was a constant interchange of legalistic protests and excuses. The notes to Britain were written for the record and there was no passion behind them.

In February, 1915, when Germany announced the creation of a war zone around the British Isles, we protested vehemently against this violation of international law. Then came the matter of reprisals. These were admittedly outside of international law but were justified on the grounds that the other fellow had started it and they were just getting even.

Both the British and the Germans were violating international law, the Germans by means of submarine warfare and the British with their blockade. The crucial difference was that the British violations concerned property while the German violations concerned human lives. The loss of American lives was the decisive factor. The climax came when the Germans announced the complete submarine blockade of the British Isles. Their note outlined in dogmatic fashion just what American ships would have to do to be recognized as neutral vessels. The order was so blunt and hopelessly undiplomatic that rejection was the only possible answer. What angered Americans most was the order to paint stripes on our ships. These were instantly labeled "prison stripes" and characterized as a humiliating indignity. The stripes were to be of a certain size and color to give American ships access to certain zones designated by the Germans and still remain unmolested. America's response to the German Navy's arbitrary order was to sever relations with Germany in February, 1917.

In January of the same year, Woodrow Wilson had made his famous "Peace without Victory" speech. By this time most Americans agreed that Germany's ultimate defeat was certain. The only question was the length of the war. In the interest of future peaceful relations among the warring powers, Wilson urged a nonvindictive peace. By that time American sympathy for the Allied cause was so strong that Wilson's proposal that Germany should not be totally crushed brought violent reaction. Many American leaders sympathetic to the Allied cause criticized the speech in the most severe terms. The French and British were bitter. Germany's militaristic reply was a brief declaration announcing the resumption of unrestricted submarine warfare.

The Germans never realized that Woodrow Wilson was a sincere idealist devoted to the cause of peace. Their diplomats misunderstood him. It should have been clear that Wilson wanted to play the role of peacemaker between the two warring factions, as Theodore Roosevelt had done in the Russo-Japanese conflict.

Wilson's "Peace without Victory" speech was out of tune with American opinion and widely regarded as pro-German. By the end of 1915, our trade with Germany had dwindled to nothing. From both the economic and moral viewpoint America was committed to the Allied cause. Wilson made this neutral speech in an effort to convince the Germans that he was going to be fair and act as an honest broker in peace negotiations. Even at this late date more skillful diplomacy on the part of the Germans might have kept the United States out of the war and thus led up to a peace more nearly based on the Fourteen Points.

Early in 1917 the Wilson administration decided that the die was cast and began to prepare public opinion for war. We published the famous Mexican note. This document, also known as the Zimmerman note, showed that the Germans sought to use Mexico as a base of operations against the United States in case of war. They tried to enlist Mexican support by promising Mexico a large piece of Texas. Colonel House, Wilson's chief advisor on foreign affairs, was, among other things, a Texan. This Mexican incident coupled with the continued sinkings of our ships and the continued loss of American lives led the United States to declare war in April,

1917. Everyone was convinced our entrance would speed the war's end and bring decisive victory for the Allies.

My own feelings were those of most Americans. Up to 1916 it had not been easy for me to formulate my position. After all my wife's brothers and half a dozen cousins were fighting on the German side. There were many things I loved about Germany. Then as time went on the ruthless way the Germans conducted the war and their stupid diplomacy turned my sympathies more and more to the Allied cause. By the time we entered the war, I was convinced that the Allies should and would win.

There was a great difference in atmosphere between World War I and World War II as regards Germans in the United States and Americans of German descent. During the two and one-half years in which we were neutral many German-Americans openly sympathized with Germany. As a result they fell under suspicion as "hyphenated" Americans. In World War I, the teaching of the German language was banned soon after our entrance. German music was outlawed. German bookstores were closed. I remember the heated debate about the famous song, "Deutschland Uber Alles." This song was interpreted as meaning that Germany should have first place in the world and dominate every other country. Actually, it meant that Germany should have first place in every German heart.

In World War I, the Army hesitated to accept anyone who had German connections. I was especially suspect not only because of my German name and because I had married the daughter of a German diplomat, but because only twenty years before my uncle, Hans von Kaltenborn-Stachau, after whom I was named, had been briefly German Minister of War. I had dropped the von from my name when I left Merrill, following my father's business practice of substituting a capital V. At Harvard they insisted on restoring the von and I let it stand until my own country entered the war. This gesture did not make me seem less German to the Army authorities whom I approached about enlisting on any basis. They were not even impressed with my top-sergeant's stripes won in the Spanish-American War.

11

My participation in World War I was from the sidelines. I continued as war editor for the *Brooklyn Eagle.* Though the Army did not accept my service offer because of my German connections the *Eagle* management never questioned my loyalty. Once during the heated prewar period Newell Dwight Hillis, pastor of famous old Plymouth Church of which I was for some years a member, delivered an impassioned attack against the *Eagle* for having me, a man of German descent, as its war editor. The *Eagle* stood by me, but to satisfy critics the publisher assigned Simon Cooper a strongly pro-Ally veteran copyreader to work with me. We got along well enough and only disagreed on the relative importance to give to rumors and unconfirmed reports. Our readers got the war news as straight and factual as we were able to present it. The headlines always overemphasized Allied victories and German defeats but this was an inevitable response to public opinion.

For the day-to-day coverage of the military progress of the war the *Brooklyn Eagle* relied on the Associated Press. It was my task to edit these dispatches and to indicate changes in the front line positions on the war maps and also to prepare short bulletins which were posted on the outdoor bulletin boards, then an essential part of every newspaper office. The A.P. wire stories were supplemented by the *Eagle's* feature stories from special correspondents such as Naboth Hedin, Guy Hickok, and Henry Suydam.

Many of the feature stories published by the *Eagle* concerned the activities of Brooklyn men serving in the American Army. Their doings were thoroughly reported while they were in the American training camps. Later when they were sent abroad the *Eagle* followed their overseas adventures. The *Eagle* always felt anything that happened to a Brooklyn man was of prime importance.

In terms of actual large-scale fighting America's participation did not begin until June, 1918. The press dispatches from the front lines gave little indication of the extensive losses suffered by our troops in the closing months of the war. The brief military communiqués reported an unending series of victories but were completely noncommittal on the cost of these victories. I have talked with German officers who told me that American field commanders were more reckless with the lives of their men than the French or British at any period of the war. This was partly due to our inexperience in the face of hardened German troops and partly to American eagerness to demonstrate courage and initiative and to achieve immediate success. The result was that in the closing months of the war we lost far and away the most men on a relatively small sector of the front. It is quite possible to argue that a good part of our losses served no important purpose. It is also debatable whether our losses might not have been smaller had we accepted the French and British pleas to integrate our troops with theirs. General Pershing reflected American public opinion in refusing to accept this suggestion.

Almost from the outbreak of war in 1914 business conditions in the United States improved. By 1917 a war boom was underway. Prices rose steadily. Fortunately for me and many millions of tenants a rent law froze rents at reasonable levels. With our two children, my son Rolf was born in 1915, we were living in a wooden frame house at 85 Willow Street in Brooklyn. It was an old house, long empty, which I had agreed to repair and keep in condition in exchange for a low rent. I accepted several reasonable rent increases but balked at what I considered an unreasonable wartime raise. Much to my chagrin my landlord hauled me into court. It was my first experience in being sued and it turned out to be a happy one. The jury was out for less than five minutes and returned a verdict against the landlord. He was a church deacon and felt so badly about the verdict that I was inclined to be a bit sorry for him. It was also my belief that landlords as a group were in a rather unfortunate position. While other prices rose with few limitations the landlords were held down to their prewar income while their costs were increasing.

There were no drastic food shortages during World War I nor was rationing extensive. We were asked to save food so that more could be sent abroad. Herbert Hoover was in charge of food conservation and we were asked to "Hooverize" our food, which meant saving food as well as chewing food properly so as to derive the greatest nutritive value. There were a great many patriotic campaigns and I participated as a speaker in the War Bond drives. I spoke on street corners and in all sorts of places urging people to buy bonds.

On November 8, 1918 when Roy Howard, general manager of the United Press News Service, cabled from France the first word that the Germans had signed an armistice, I was working on the *Eagle's* war desk. His report was headlined by all papers carrying U.P. service and started a whole series of premature peace celebrations. In checking his dispatch with the latest Associated Press reports I became skeptical. The German delegation which had been given the surrender terms had not had time to get back to the appointed rendezvous on the basis of the distances which I had checked on my war maps. As a result the *Eagle* held out against printing news about the false armistice while the *Standard Union* bulletin board across the street from the *Eagle* building carried a huge announcement of the war's end. Violent arguments developed in the huge crowds that read both the *Standard Union* bulletin and the sober *Eagle* announcement, "Armistice still unsigned." At one point the assistant pastor of Plymouth Church headed an angry crowd that burst into the *Eagle* newsroom and demanded that we announce the war's end. I stood my ground and the *Eagle* management stood by me. It turned out to be a great prestige victory for the Associated Press.

The enunciation of Woodrow Wilson's Fourteen Points in January of 1918 was an important factor hastening German surrender. The Fourteen Points were publicized to the German troops by leaflets and loud speakers. Radio was just being introduced as a means of communication and the American forces made a great point of beaming the Fourteen Points over to the German receiving sets. There is much evidence that this "peace with honor" propaganda helped weaken German resistance. When the Germans did surrender in November, 1918 it was on the basis of those Fourteen Points and the "just peace" they were supposed to represent. All our presurrender propaganda was forgotten when the time came to draw up the Treaty of Versailles.

Many history books now hold that the Treaty of Versailles sowed the seeds of future wars. That may be so. But if Versailles paved the way for Hitler and Company, then the Kaiser and his ruthless conduct of the war paved the way for Versailles. Even before the Germans surrendered there was a strong element in all Allied countries that urged a harsh peace. The British election that followed the Armistice was known as the "Khaki Election" and was conducted in a vindictive atmosphere. "Hang the Kaiser!" was the successful Lloyd George slogan. That spirit of revenge characterized the atmosphere in France and to a considerable extent in this country. It was heightened by the appalling loss of life in the war.

The bitterness against Germany was accentuated by the feeling that the Germans had not really suffered. Their territory had not been invaded or occupied except for East Prussia and we knew little about German food shortages or the large proportion of German soldiers who had been killed or crippled. The resentment against Germany was particularly strong in Belgium and France, the two countries that had suffered occupation. The Fourteen Points and a "fair and just peace" made no appeal to the war-weary and embittered Europeans when it came to dealing with a traditional enemy completely in their power.

When Woodrow Wilson sailed for Europe he was looked upon as a savior. He was the outstanding champion of a League of Nations seen by the peoples of the world as a way of maintaining peace for all time. Knowing of Wilson's devotion to the League idea the hardheaded realists like Georges Clemenceau of France and Lloyd George of Britain managed to get his acceptance of the harsh terms of the Versailles Treaty in exchange for their acceptance of the League.

The sad story of Wilson's failure to get America into the League should be a lesson to future presidents. Wilson could have secured the acceptance of the League by the U.S. Senate if he had been willing to accept a reasonable compromise in the language of the Covenant. We know now that the proposed reservations could have been accepted without interfering with the League's work. What a strange paradox that Wilson who had made so many far-going concessions to foreign diplomats at Versailles would make none to American senators in Washington.

Wilson's inflexibility on phraseology led to the rejection of the League by the Senate. The Republicans had accepted the spirit of the League but were not willing to accept Article X which bound members to guarantee one another's territorial integrity and political independence. Wilson called this the heart of the Covenant and would not accept a reservation with regard to the implied obligations. As it turned out every member of the League felt free to make its own interpretation of the obligations it assumed in signing the Covenant.

The rejection of the League by the Senate was the first of several unfortunate postwar developments. We had a serious "Red scare" and there was a concerted effort to deport all "dangerous" aliens. The Russian Revolution in the spring of

1917 which brought the moderate Alexander Kerenski regime to power was greeted with friendly enthusiasm. There was justifiable hope that, with the overthrow of the Czar, Russia's democratic forces would maintain control. Americans never approved the Czarist regime, but they felt almost equal antagonism toward the ruthless revolutionists who overthrew the Kerenski regime in November, 1917 and set up the Communist dictatorship. Our newspapers featured the violence and bloodshed that followed. This helped develop a wave of hostility toward Communists and communism. It was climaxed by news of the execution of the Czar and his family.

Years later I visited the Sverdlovsk cellar where the Romanoffs met their death. My visit was in the company of a Bolshevik leader who said he saw them die. He told me that the hysterical weeping of the women so unnerved the execution squad that half the shots went wild and he pointed out the bullet holes high up on the wall. He claimed to be one of the few who knew where the bodies had been buried.

Premier Georges Clemenceau for a long time advocated what he called a *cordon sanitaire* to isolate Soviet Russia and keep the virus of Bolshevism from infecting the rest of Europe. It was to prevent the spread of Bolshevism into the United States that Attorney General Palmer began his indiscriminate raids. Union leaders and liberals were arrested and given little chance to defend their reputations. The Attorney General used war powers to exploit the fear of Communist penetration. The innocent suffered with the guilty. Foreigners were particularly suspected and the unfair treatment some received shows what can happen in a democratic country once a hysterical witch hunt really gets underway.

Although America turned thumbs down on joining the League of Nations this country always had a great interest in League affairs. There was a League of Nations Association and Americans played a great role, officially and unofficially at most League meetings. In 1921 I was sent to Geneva to cover the League Assembly's September meeting for the

Brooklyn Eagle. At once I was struck by the extent of American participation in various League activities.

Official and unofficial American observers attended most council and committee meetings. A good many Americans were League employees and some held important positions. The United States was actively co-operating with a dozen different League organizations. To avoid stirring up political controversy at home Washington did not publicize its close relations with League activities.

Foreign correspondents from newspapers all over the world played an important role at the League meetings. Everyone knew that League success depended to a great extent on promotion and publicity so the press was given every facility. It was possible to get interviews with a dozen outstanding world leaders by merely moving from one hotel to another. The League had its own radio station and sent short-wave radio broadcasts to all parts of the world. I served for a short time as consultant for this station and vainly tried to get some showmanship into its programs.

Geneva thus became an international meeting place where all outstanding world problems were discussed. I soon learned how much the informal exchange of opinion among diplomats could contribute to international understanding. The League provided an international friendship house where through informal talks or more formal agreements differences between countries could be settled or a foundation for later settlement could be laid.

My first visit to the League was in September, 1921, as the League was just getting underway. The atmosphere radiated hope and enthusiasm. Eduard Benes, then Czechoslovakia's Foreign Minister, was a great League figure. He once told me that the problems of the League reminded him of tennis, a game we both loved. You were frequently behind, according to the score, but you must learn that this did not count until the final point was played. Being behind did not mean eventual defeat. The score might be love-forty against you and you could still win the game and frequently did. The battle for peace was sure to be hard and long but it would be won in the end. I liked his optimism.

Many people thought that the mere existence of the League would stop war. History proves they expected too much. The danger was that having failed to attain a peaceful world through this first real attempt at uniting against war the nations would give up further efforts.

My own head which had been in the clouds at Geneva cleared up when I visited postwar Germany and France. The emotions of the war were still very much alive. The French hated and still feared the Germans and the Germans rather looked down on the French. The Germans felt that they would have easily defeated the Allies if the United States had not intervened.

In Germany the new republican government established at Weimar was not supported with enthusiasm. Left wing Communists and right wing militarists and monarchists were well organized and active. They took advantage of the unsettled conditions that prevailed throughout Germany. There was widespread disillusion. The fact that Wilson's Fourteen Points had not been translated into the peace treaty was brought up in every conversation. Again and again Germans asked me whether I did not feel guilty because the peace had not been written on the basis of President Wilson's promises to the German people.

Germany's living standards were down at least fifty per cent from the prewar period. There were food shortages of all kinds. The humiliating defeat, the growing inflation and the generally uncertain future made Germans sorry for themselves and unfriendly to all other nations. Germans have never been able to see themselves as others see them. As for the Weimar Republic they regarded it as an enemy creation and refused to give it wholehearted support. The government never recovered from having had to sign the ignominious Treaty of Versailles which imposed impossible reparations and forced Germany to assume the exclusive moral guilt for the war.

Austria was even worse off than Germany. The peacemakers at Versailles redrew the map of Central Europe and doomed Austria to a position of economic hopelessness. The loss of former markets, former sources of raw materials and new tariff barriers contributed to Austria's economic impotence. Inflation began in Austria even before it began in Germany. Austria-Hungary had been a logical economic entity even though a political and ethnic hodgepodge. Postwar Austria could only exist as an independent power in an impossible world where all tariff barriers were eliminated. To feed her people Austria had to import far more than she could export. In dividing up the Austrian Empire the Allies created a political separation which had a logical basis but at the same time they produced divisions that disorganized economic life throughout the heart of Europe.

Vienna appeared to me the saddest city of Europe, perhaps because it had once been the gayest. It was the capital of a nation reduced from sixty million people to six million. The enormous governmental palaces from which the Hapsburg emperors had ruled their turbulent empire were half empty and rundown. There was still architectural beauty, but everything within and without spoke of past glories and present neglect.

Austria was entirely dependent on outside aid. The League gave some aid and we helped with food. I visited installations for the feeding of Viennese children established through American aid. These emergency centers kept thousands of children alive. This American enterprise like so much else in the way of emergency supplies for postwar Europe had been organized by both the Quakers and the Hoover Relief Committee. This aid was well administered and was not misused for political purposes. The Austrian people were genuinely grateful to Americans for the aid they received.

Inflation was still rampant. One American dollar went a long way. The exchange rate was some fantastic sum like seventy thousand Austrian crowns to the dollar where formerly it had been about six to the dollar. Whenever I exchanged dollars I had to wrap up in a newspaper a huge quantity of Austrian paper notes of low denominations.

One of the vivid memories I retain of Vienna in 1921 is of a walk along the Danube one evening. My wife and I came to a bridge and heard a few people cry out. We asked what was wrong. "A man has just jumped into the water!" "Can't we try to save him?" I asked.

"Oh, no" was the sad-voiced answer. "He jumped in deliberately. If a man wants to take his life these days he is entitled to have his way." That was the philosophy of postwar Vienna.

Yet, in spite of it all, the Austrians were still able to laugh and joke. In the cabarets comedians poked fun at political and economic conditions. The Austrians have always taken life more lightly than the Germans. The Austrian attributes to a German the well-known remark, "The situation is serious but not hopeless," while the Austrian says, "The situation is hopeless but not serious." This familiar story underlines an important difference between the two peoples.

There was one man in Vienna whom I particularly wanted to see and that man was Sigmund Freud. His writings had achieved world-wide acclaim and immediately after the war the Freudian doctrines of psychoanalysis were widely discussed in the United States. Dorothy Thompson, who at that time was Vienna correspondent for a group of American papers, helped me arrange an interview with the great psychoanalyst who rarely saw members of the press. He refused to see anyone who did not speak German since he had much cause to complain of misunderstanding and misinterpretation due to faulty translation.

When I came to his comfortable but unostentatious home which was also his office his businesslike secretary told me I could have exactly five minutes. She then ushered me into his presence. He was a handsome man with a high forehead, tall, sharp-nosed, keen, and alert. He seemed to me a man almost devoid of emotion. The moment I met him I felt he was subjecting me to cool appraisal and self-consciously I wondered what complexes he attributed to me. I had read his essay "Reflections on War and Death" and was especially anxious to learn his views on the political and economic consequences of the war. He waved such questions aside and said that he would only talk about his psychoanalytic doctrines. Still I asked him if he were planning to lecture or teach in the United States. "I am not going to America" was his quick reply. "Let those who will, come to me."

Americans in great number were coming to him and he told me of some of the American doctors who were studying with him. I asked him about one man who had attained a good deal of money and publicity in New York by his popular writing and lectures on psychoanalysis. At the mention of this man's name he showed the first sign of emotion. "That man is a thief!" he said. "Did he steal your ideas?" I asked. "My ideas belong to the world and he is welcome to them," he said, "but that man stole the text of two of my articles, combined them into a book and signed his own name to it. I regret to say that under American law that kind of stealing seems to be permitted."

Then he went on in an angry denunciation of fakers who pretended to know something about psychoanalysis and who prey upon gullible men and women. He said that people should only deal with psychoanalysts who had had direct contact and training with him.

The opposition that Freud's ideas on sex and psychoanalysis encountered particularly in the early years seemed to have hardened him into something of an authoritarian. I sensed that he was a man who would brook little opposition and I can well understand his denunciation of former students who developed psychoanalysis in their own way and dared to criticize some of Freud's ideas.

Although he has done much to alleviate human suffering by making possible new cures for mental illness Dr. Freud did not give me on this brief meeting the impression of a sympathetic person. He was altogether curt and businesslike. Later I learned from those who knew him well that behind this brusque exterior he was a most genial and compassionate human being. Certainly he is one of the most outstanding and influential men of our century.

Before returning to the United States my wife and I went to Italy to revisit briefly the scenes of our honeymoon. On the surface Italy gave the impression of having achieved a certain degree of stability. The reports I sent back to the *Eagle* on the basis of this 1921 visit were optimistic in tone. It looked as though Italy had been able to overcome the threat of revolution from the left. Immediately after the war various Communist and Fascist groups—the distinction between them was not always clear—had seized factories in northern Italy and had tried to operate them through workers' committees. When machines broke down or raw materials ran out they asked the original owners to resume control and assure a continuance of their jobs. This failure of communal ownership was widely hailed as heralding the decline of left-wing radicalism. The Italian government felt confident that, having survived these radical uprisings, it could deal with such further problems as might arise. In the Italy of those days not much was heard about Mussolini. He had been a Socialist editor in Milan, who with his Fascisti claimed credit for putting down certain left-wing uprisings, but no one took him very seriously.

On this trip I paid my first visit to the Vatican. My wife was with me and purely through accident became one of the few women to penetrate into the private chambers of the Pope. We had been cleared by the Swiss guards for a previously arranged early evening interview with Cardinal Gasparri, then the Papal Secretary of State. We started walking down some of the endless corridors but since this was an hour when some of the guards were off duty we were soon lost. The great halls were empty and we found no one to guide us. We kept heading into what we thought was the general direction of the office of the Papal Secretary and at the end of a long corridor we opened a door and found ourselves in a beautifully furnished room much more homelike than anything we had seen. We were there but a moment when three Papal guards differently attired from those at the entrance appeared and with stern faces warned us back. They informed us that we had trespassed upon the private apartments of the Pope where no woman is supposed to enter. Quickly they guided us out and one of them made sure that we would not again lose our way. He remained at our side until we reached the Papal Secretary's apartment.

Cardinal Gasparri, a genial corpulent individual, looking for all the world like one of the good-natured monks depicted in many paintings, outlined for my benefit the Pope's wartime efforts on behalf of peace. He had a wonderful sense of humor and saw nothing incongruous in picturing the Pope as walking on a tightrope while the Central Powers were trying to pull him down on one side and the Allies on the other. He pointed out—and this was his purpose in granting the interview—that the United States was in a unique position to help bring peace to the world. The Vatican is equipped with widespread and competent information and intelligence services. The Catholic church leaders have always been quick to recognize shifts in the international balance of power. Cardinal Gasparri was the first statesman in Europe who stressed to me the great new role which the United States would play in the postwar world. Thereafter, many others emphasized the same thing, but not until then had I been led to give serious thought to the wide international significance of America's new position. We were little aware of this in the United States and it took this trip to Europe in 1921 to impress it upon me.

Commenting on the postwar era, Cardinal Gasparri said, "We have peace but no pacification." In parting, the Cardinal complimented President Harding for issuing the call to a general disarmament conference scheduled in Washington for the winter of 1921-22. He saw it as a happy augury for a peaceful world.

12

LIMITATION OF ARMAMENTS WAS A POTENT SUBJECT immediately after World War I. Armaments were held to be one of the major causes of that war. The United States had taken the lead in calling for a general disarmament conference to be held in Washington in the fall of 1921. Also to be considered were certain problems in the Pacific, particularly the territorial integrity of China. All major countries sent representatives who were accompanied by large staffs and a great number of foreign correspondents.

During some of the press conferences held in Washington, which I attended as special conference correspondent for the *Eagle,* I had occasion to watch President Warren Harding in action. He was a handsome man, always genial and friendly, but it soon became evident that he was not too well informed on foreign affairs. He revealed this ignorance when, at one of his meetings with the press, he assumed that the Japanese home islands were included in the treaty restrictions which were being applied to island areas in the Pacific. It remained for the State Department to clear up his mistake.

In this respect the contrast between President Harding and his Secretary of State, Charles Evans Hughes was most marked. Secretary Hughes was the dominant figure of the conference from its inception and displayed a high degree of statesmanship. His conduct as presiding officer reflected great credit on the United States. The attitude of coldness and aloofness that seemed to characterize his public appearances in 1916 had disappeared. If he had run for President after 1922 he would have had a better chance of election.

The disarmament conference was opened with a dramatic United States proposal for a drastic reduction in naval strength. For the first time in history a responsible representative of one of the Great Powers made a specific concrete proposal not only to limit but to reduce armaments. The Hughes proposal involved the scrapping of a certain number of battleships and the canceling of construction on other ships already on the way.

Within this country there was considerable opposition to such voluntary limitation on our naval strength. The United States could well afford to build up its naval strength to a point where it would surpass that of Britain. Many Americans felt that we should build the greatest navy in the world. In 1922 Great Britain was still supreme in naval power. For centuries Britain had been mistress of the seas and for years had maintained a two to one ratio with the next greatest naval power. For Britain to accept parity with the United States was to admit that she no longer held this position. Thus it represented an immediate British concession while it showed us willing to forego our right and our ability to become the world's greatest naval power. Lord Balfour, experienced head of the British delegation, at once accepted the Hughes proposal "in principle" and the conference was off to an auspicious start.

Of all foreign delegations at the conference the British were by far the most skillful in their press relations. They held daily press conferences and always managed to provide factual information for news-hungry reporters. Most of the other foreign delegates and their press representatives were formal and secretive. The British understood the problems of newsmen and went out of their way to provide members of the working press with some kind of a daily story. Without violating any British secrets their press relations officer always managed to dig up something. They were most helpful in providing valuable background information. They had an excellent staff of competent researchers who were always ready to dig up facts, history, and statistics. The British press headquarters thus gave the impression of being primarily an information service and only secondarily a propaganda office.

Some thirty-two Japanese correspondents covered the conference. One of them I noticed, spent twelve hundred dollars on a single cabled report back to Tokyo. As a group they held themselves aloof and were not communicative. Public opinion in Japan was by and large opposed to any reduction in naval armaments. The Japanese diplomats at Washington who agreed to the 5-5-3 ratio of limitation did not have an easy time explaining this "humiliation" when they returned home.

One general result of this conference was that the United States emerged as the dominant world power. We got virtually everything for which we asked in return for taking an affirmative role in world affairs. In a sense we were reversing the position we had taken on the League of Nations. We emerged as an important Pacific power and our position of influence in European affairs was guaranteed. Even in those days of 1921-22 when normalcy and isolation were supposedly in full bloom these treaties committed us to exactly that type of foreign entanglements against which we were always being warned by Americans who still dreamed about a provincial past of isolation that was gone forever. It was proof of our manifest destiny that the very time when we proclaimed our isolation from Europe we organized a conference that drew us more deeply into world affairs.

The Washington Conference showed the possibilities of international agreements. Despite conflicting national interests, nations could agree on such a delicate subject as armament balance and reduction. This presupposed a certain fundamental understanding among powers, a respect for one another, and a willingness to discuss mutual problems in a spirit of give-and-take without which there is little hope of success for any diplomatic meeting.

This conference stands as a landmark on the road to peace as the only conference where governments agreed to destroy arms by mutual consent. Large armaments may not be the direct cause of war but they inevitably contribute to international tension. They provoke fear, fear provokes hate, and hate leads to war. Therefore, any agreement to limit armaments is really an agreement to live in peace. Arms reduction is one of the most practical approaches to peace. Every agreement to reduce or limit arms brings with it a larger confidence that war can be avoided. Limiting arms is one of the best practical and psychological approaches to the elimination of war. It is not enough in itself, but it is a long step in the right direction.

The social side of the Washington Conference was a marked success. The capital hostesses vied with one another in giving elaborate parties and dinners. There were many brilliant gatherings and the conference was the most important and colorful international meeting ever held in the United States. One of the most pleasant parties was an open air barbecue given by the publisher of the *Baltimore Sun* at his country home in Maryland. The outstanding personalities of the newspaper and diplomatic world came out to witness a rodeo which was the feature event. I sat near roly-poly H. G. Wells who was acting as correspondent for various British newspapers. He was most intrigued by the bulldogging and calf-roping, and was greatly amused to observe the effects of American bootleg liquor on some of his ordinarily sedate British colleagues. Some of them and even more of their American friends had imbibed freely and a few rolled off into the grass from the rickety arena seats erected for the occasion.

The foreign correspondents were most amazed at the open press conferences with the President and Secretary of State. Such free and easy contact and exchange of informal question and answer were for them an unusual experience. In

Europe correspondents very rarely get beyond the press officer of a government department. President Harding, although he had been a newspaperman, never excelled at these press conferences. But Harding was such an agreeable and pleasant personality that the reporters were nearly always ready to cover up his shortcomings. His charm and good nature were his greatest assets. Eventually these proved to be his undoing.

Back in 1915 I had helped organize one of the first of a series of travel tours to be sponsored and conducted by the *Brooklyn Daily Eagle*. These tours enabled me to see much of my own country and the world which I could not afford to see on my own time and money. They took place during the summer months when news was apt to be slack and provided me with a welcome opportunity to do what I loved best—travel. The *Eagle* tours were fundamentally conceived as a promotion enterprise for the paper. If they made money—which they did—so much the better but that was not their primary purpose.

The 1915 hegira was called "The California Exposition Tour." It was thought up by Herbert F. Gunnison, business manager of the *Eagle* and originator of the *Eagle* tour idea. He was with me on this first tour and taught me something about the fine art of keeping tourists happy. I soon developed my own techniques and always followed two primary rules: "Keep them fed" and "Keep them moving." Our 1915 destinations were the expositions being held in San Diego and San Francisco. The *Eagle* publicized the proposed trip and we soon had more than enough applications to fill our special *Eagle* tour train. The railroads gave us a flexible schedule and we could stop along the way as we saw fit. Chambers of Commerce along the route were only too eager to show Eastern visitors their industries and their real estate. They were happy to sell the West to the East. They bragged about their growing population, their scenic attractions and their commercial opportunities. They arranged side trips and organized luncheons and dinners that featured local products ranging from hazelnuts to brook trout. The West was just beginning the vast irrigation projects that have helped develop Western agriculture. Not one single Western Chamber of Commerce president failed to proclaim, "We have made the desert to blossom like the rose." On those rare occasions when there was an unscheduled stop at some small town because of an engine breakdown or a traffic delay an alert Chamber of Commerce secretary could do much on short notice. Even the dullest-looking town would organize a drive or a picnic that gave us a good time and gave our hosts a chance to explain the magnificent prospects of their area.

This Western tour was my first journey west of Wisconsin and it gave me a deep respect for the size and vitality of my country. The state of Utah I found particularly exciting because I knew less about it than about California. I was much impressed with the remarkable accomplishments of the Mormons, who combine a shrewd business sense with a deep religious feeling and a strong social conscience. The members of the Mormon church are remarkably skilled in handling communal problems. They are masters in the difficult art of municipal administration. Some of their self-help accomplishments could well serve as an example to other sections of the country that rely too much on government handouts.

In 1919 I had organized a National Parks tour which gave me my first view of such magnificent national reservations as Rocky Mountain, Yellowstone, and Glacier Parks. I was happy to co-operate with the National Park Bureau then under the far-sighted direction of Stephen T. Mather. He, in turn, would give the *Brooklyn Eagle* party an official invitation to lead in some ceremony or dedication which helped our publicity and dignified our tour.

It was on this tour that I collected from the members of the *Eagle* party enough money to complete a necessary piece of road linking the Blackfoot Indian Reservation that adjoins Glacier Park with the Blood Indian Reservation in Canada and the Canadian road system. As a reward the Blackfoot Indians came to our hotel in the Park to give us a war dance and make me a member of the tribe. Chief Curly Bear and Chief Two Guns White Calf, whose head is on the Buffalo nickel, presided at the ceremony. A beautiful feather head-dress was placed on my head, my face was daubed with the ceremonial paint, and I was given the flattering name of Mis-tuksihna, meaning Mountain Chief. I was then invited to participate in the war dance. Somewhat reluctantly I essayed the steps which were not too difficult until the pace was quickened. My feathered war bonnet wobbled about in a way that worried me but delighted the Brooklyn Eaglets who were looking on until dinner was announced. Then they went into the dining room leaving me still dancing. As guest of the occasion I was waiting eagerly for my Indian hosts to signify the end of the dance. What I did not realize was that they were waiting for me as the honored guest to give this signal. With perspiration streaming down from under my war bonnet I grimly continued until the train whistle signaled our early departure and I finally indicated to my hosts that I had to stop. No one was more eager to depart than I, and none more anxious to see me go than those tired Indian braves.

In 1921 the *Brooklyn Eagle* tour ventured as far as the mid-Pacific to dedicate the great volcanic area on the island of Hawaii as a national park. This was a heavenly trip which enthused every participant. The Hawaiian Islands kept their much advertised promise. Few spots combine so perfectly great scenic beauty, perfect climate, native interest, and complete modern luxury. The islands are also a great laboratory in race relations and race amalgamations. Here the most diverse racial strains live together in amity and understanding. There is constant intermarriage between different races and groups. The Hawaiian-Chinese unions produce children that unite most happily some of the appealing gentleness of the Hawaiians with the more sturdy traits and the sense of thrift peculiar to the Chinese. Then as now there were many Japanese on the islands yet every American assured me that those Japanese who were born under our flag would always prove loyal to the United States. The events of World War II gave ample proof that they were right. The highlight of the trip was looking down into the lake of living fire on the side of Hawaii's great volcano.

In the summer of 1922 we visited South America. Brazil

was having a Centennial Exposition which was the chief objective of this tour. In the course of the journey we met some of the presidents of South America. In several countries a small aristocratic group dominated both government and business. The great mass of the population was most often poor, largely illiterate, and a prey to disease. The common people had little opportunity to better themselves. It is this inequality between the classes that makes dictatorship and revolution endemic. Few South American countries have had any experience with what we would call true democratic government. The revolutions that succeed one another are often palace revolutions started by military cliques. Where the great mass of the population is illiterate and excluded from actual participation in government some form of dictatorship cannot be avoided. Uruguay, with its unified population and its advanced social legislation, is an outstanding example of democratic progress.

We were well received throughout our long journey down the west coast of South America, across the Andes and the pampas, and north from Buenos Aires. Relations between North and South America were good. The South Americans were becoming less hostile toward the "Yankee imperialists." There had been a suggestion that the Monroe Doctrine be made multilateral. The South American countries should agree to help protect the United States from any foreign attack in return for our agreement to help protect them. The military assistance they could provide was negligible but our willingness to abandon the unilateral aspect of the Doctrine would be an important concession to Latin-American pride. Years later this mutuality was incorporated into Pan-American agreements.

In 1923 an *Eagle* tour to Alaska just about rounded out my travels throughout North America. Alaska had almost ceased to be the land of gold, yet we were still able to see the old process of washing out gold nuggets at a small mine near Fairbanks. The mosquitoes were omnipresent in frightening numbers. In some places it was necessary to be dressed like a beekeeper to escape them.

Alaska is still a forbidding country and few of the many

projects to tap its resources have been financed. Forbidding climate and lack of transportation are the reasons. Even the area along the new railroad line from Anchorage to Fairbanks is not attracting settlers. Nevertheless, the hunting and fishing in Alaska are unbeatable. For future generations the coastal forests should provide an inexhaustible supply of lumber.

When I danced with the wife of the Mayor of Fairbanks —her history went back to gold-rush days—she forgot her previous stiff, conventional politeness. She clapped me on the shoulder and exclaimed, "Boy, you're some spieler!"—a compliment I still cherish.

On April 4, 1922 I made the first of what later became a regular series of radio talks on current events. The year before I had talked briefly from an experimental station in Newark, N.J. addressing a Chamber of Commerce group that had gathered in Brooklyn for a demonstration of the new invention. "We heard you—your voice came in clear as a bell" was the amazed reaction when I got back to the Brooklyn meeting.

The current events talks that I delivered on the air were something entirely new. They were the first spoken editorials ever heard by a radio audience. News was still the monopoly of the newspapers but they feared the new competition. A few publishers owned stations but no press association would permit its news service to be used regularly on the air. Radio itself was extremely timid. There was fear that the expression of opinion on the air might have dangerous repercussions and might even jeopardize the future of broadcasting.

The first thing I missed in my radio talks was an audience. The impersonal and unresponsive microphone was a poor substitute for the eager attention of visible listeners. The complete indifference of the technicians behind the glass window that separated them from the studio made it even harder. I felt extremely self-conscious while broadcasting, and whenever I finished my extemporaneous thirty-minute talk I was bathed in perspiration. As on the lecture platform I used only brief notes. Radio speaking required a new kind of mental concentration that went far beyond what was necessary when speaking to a live audience. My early radio talks made me realize how much the visible listener helps the speaker. One does not sense the great encouraging value of an occasional responsive smile or look of understanding until one first talks to the unresponsive microphone. The radio speaker also misses the valuable warnings such as signs of inattention or a negative reaction. Mistakes of fact or judgment will go unnoticed until the dancing lights of the telephone switchboard bring in listener protests. That is one reason why so few radio talks are extemporized. During my early microphone appearances I often had a panicky feeling that no one could be listening or that something had gone wrong with the mechanism. Even when fan mail began coming in it was still hard to visualize that I was really talking to tens of thousands.

In radio speaking there are no easy props such as taking a drink of water or pacing a few steps on the platform to get the effect of pause or gain time to think through an idea. On the radio there is nothing but dead air when the voice is still. That is one reason I delivered most of my radio talks standing up. When sitting down I had a tendency to relax and I just did not dare relax in front of a microphone. Standing also gave me more of a sense of being in front of an audience. For the same reason I continued to gesticulate while talking into the microphone. This was a source of constant amusement to those who watched me broadcast. I didn't care because I found that physical expression released emotion and reduced tension.

The lack of sensitivity in the early microphones also made it necessary to control physical exuberance. Any turn of the head away from the carbon mike would make some words inaudible. For a few early broadcasts my head was placed in a frame, similar to that used by the old-fashioned photographers to prevent movement. This was so exasperating that I insisted on getting on without it. A chalk-marked square on the floor designated the area within which I had to keep my feet. The studios were all heavily draped with curtains that covered the walls from the ceiling to the ground. Their purpose was to deaden sound and prevent echoes. In the summer these studios were unbearably hot. Air conditioning came years later. Most of my hot-weather broadcasts were delivered in shirt sleeves with sweat pouring off my face.

No one cared much about exact timing in those early days. My half-hour current events talks frequently ran over one or two minutes. Less often they ran short. There was always a pianist stand-by, who played a few bars between programs and filled in if a speaker was late or didn't fill out his time. The pianists prided themselves on their ability to play something appropriate, like "How Dry I Am," when I had talked about prohibition. No one worried much about coughs or sneezes. These were actually welcomed as adding a touch of realism. My children took delight in greeting me with such a comment: "Dad we heard you cough today!" To my regret this was more important to them than my editorial expositions. But it helped me not to take myself too seriously. I soon learned that naturalness on the air was more important than meticulous exactitude. When the studio door was left open I simply called over to the announcer and asked him to please shut the door. Broadcasting was informal in those early days.

Because no one was accustomed to hearing controversial issues discussed on the air I got into all sorts of trouble during the winter of 1923 when I did a regular series of weekly talks over station WEAF in New York City. This station was then owned and operated by the American Telephone and Telegraph Company on an experimental basis. The *Brooklyn Eagle* was sponsoring my current events talks and since I spoke as an *Eagle* editor I assumed that I had the same editorial freedom on the air that I enjoyed on the *Eagle*. On one occasion I criticized the decision of a New York judge. It so happened that this judge was about to preside over an important rate case involving the A.T.&T. The Vice-President-in-Charge-of-Litigation suggested to the Vice-President-in-Charge-of-Radiobroadcasting that it was suicidal for the telephone company to lend its facilities to a radio commentator to criticize an important judge whose ill will might prove very expensive to the company. This delicate situation was explained to me by the Vice-President-in-Charge-of-Radiobroadcasting. I responded by telling him that I was saying on the *Eagle's* editorial page the same things that I was saying on the air. He shook his head sadly and adjured me to be more careful.

The next week I was again in trouble. I had taken an editorial stand on a strike against the public interest which proved offensive to an important New York labor union official. Immediately the Vice-President-in-Charge-of-Labor-Relations for A.T.&T. called in the Vice-President-in-Charge-of-Radio and demanded that I be put off the air. He pointed out that my comments were seriously jeopardizing the telephone company's labor relations. Again the Vice-President-in-Charge-of-Radio came to me for another one of our friendly little chats. Again he urged me more strongly to be careful not to get him into any more trouble. My talks he said were popular and he would hate to lose them but he had to live with his company.

The next time I offended Secretary of State Charles Evans Hughes. I had criticized his curt rejection of the Soviet Union's plea for diplomatic recognition. My point was that the rejection could have been more courteous. I also believed that we could recognize the Soviet Union as the stable government of Russia without thereby expressing approval of the internal policies of the Communists or of the methods by which they came to power.

It seems that Secretary Hughes was listening to my talk in his Washington home in the company of a group of distinguished guests. At that time WEAF programs were already being carried by telephone wire to station WRC in the nation's capital. Secretary Hughes did not like what I said particularly since my opinions were expressed in his own home in the hearing of his guests. He communicated directly with the president of A.T.&T. who expressed his serious displeasure to the long suffering Vice-President-in-Charge-of-Radio in New York. Once again the harassed director of A.T.&T. broadcasting talked to me and this time he laid down an ultimatum. My talks were to be discontinued at once unless I agreed to cease all editorial comment. Naturally I refused and the station notified the *Eagle* that it was canceling all further broadcasts. The *Eagle* management responded by telling the A.T.&T. that it would have to announce in its columns the reasons for the cancellation. This brought about a reconsideration of the issue in the A.T.&T. office and the Company finally agreed to let the program complete its scheduled course. Then, when the contract period expired, the telephone company politely indicated that "because of the pressure of other programs" it would not be "convenient" to renew the *Eagle* contract and I became what the famous Roxy characterized as "the wandering voice of radio," because of my frequent shifts from station to station.

When my first series of talks was thus terminated the *Eagle* printed two full pages of letters received from listeners who deplored the ending of the series. In the space of a week some fifteen hundred letters came in asking that the talks be continued. A good many were from prominent citizens and representatives of large organizations whose membership had voted for a resumption of the series. These letters were not in response to any request for mail but represented a spontaneous reaction of an audience that wanted something more than music and entertainment. Blind people, cripples, shut-ins, older people wrote expressions of thanks for the way in which these talks had kept them informed on current affairs. Radio was so new and to them it had already come to mean so much. It was a heartening response and a graphic demonstration of the size and interest of the rapidly developing radio audience.

For reasons that can be readily understood the telephone company soon gave up the broadcasting business. This great corporation has always been deeply aware of the necessity for good public relations and could not permit its broadcasting activities to jeopardize the good will they were trying so hard to build up.

The abounding evidence of listener interest in radio talks on current events prompted the *Eagle* to make arrangements to continue the series in the fall over another station. But before long the same difficulties that had plagued WEAF began to reappear. Protests were sure to develop whenever I commented editorially on some aspect of the news. When these protests became too intense or when they came from particularly influential people the station would become alarmed and after a time would drop Kaltenborn "because of the pressure of other programs." But some other station was always ready to carry on not because my talks were so good but because of the great advertising value of *Brooklyn Eagle* support. Station WOR in New Jersey proved to be the first one powerful enough and with a sufficient spirit of independence to refuse to be intimidated by pressure or disapproval. They held that since I spoke for the *Eagle* as an *Eagle* editor I had a right to voice opinion. Even when Mayor Jimmy Walker's associates at New York City Hall threatened to bar station WOR from broadcasting important municipal events until I stopped criticizing the Mayor, WOR's executives put no pressure on me to ease up. I have always had a feeling of gratitude for this station because it was the first to provide "the stormy petrel of the air," as I have been called, with a permanent home.

Radio has been timid about controversial material from its earliest beginnings. The fact that broadcasting stations depend on a government license to broadcast at all and because of radio's total dependence on advertising for its financial existence station management has feared to give offense. The broadcasters were cautious about offending the political party in office and the advertisers naturally did not want to antagonize anyone. Because the expression of controversial opinion was the very essence of my talks I was always giving offense to some group or individual.

Hardly a week went by in which there was not some threat to have me put off the air. In those early days it was my association with the *Brooklyn Eagle* that helped keep me on the air. The threat of publicity is often an effective answer to the demand for censorship.

In the twenties many radio stations were not well enough established or sufficiently sure of their own power and authority to challenge the special interests that protested against specific broadcast material. The easy answer was to substitute something else. Not until the thirties did most stations become sufficiently profitable and sure enough of their own rights to ignore pressure. Not all radio stations were timid, but the tradition of independence and public service was not yet well established. While the great majority of stations defended free speech they also took care to avoid comment that stirred up controversy or that contradicted the opinions of advertising sponsors or station owners. Someday I may try to write a book on the history and progress of free speech on the air.

13

"Woe to the vanquished!" is an old Roman proverb. Just how much woe in the form of reparations was to be inflicted on the vanquished Germans was the problem that plagued the victorious Allies for twenty years. At the Versailles conference astronomical figures were discussed. Civilian losses, destruction of nonmilitary property, and even military pensions were to be included in Germany's reparations bill. Not until 1921 were the Allies able to agree upon the then fantastic sum of $31,500,000,000 which the Germans were to pay not in German marks but in gold or foreign currency. The Allies had little confidence in the value of the German mark, a distrust that was shared by the Germans. The value of the mark began a steady decline which soon developed into a disastrous inflation. This inflation wiped out Germany's internal debt and with it the well-being of the middle classes, the basis of German stability. The consequent economic stagnation dimmed any prospects the Allies had for collecting reparations except for those deliveries in kind which were also stipulated in the treaty.

The Treaty of Versailles provided that if Germany failed to meet its reparations her territory could be occupied until her creditors were satisfied. It was a failure to deliver some telegraph poles that brought French and Belgian troops into the Ruhr basin, Germany's richest industrial area on January 11, 1923. (France and Belgium were to receive sixty per cent of German reparation payments because their countries were most heavily damaged by German occupation.)

From January to September, 1923, there was a state of cold war between France and Germany. The German Government encouraged the inhabitants of the Ruhr in their campaign of resistance with heavy financial subsidies which advanced inflation. The German people resisted passively and actively by sabotaging French efforts to remove coal and timber from the Ruhr. There was occasional violence in which lives were lost.

I went into the Ruhr that year to study this use of force to collect reparations, and found a tragic situation for both French and Germans. The costs to the French of their occupation far exceeded the value of the reparations they were able to extract. Without the co-operation of the German technicians and workers the French were unable to run most of the factories and mines. There was bitterness and reprisal on both sides. The French soldiers hated their job and the Germans hated the French soldiers. The French franc also began to fall as the German mark collapsed. It was only the continuance of wartime hatred that prompted the French to continue their futile effort. The French wanted to make sure that Germany could never recover enough economic strength to threaten France. The French did not realize that a prostrate Germany was also a threat to European well-being and political security.

The German Communists and the Nazis, who later co-operated to overthrow the Weimar Republic, gained their foothold in these years. The French occupation policy helped create those forces which were to overrun France once again. I visited Nazi headquarters in Munich and was amazed at the power and organization which Hitler's private army had already achieved. His attempted Beer Hall *Putsch* in

1923 failed but his party carried on while he was writing in jail the Nazi Bible *Mein Kampf*.

The British were fundamentally more realistic about the reparations problem. Much as England wanted revenge for its tragic losses in manpower during the war she realized that an economically stable Germany would contribute to the well-being of Europe. World trade was essential for British economic recovery. The British had not participated in the Ruhr occupation but tried to arbitrate between Germany and France. At British insistence a new reparations commission was created to study Germany's capacity to pay war damages.

An American banker, Charles G. Dawes was appointed chairman of this reparations commission. Here was another important American participation in world affairs. The new body proposed a compromise settlement which became known as the Dawes Plan. This was accepted by both the French and the Germans. It provided for a temporary easing of Germany's indebtedness and a total reorganization of Germany's financial structure under foreign supervision. A series of loans was arranged, principally from the United States, which stimulated German recovery. Germany resumed reparation payments and the tension between Germany and France was eased.

In December, 1925, at Locarno, Switzerland, representatives of France, Germany, and Britain exchanged solemn pledges of peace and guarantees of existing frontiers. For the first time since the war the peoples of all Europe began to look confidently toward the future. The era of good feeling that followed became known as the "spirit of Locarno." The new, more peaceful atmosphere was due in great part to three great liberals who guided the policies of France and Germany during this period. France's Edouard Herriot, who became premier in 1924, and Aristide Briand, premier and foreign minister in many cabinets, helped turn their country away from the *revanche* policies of Clemenceau and Poincaré. Herriot had an international point of view. His moderate attitude and the tact and skill with which Briand handled the case of France at Geneva helped inaugurate the new era of better relations between France and Germany.

In Gustav Stresemann Germany was equally fortunate. He was an unusual German in that he was an extremely skillful diplomat who was careful not to open any old wounds. In both countries these men strove earnestly and successfully to make peace possible.

The year 1926 marks the high point in the history of the League of Nations. This was the year in which Germany was admitted. How well I remember the solemn moment in Geneva when the German delegates formally entered the League Assembly hall. Led by Gustav Stresemann, the foreign minister of Germany, the delegation marched in with dignity and typical German correctness to be greeted with polite applause. Stresemann made the first speech, the first German to address the League, and he did so in his native tongue. With his bald bullet head and stocky build he looked like the typical, much-caricatured German. His gestures were close and rather awkward. He read his speech with care and precision, knowing full well he was speaking to the world. He urged world-wide disarmament and the reduction of economic barriers. He praised the Locarno treaties and was optimistic about the future of peace. His address was well received but aroused no enthusiasm.

The speech that followed was delivered by Aristide Briand. It stands out in my mind as one of the greatest oratorical efforts I have ever heard. The French statesman walked up to the speakers' platform with his characteristic slouching gait. As usual, his shaggy hair was unkempt, his clothes were baggy and ill fitting. His almost apelike figure was not one that commanded admiration. But when he began to speak in a low tone and with slow pace the audience settled down instantly to absolute quiet. Briand had a wonderful, organtoned voice and was able to produce an amazing variety of tonal contrasts without apparent effort. Even when he spoke in a whisper he could be easily understood. Gradually he moved upward from one emotional level to another until at the climax the audience was quivering with excitement.

It was a compelling hymn of praise to the Goddess of Peace. "Peace in Europe," he said, "will be maintained when France and Germany work together." He reached his climax with these words that will always ring in my ears, *"Arrière, en arrière les fusils, en arrière les canons, en arrière les mitrailleuses. En avant la démocratie, en avant la liberté; en avant l'esprit de la paix!"* Briand delivered them with dramatic gestures and with an emotional fervor that brought the delegates to their feet in a long-continued tumult of applause. His speech embodied and dramatized the longing of the world for peace. Everyone in the great hall was moved and shaken by this great oration. Rarely have time, place, and circumstance combined so perfectly to give a great speech its full effect. To us assembled in Geneva it looked as though men's dreams for peace were coming true.

After the formal Assembly meeting came the annual League of Nations press luncheon in which we reporters joined to entertain the principal delegates and League officials. When Stresemann and Briand clinked glasses and drank a toast to one another's country the luncheon guests broke into another roar of approval. Speeches followed. Briand spoke only briefly and quietly; he was too old a hand to try and repeat a supreme success. Stresemann on the other hand, who in his morning speech had spoken cautiously from a prepared manuscript was completely at his ease and spoke freely without notes. He emphasized the importance of Franco-German amity and pledged himself to work for it with all his heart. He carried off the oratorical honors of the afternoon and brought a great occasion to a happy end.

It is always a memorable moment in history when two nations that have been marching toward war can agree to reverse this direction and march toward peace. It is particularly fortunate when their agreement has a sound and practical basis. The age-old hostility between France and Germany has always seemed to me to be tragically unnecessary. I know and love the people of both countries and realize how much they could do for one another. They supplement each other and have always needed one another. Frederick the Great, an admirer and friend of Voltaire, realized and admitted

Prussia's need of the refining influence of French intellect and culture. He tried to infuse some of it into the Prussian government, though alas, with little lasting success. The enmities that were stirred up by the imperialistic and militaristic leaders on both sides led to terrible and unnecessary wars which bred more and more hate. A united France and Germany working together for a peaceful stable Europe has long been the aim of men of good will. For a little while at Geneva, in 1926, it seemed about to be realized.

The feeling that at last the world was on the road to peace helped persuade America to participate in advancing the good cause. As the result of an exchange of notes between Aristide Briand and American Secretary of State Frank B. Kellogg regarding the renunciation of war as an instrument of national policy, the Kellogg-Briand Pact to outlaw war was signed in Paris in August, 1928.

I was in Paris in 1928 for the signing but did not altogether share the mood of optimism and enthusiasm that was prevalent in the French capital. My best hope was that the pact would at least give the nations that participated the sense that they were promising to keep the peace. It was a recognition of the wickedness and futility of war. There was then still a great deal of confidence in pacts and agreements. The most powerful nations in the world could at least agree to maintain peace. The Washington Conference (1922) decisions were still being carried out and there were hopes for further progress toward disarmament. The Kellogg Pact was a disarmament gesture on the political side.

Europe also welcomed the fact that this pact represented further participation by the United States in world affairs. Aristide Briand told me at the time he felt the pact marked America's definitive re-entry into the larger world stage. He thought it showed clearly that the United States would unite with the other signatory powers to take effective steps to check aggression. While the pact did not provide any punitive measures against an aggressor it did call for consultations on what could or should be done. This in itself was an important step for the United States, and Briand frankly hoped that it would serve as a check on any potential aggressor.

In his brief address at the signing of the pact Briand made a point of quoting an earlier statement by President Coolidge: "An act of war in any part of the world injures the interests of my country." Coolidge was expressing a truth but a truth which had not been implemented by any previous commitments to co-operative action. Two years before when I talked with President Coolidge at the White House he said to me in response to my question about further American participation in European affairs, "I think we are very snug as we are." The substitution of the letter *m* in the word snug would have made this an aphorism.

The British, as usual, were more alert to the state of American public opinion than were the French. They felt that it was unwise for Briand to exaggerate and emphasize this increasing participation of the United States in European affairs. At a press conference the night before the pact was signed Lord Cushenden, the British plenipotentiary, dissented sharply from Briand's remarks. I noted in my story to the *Eagle* that he said, "The part Secretary Kellogg played indicates no modification of the American policy of aloofness from European affairs. We might wish it otherwise, but we will disappoint ourselves to assume that there is a change. The pact carries no implication that the American people will concern themselves with European affairs."

Lord Cushenden knew that the pact did actually indicate a larger concern by America with the world scene but he did not want to frighten American isolationist opinion. That is why he played down the implications of the pact.

The American Secretary of State Frank B. Kellogg was not well suited by temperament or experience to act as chief American plenipotentiary at any international gathering. He always appeared ill at ease at the meetings of the many foreign diplomats. His nickname at home was "Nervous Nellie" and I could see why this rather cruel characterization was used. The newspaper dispatch I filed from Paris about signing the pact began with this sentence, "The most silent, the most unresponsive, the most awkward and the most embarrassed of those who signed the antiwar pact was one of its authors, Secretary of State Kellogg."

Arrangements had been made for Secretary Kellogg to deposit a wreath at the tomb of the Unknown Soldier. The Secretary was clearly moved by the sight of the eternal flame that burns by the tomb under the great Arc de Triomphe. After depositing the wreath rather awkwardly he stood there for a moment, and then spontaneously dropped one knee and bowed his head. Those of us who had not been overly impressed by his conduct at press conferences and at the other gatherings recognized that simple unpremeditated gesture as a sincere expression of the real wish for peace that lay behind his sponsorship of the almost forgotten antiwar pact that bears his name.

14

EVER SINCE THE RUSSIAN REVOLUTION I HAD BEEN eager to visit Russia and see the Communist experiment at first hand. In the summer of 1926 I applied for a visa. It was not hard to get. Few newspapermen were stationed in the country. The only visitors were either businessmen, engineers, or social science students interested in the Communist experiment. The violence of the revolution and the unsettled conditions deterred others.

I entered Russia through Finland, and my first contact with the Communist way of life came at the border. Because of the mutual suspicion and hostility between Russia and Finland it was impossible to buy a through ticket to Leningrad. After the train crossed the "no man's land" between the two countries I had to leave the single coach on which I crossed over as the only passenger and buy a Russian railroad ticket to Leningrad at the Russian station. "How much for a first-class ticket to Leningrad?" I asked. The ticket clerk looked at me coldly and snapped back, "We have no classes on the Soviet railroads." I tried again: "Please give me a ticket to Leningrad." That mollified the agent. "How will you have it?" he asked. "Soft seat or hard seat?" After buying myself a soft-seat ticket at three times the cost of a hard seat, I found that the soft-seat cars were much like the second-class cars in European railways. The hard-seat cars were extremely dirty and had wooden benches as seats. I soon learned that in the classless Soviet Union there are many unacknowledged class distinctions. Officers are called Commanders. Autocratic department heads were the People's Commissars. Private property had been abolished but there were plenty of ways to acquire it.

Drabness, dinginess, and dirt were my first impressions. Everything seemed run down and worn out. The universal poverty was a great stimulus to theft. When I asked why large rolls of paper, which in Finland were transported in open cars, were transferred into closed sealed cars when they entered Russia the answer was that in Russia everything had to be transported in closed cars lest it be stolen. We arrived in Leningrad in the late evening, but it was still light and I experienced one of the famous white nights of the former Russian capital. Outside the station stood a few old one-horse cabs. One of these took me to my hotel. Fog was coming up from the river Neva and gave everything a gray-white color. We drove past great palaces with broken windows and only a few rays of artificial light streaming from the cellars or the first stories. All walls had remained unpainted for years. As we drove through the wide cobblestone streets and across the great squares decorated with monuments we met only a few bicycles and one or two automobiles. The uniformed old porter at the hotel was a holdover from the Czarist regime—uniform, white beard, and all. The hotel help worked on strict union hours. The waiter worked from nine until five, after which there was no dining-room service. No one had thought of a double shift although there were plenty of unemployed. The manager told me he was anxious to pay for overtime but was not permitted to do so because that was regarded as capitalist exploitation of labor.

At the great Kazan cathedral on the Nevski Prospect I talked with some of the priests who spoke French or German. The churches were still open but attendance was sparse except on holidays. The rich silver decorations, the candelabras, and service vessels had not been confiscated. The Russian priests were convinced that religion would survive even under Communist control. Religious teaching was closely circumscribed and had to compete against government supported antireligious propaganda. The Church was in financial difficulties since it depended on voluntary contributions from the few faithful. These were largely older people who had little money to spare. At seven in the morning and seven at night the faithful were summoned to prayer by the great bells of Leningrad whose plangent sound still rings in my ears as I recall that first contact with Russia.

When I visited the great Leningrad library originally built in 1800 I learned something about Soviet censorship. There were four million books, including Voltaire's original library which had been purchased by Catherine the Great. Only a small fraction of these books were available to the public. To read books in a foreign language or books not specially approved by the local censor, permission had to be secured from the chief librarian. Only students who had proven their sympathy with the Soviet regime were permitted access to these restricted books.

As I walked through the library I noticed that most of the portraits of the Czars were curtained. For some reason the features of Catherine the Great were uncovered. I was surprised to come upon an excellent portrait of George Washington. "Do you know that George Washington was a bourgeois and a capitalist?" I said to the guide. "Ah, yes," was the reply, "but he was also a great revolutionist."

The greatest tourist attraction in Leningrad was the enormous Winter Palace of the Czars. The Communists kept this palace and many others intact and converted them into museums. The sole purpose of these museums, as of so much else in the Soviet Union, is to teach communism. The guides pointed out the wealth, the luxury, and wasteful habits of the former Russian rulers. The first thing the guide told me was that the Czar had two thousand servants including eighty furnacemen. There were twenty cooks just for the Czar. Since he feared poison there were cooks whose only function was to taste whatever dish was prepared. According to the guide the cooks employed by the last of the Czars, Nicholas II, were better paid than ministers of State. After showing the opulence of the Czar's living quarters the guide took me to the miserable cellar rooms for the servants. The eager young girl guide who showed me around told me that her greatest joy was to point out to visitors the contrast between what the Czars did to the common people and what "We Communists are now doing for the common people."

The problems that faced every industrial manager under communism became evident during a visit to a textile factory. The plant director who received the same wage as one of the skilled workers was a sincere and hard-working individual. Before making any important decision he had to consult with a shop committee. These decisions were debated at full length and if the committee failed to agree with him there was nothing he could do about it. This system was later abandoned when it became clear that it was a serious handicap to efficient production. The committees remained but more responsibility and authority were transferred to the manager. Every head of a Soviet plant was in an uncomfortable position. From the top he was squeezed by directives from his superiors in the Communist economic planning unit who demanded greater output and more efficiency. From the bottom he was squeezed by the shop committee who resented his suggestions for stepping up output. If the factory fell behind in its production schedule the manager would be blamed by his superiors. If he put in his more efficient methods his shop committee would do its best to sabotage them.

The Communists did succeed in giving the workers a greater sense of communal participation in an enterprise. The Government did its best to encourage this sense of participation. What was known as the "wall newspaper" fulfilled an important function in every factory. Written by the workers and posted conspicuously it gave them a chance to criticize superiors and suggest improvements in working conditions. No criticisms of Communist doctrine or of Communist leaders was permitted, but the wall newspaper gave workers an opportunity to vent minor grievances. The great majority of Russians have no conception of or interest in the American tradition of free speech because they have never known it. Grievances which affect details of daily life are more important to them than the freedom to discuss the merits of democracy versus communism. The wall newspaper also served to supplement the spy system. It enabled the Moscow leaders to check up on the work of factory managers in different cities. Copies of all wall newspapers were forwarded to Moscow for analysis.

During my entire 1926 visit I found the Russians most friendly and curious. The Communist officials I interviewed were co-operative. I encountered virtually no antagonism toward the United States. There was tremendous respect for American achievement, particularly American industrial techniques and mass production. Henry Ford, though a great capitalist, was a great hero to Russians of that day. He was one of the first to sell cars to Russia and it was his cars they copied in their own plants. When I walked through one of the industrial plants in Stalingrad word got around that Henry Ford had come for a visit, and I was mistaken for him. The workers gazed at me with rapt admiration and some applauded me. I did my best to point out their error but with little success. The plant officials did nothing to disabuse them of their mistake.

There were then twenty-four radio stations scattered throughout the Soviet Union. The Communists were using radio most efficiently as a propaganda medium and to transmit news and directives to the farthest reaches of Russia. Telegraph lines were few. Tass, the central Russian news agency, had no teletype or telegraph service. Twice each day a radio announcer read dispatches slowly enough to be taken down by hand. In that way press service news was transmitted all over the Soviet Union. Since there were few home radio sets, radio's chief purpose was to serve working men's clubs, reading rooms, and outdoor loud speakers. People listened in groups to the lectures, news, and musical programs that made up the daily fare. Many of the operas and plays then being performed on Moscow stages were transmitted unabridged over the air. All Red Square demonstrations were broadcast. Church music was never aired. A popular feature was the regular midnight broadcast of "the noises of the city of Moscow." Microphones were placed in the Red Square to catch the sounds of passing traffic and especially the ringing of the great bells of the Kremlin. The Kremlin had always been a kind of holy center for the Russian peasant so this served as a link between Moscow and the rest of the country.

When I asked the program director of the Moscow station what type of programs his listeners liked most, he hesitated and then said, "Well, most people like cheerful music." Then, as he looked up at the omnipresent big pictures of Lenin and Stalin on the wall he quickly added, "But they also like to hear the Big Leaders speak."

In the early days of the Soviet experiment the Communists decided to institute prohibition. They did not want the workers to waste money, time, and energy on vodka but to keep their minds on the serious business of building socialism. The Commissars soon discovered as we did in the U.S. that enforcement was impossible. The vodka drinking peasants refused to co-operate. They built their own stills where they made strong vodka. The Russians abandoned prohibition in October, 1925. I talked with the Commissar for health who had been in charge of the noble experiment. "With our people," he said, "vodka drinking is an ingrained habit and we simply cannot wipe it out. It is one of our fundamental habits. We can't change this overnight. All we can hope to do is slowly to educate the people away from it. Maybe in time we will come back to prohibition, now we promote temperance." The vigorous campaign against liquor then in progress consisted of speeches, lectures, radio talks, posters, and films. The moving picture against drunkenness was an entertaining masterpiece. A comical peasant was shown staggering drunkenly through traffic and missing death by the narrowest of margins. A drunken painter was shown teetering precariously on a high ladder. He lost his balance and crashed to his death in the street below. Gruesome realism and uproarious humor alternated.

This film did not cure me as effectively of my taste for vodka as did an experience in a Moscow restaurant. I was very thirsty and in my haste mistook a carafe of crystal-clear vodka for a carafe of water. I gulped down a large quantity before I realized what had happened. It was a burning shock—and left me with a decided preference for water.

One important reason why the Communists abandoned prohibition was that the peasants in their illict stills used much precious grain which was in short supply. Legal vodka can be made from the more plentiful potato. The Communists also tried to cut down drunkenness by limiting the alcoholic content of legalized vodka. They found, however, that whenever they dropped the alcoholic content below forty per cent the peasants went back to making their own. The peasants like it at sixty per cent, but the authorities were working out a compromise between forty and sixty. The abandonment of prohibition was another proof of the flexible and practical nature of the Communist experiment in its early stages.

In Russia in 1926 I saw many truly outstanding theatrical productions. The Russians have a remarkable sense for the theater. Although I understood virtually nothing of the dialogue the acting was so expressive that it was entertaining in itself. Stanislavski was directing and teaching in the Moscow Art Theater at that time and I had the privilege of sitting in on one of his rehearsals. During this rehearsal one actor had to deliver one line thirty times so that the stage manager could work out individual reactions for each of thirty other actors who were supposed to be listening to him. Stanislavski managed to make each participant in the crowd scene stand out and become an individual, yet never allowed him to dominate the scene. The actors agreed that it was a joy to rehearse with Stanislavski. One said to me, "He inspires us, he knows exactly what he wants to accomplish, and we love to do our best to give him what he wants." After the rehearsal I told Stanislavski how impressed I was with the careful detail with which he rehearsed his productions. He said that this was only possible because the State supported the theater. "In your country," he said, "the cost of such lengthy rehearsals would be prohibitive for a theater that must be self-supporting. State aid is the only answer. Even in the hardest times here the State gave us support." I asked him about American plays. "I have never seen an American play that I would like to produce," he replied. "Your plays are too local and not in our tradition." I asked him further why his troupe on their American tour would not play Shakespeare. "That would be too much like carrying wood into the forest."

For a long time Moscow's most revered shrine was that of the Iberian Virgin at the entrance to the Red Square. For many years this had been the most sacred ikon in Russia. It stood just underneath a government building on the wall of which was inscribed "Religion is the opium of the people." I watched several women kneel before the Virgin and as they looked up into her face their eyes may have seen the Communist slogan but their minds and hearts were concerned only with the hope that is inspired by belief.

On the way out of Russia I traveled from Moscow to Berlin and shared a compartment with the man who had embalmed Lenin's body. Only after a good many hours of travel and shared drinks in the dining car did my traveling companion make known to me his greatest claim to fame. Dr. Vladimir Worobjow was at that time the director of the Anatomical Institute at Kharkov. In the course of our train trip he told me the macabre story of how he came to embalm Lenin. He said that the original embalming was intended to last only seven days to accommodate the great crowds they knew would come to the Lenin funeral. But the mob continued coming for three months and since the body had apparently been well embalmed the crowds were allowed to keep on coming. No change in the condition of the body was noticed until near the end of the third month. At that time a few brown spots appeared on the cheeks. The question then arose in the Politburo as to what steps could or should be taken to preserve the body for a longer period. Stalin and his followers realized what a marvelous propaganda instrument they had in their hands and what a wonderful "relic" for worship it could become. After much discussion Professor Worobjow was called in for consultation as to whether more permanent embalming was possible. He told me he thought it wiser to say preservation was not possible because if he had given an affirmative report and then failed, his own life might well have been forfeited. He knew the veneration in which Lenin was held and how important it was to succeed. But the members of the Politburo were not to be put off. They understood the Professor's hesitations and reassured him that if he tried and failed they would not hold him responsible. They gave him carte blanche and said they would pay whatever costs might be involved. Reluctantly the Professor agreed and began his work. To make his position with the Politburo more secure he called in a dozen other top-ranking embalmers, physiologists, and chemists to share responsibility. The biggest problem according to the Professor was not so much the preservation of the body as the elimination of those brown spots on Lenin's face where decay had already set in. The technique of embalming had been known ever since the Egyptians, but restoration was a different matter. His problem was further complicated by the insistence of Stalin that Lenin's body should be prepared so that it would not have to be put under a glass case. This would make the showing dramatic and effective. Exposure of the body to air and to varying temperatures naturally makes the task of the embalmer more difficult. For three months the Professor and his assistants worked and in the process developed a new embalming technique which he told me he has since patented. After months of work the Professor informed the Politburo that the work had been successfully completed and that Lenin's body would last for one hundred years. Occasionally the tomb is closed while the Professor and his assistants give the body certain attentions. Every effort is made to keep heat from penetrating the chamber where the body is kept, and on hot days the tomb is closed.

After we had talked for some time with a bottle of vodka on the table the Professor told me frankly that he did not like life in Russia. "Before the Revolution I used to travel to Berlin quite frequently," he said, "but now they only let me out for a brief period once a year. But the three weeks in Berlin when I can enjoy wine, women, and song are the happiest weeks of my life."

The Professor had dreams of coming to the U.S. and continuing in the embalming business in this country. He told me that he could repeat the process he had developed for Lenin's body for something like twelve thousand dollars. He recalled the embalming of Caruso's body and was enthusiastic about the business he might do in Hollywood. With him embalming was a passion but when I saw him gazing with fascination at the brown freckles on my nose I thought it was time to end our conversation. He continued on the train for his annual Berlin vacation while I got off at Warsaw.

15

In the summer of 1927 I sailed from San Francisco on a Japanese ship for my first visit to the Far East. The voyage itself gave me an enlightening introduction to Japanese ways.

I love shipboard games and habitually enter them with much gusto. This fact was not lost on the ship's officers and I was soon made chairman of sports contests. Had I known what this would involve I would never have accepted the honor. Part of my duty was to provide prizes for the winners of the deck-tennis, ping-pong, quoits, and shuffleboard tournaments. The participants each made a small contribution to the prize fund and the ship also contributed. When my committee discussed the matter of prizes I made what I considered a practical suggestion—instead of worrying about selecting appropriate prizes, I proposed we give the winners cash and permit them to select their own. Very politely, but very emphatically the Japanese members of my sports committee said no. They explained that the winning of a contest was a great honor and prizes had to be selected and awarded formally. They assured me that there would be great displeasure if the winners were merely given the money and permitted to buy their own prizes. Outvoted I gave in.

More difficulties lay ahead. The Japanese, again very politely, pointed out that we had made no provisions for prizes for the members of the winner's family. It was explained to me that unless every single child in the prize winner's family received a prize both the winner and his family would be very disappointed. The assumption was that he had won the tournament more for the honor of his family than for his own glory. All this necessitated lengthy consultations especially since there were not only first and second prizes, but third, fourth, and fifth prizes. No one who participated in the tournaments could be permitted to lose face. As a result, no one got off the boat without a prize. I still have a little porcelain vase with a picture of Mount Fujiyama to prove that I won fourth prize in ping-pong. My experience as sports chairman taught me that the Japanese rarely oppose any suggestion directly—they merely fail to give consent. It was necessary to question them politely and patiently to find out why they had failed to consent.

Japanese participants in the games hated to lose. They felt that losing lowered them in the estimation of others. Whenever I happened to beat a Japanese I sought to make defeat more palatable by attributing it to my good luck.

On landing in Japan I was at once impressed by the sharp contrast between medievalism and modernity so characteristic of the Japan of that day. Men dressed in traditional Japanese costume walked side by side with those in Western business suits. The flimsy bamboo houses stood close by solid business buildings constructed after the earthquake. The art museums displayed the delicate ancient Japanese art alongside inferior imitations of paintings in the Western style. The gardens and general landscape had not been modernized and were a never-ending source of delight to Western eyes.

Admiral Nomura, who later became Ambassador to the United States in the historic year of 1941, introduced me to my first formal Japanese dinner. My famous fellow Brooklynite, Elmer Sperry, whose gyroscope was then being introduced in the Japanese Navy had given me an introduction. It was a most elaborate ceremonial occasion in the Japanese style. We sat on the floor and ate with chopsticks. The meal began with crisp, fried grasshoppers. Now if they had been disguised and had not looked like grasshoppers, I would probably have enjoyed their rather pleasant crisp taste. But appearance and memory both play a dominant part in the enjoyment of food. Many strange dishes all most charmingly served followed in swift succession. Fortunately the portions of strange nuts, seeds, and raw fish were small, and I was expected to do little more than taste them. The delicious dry-cooked rice provided a solid foundation for the meal. The Orientals are connoisseurs of good rice and keep their best varieties for their own consumption. Inferior grades are exported to the less discriminating West.

After dinner Admiral Nomura took me to a traditional Japanese play. The performance began at four in the afternoon and ran until eleven. I was told that the current play would not be completed for several weeks. It was completely formalized and exasperatingly slow in action. I stayed for only an hour. The strict forms and rigid classical traditions that governed costume, facial expression, gesture, and movement meant much to Japan's theatergoers but nothing to me. The leading actors were extremely popular, and were idolized throughout the country. Pictures and costumed replicas of the star performers were on sale in the lobby. The audience seemed appreciative but restrained its demonstrations of approval.

In 1927 the militarists were slowly coming into control. I talked with Baron Tanaka, later described as the last moderate prewar premier of Japan. He favored what he called a "positive program" in China but decried active military intervention as against Japan's best interests. He reviewed the economic situation and discussed Japan's imperative need for the vast China market. "The unsettled conditions in China are deplorable," he said, "all we want to see established there are conditions of peace and stability. It is therefore utterly out of the question that the Japanese attitude should be aggressive against the Chinese people, as has sometimes been erroneously reported. Japan merely wants to help China's economy for mutual benefit. However Japan cannot tolerate the breaking of treaties and is compelled to protect her legitimate rights and interests in the face of continued disturbances in China. To accomplish this, Japan wants to co-operate with other foreign powers, especially the United States." This was a period when we were not ready to co-operate with other countries for the maintenance of peace. As we study the history of our Far Eastern policy we must admit that the failure to take positive action on behalf of peace can have much to do with promoting war.

Everywhere in Japan there was multiplicity of government controls. Railroads, telephones, telegraphs, radios, trade in tobacco, in camphor, in salt, and even the red-light districts in the big cities were operated or closely controlled by the government. Strangely enough alcoholic beverages were exempt. I was told that the private sake industry was too diversified to be taken over by the government.

It was not generally realized that government supports and props to an unsound economy can be continued for years before the inevitable ultimate crash develops. They are like drugs that alleviate pain while the cancer continues to destroy healthy tissue. Government controls necessarily involved a sacrifice of independence by Japan's business enterprises. It led to the development of a totalitarian economy that turned to foreign conquest as a way to avoid the normal operations of economic laws. These always operate more slowly than impatient man expects. The bust that follows the boom can rarely be avoided but it can be postponed longer than we think and government action can soften the impact.

In Japan at that time there was a small but active group of democratically inclined Japanese politicians. They opposed the rising militarism but operated under great handicaps in a country that was far from democratic. They were never able to control the general course of events. One reason was that they were barred from the normal means of communication. Radiobroadcasting was a tight government monopoly.

Talks critical of the government were not tolerated. Opposition parties had no access to the air. The government just about equated communism and true democratic methods. It opposed both. Anyone who criticized the government was dangerous—a radical. There was no free-speech tradition.

Emperor worship was part of Japan's religion and proved a most effective way to control the law-abiding Japanese. The interpreter, a reporter on the Japan *Advertiser,* who was my guide in Tokyo was himself a Socialist and extremely critical of the government. One day, as we were passing by the entrance gate to the Emperor's palace, he surprised me by stopping and bowing low three times in the direction of the palace. When I asked him how he, a Socialist who stood against the Government headed by the Emperor, could go through with this ceremony of obeisance he said that he couldn't help it. He had learned Emperor worship as a child and there was something in him that prevented him from passing this gate without bowing. He said it was instinctive and failure to respond would violate something that was very deep in his heart and mind. This incident taught me something that everyone who lives in Japan is sure to learn.

My most thrilling experience in Japan was a climb up the sacred Mount Fujiyama. There are ten wayside stations where weary pilgrims rest while the wooden staffs they carry are branded with each station's symbol. The stations near the top were not yet equipped for travelers since it was early in the season and the mountain was still snow-covered. But at one I was happy to be offered "white tea" which turned out to be hot water. The sunrise that followed a cold night in a mountain hut compensated for all hardships. To see a vast area of Japan from the top of Fuji is to understand why this mountainous country has less arable land on all its home islands than the single state of Kentucky. Writing for the *Brooklyn Eagle* I summarized Nippon's problem in this sentence: "With her population increasing at the rate of one million a year Japan must have industry, markets and a merchant marine."

While my climb up Mount Fuji was a succession of spectacular vistas my slide down the snow-clad slopes with a straw mat serving as a toboggan proved a memorable quarter-hour. I should have broken a few bones. Actually, as my young guide proudly informed me, we set a new speed record in our quick descent.

The first Chinese city I visited was Hong Kong, that beautiful and picturesque island of greenclad hills which slope down to the blue waters of one of the world's finest and loveliest harbors. The well-built and substantial business district, so solidly British, stands in marked contrast to the slums where the Chinese live. The difference in the standard of living between the Far East and the West must be seen to be understood. It comes as a shock to every American traveler who contrasts the world's highest with what is probably the world's lowest standard of living. This trip to China in 1927 was my first contact with the miserable poverty in which some of the peoples of the world exist.

The British Governor-General of Hong Kong, an able civil servant, told me some things about China which I have always remembered because they were confirmed by later experience. He had lived a long time in the Far East and through the years had come to know China.

"China is nothing more than a geographical expression," he said. "There is no unity. There are no connecting roads or railroads that run from one end of the country to the other. There is no exchange of population, no common language. Sometimes the Chinese do not even understand the language of their countrymen who come from a village two hundred miles away. They have lived in the same provinces and villages for centuries and do practically no traveling. They have only the beginnings of a sense of nationalism. Fundamentally the Chinese are a series of provinces very loosely related to a government in Peking, ruled by local overlords who exercise absolute authority over a limited area. These provincial autocrats collect the taxes and make a small contribution to the national government which responds by leaving them alone."

These views were borne out by what I saw in China nearly a quarter century ago, and China changes slowly.

I entered Canton just after a Communist rebellion had been put down. I was warned not to wander about as armed bands of Chinese triggermen were patrolling the city looking for certain Communist leaders. Foreigners were supposed to remain behind the barbed wire which surrounded the foreign settlements on Shameen Island. I was sure that dressed in my American business suit and a newly acquired Panama hat I could not possibly be mistaken for a Communist. So I felt it safe enough to disregard warnings and go for a walk with the American president of Canton Christian College.

As we were walking along a group of Chinese triggermen swooped down upon us. They were not interested in my friend who spoke fluent Chinese but told him they recognized me as a Communist agent and started to hustle me off. My companion did his best to identify me as an American newspaperman but to no avail. The leader was all for an immediate execution and nothing I could say in French, German, Spanish, or English—I tried them all—had the slightest effect.

My companion said he would get the authorities to intervene and left me with my trigger-happy guardians. Sadly I watched his departing figure. He had warned my captors that he would bring a superior officer and woe to them if anything happened to me before he returned. He told me not to worry but I did worry especially when I was hustled off to a nearby hut and my captors closed around me in a circle to get a better look at a dangerous Communist. What disturbed me most was the way they kept jiggling their fingers along the triggers of their rifles.

Suddenly I had an inspiration. Back in my Wisconsin boyhood days I had developed a juggling act for an amateur minstrel show. For weeks I practiced in the cellar of my father's home, using empty Rhine wine bottles as Indian clubs. After a few weeks of breaking bottles I became fairly proficient in keeping three balls or bottles in the air and in balancing anything from straws to chairs on my nose or chin. Fortunately I carried with me a few oranges to satisfy thirst because the drinking water was unsafe. I began to juggle these oranges. The triggermen gazed at one another and then at me in utter amazement. Then the ice broke and they first smiled, then roared with laughter. Hearing this other Chinese crowded into the hut to see the fun. Having exhausted the juggling possibilities inherent in the oranges I next balanced a straw on the end of my nose. This made an even greater hit and when I took off my right sock and shoe and balanced a stick on my big toe my success was complete. They shrieked with laughter. They even put down their guns and seemed to regard the juggling act as a convincing demonstration of anticommunism. When my friend returned a few minutes later with a Chinese officer my captors and I were on the best of terms. The moral of this story, if it has a moral, is—when in danger don't stand on your dignity.

That night on a back street in Canton I saw the most revolting exhibition of human depravity that has ever come before my eyes. Miserable old hags were selling nine- and ten-year-old blind girls for prostitution purposes. The plentiful opium dens and their sodden victims were nothing in comparison. I tried an opium pipe but enjoyed no dreams and instead felt rather sick.

From Canton I traveled north by British tramp steamer to Shanghai. Life in Shanghai for the foreigner or for the wealthy Chinese was about as luxurious as could be found anywhere in the world. Magnificent clubs, wonderful service—and by Western standards all at a very low cost. The clubs were beautifully equipped with swimming pools, tennis courts, golf courses, and luxuriously appointed dining rooms. Yet underneath all of this splendor I sensed the latent rumbling power of Chinese discontent. The general feeling in Shanghai was that if and when the Chinese Nationalist movement succeeded, it would mean the end of foreign rule and the special privileges that went with it. The foreign settlements were surrounded by barbed wire and kept under constant guard. Foreigners lived in constant fear of an antiforeign uprising.

Chiang Kai-shek has been the dominant figure in China for the past twenty-five years. In the summer of 1927, he had just resigned his leadership of the Nationalist movement and was living in temporary retirement in a Buddhist monastery near his native village in Ningpo Province across the bay from Shanghai. With the Far Eastern correspondent of the *New York Times,* Henry Misselwitz, I made a two-day trip inland to have an interview with him. Armed with a letter of introduction from Chiang's brother-in-law T. V. Soong, we set off on what proved to be an arduous journey. We were helped along our way by representatives of the Standard Oil Company in Ningpo whose steam launch saved us a wearisome overland trip. The Standard Oil Company had outposts deep in the interior and the Shanghai officials of the company gave me a letter which asked their representatives to help us along. Even in areas where foreign diplomats and missionaries had left their posts to avoid possible attack the Standard Oil people stuck to their posts. They kept selling oil even when they had to take native products in exchange. The organization was remarkably flexible and gave considerable autonomy to its local agents. They employed Chinese whenever possible. Their officials and representatives were well trained and fully conversant with Chinese customs and language.

We started from Shanghai on a small Chinese steamer which was jammed as usual with hundreds of passengers. The few public conveyances in China are always hopelessly overcrowded. Every trip looks like an emergency evacuation. From Ningpo where we left the steamer a Standard Oil Company launch carried us some thirty miles up the river where we transferred to rickshas. We spent the first night in the small Chinese village where Chiang Kai-shek was born. As we arrived a celebration in his honor was underway. There was a fantastic lantern procession of the village children whose lanterns bobbing from bamboo sticks were in the shape of real and imagined animals.

We, too, provided the villages with a spectacle the like of which they had never seen. Desperately hungry after our long trip we sat down in the open and began to prepare a meal from the canned goods we carried. When we started to eat with knives and forks a group of youngsters who had eagerly watched our preparations ran off to alert the rest of the village about this fantastic exhibition. Soon the village population crowded about watching with amazement as we ate. They had never seen anyone eat with knives and forks and found the spectacle enormously amusing. Too polite to laugh directly at us they would cover their faces and turn away until they could compose themselves again.

On the next stage of our trip we shifted to sedan chairs. A crew of five carriers was assigned to each chair. Four would carry while the fifth rested. It was no easy task to carry us up the fairly steep mountain we had to ascend. Riding in the chair was also far from comfortable. It rocked from side to side as we covered the rough and uneven ground. When we became too stiff and uncomfortable we tried walking. But in the heat that was even worse.

We arrived at our destination, a picturesque Buddhist monastery, in the late evening and sent in our credentials. Chiang Kai-shek sent back word that we were to be admitted and made comfortable and he would be happy to see us in the morning. We slept soundly and were awakened by the weird temple bells that summoned the monks to prayer. We received word that to do honor to his American guests the Chinese leader was sending us a special American breakfast. When it came we found it consisted of California oranges and a box of San Francisco chocolate drops.

Our host was an altogether charming human being. He was slim, fairly tall, youthful in appearance, intelligent, and modest. He wore a kind of khaki uniform with a brilliant red fountain pen clipped to the tunic. He was most solicitous about our comfort and clearly pleased that we had come so far to see him. He explained that he was in this Buddhist monastery for a brief vacation and indicated that his retirement from leadership was temporary. He explained that the first stage of the Nationalist revolution had now been completed. The next phase was to be the march through Shantung Province up to Peking. There Chang Tso-lin, an elderly Manchurian war lord, controlled the richest province of China. For many years he had been a dominant figure in North China. Until that highly important area came under Nationalist control Chiang Kai-shek's regime could not be considered an all-China movement. He was vague about the date of his march against Chang Tso-lin and explained that he had learned from the Russians the value of preparing the way for the army by propaganda. He told us he was sending propaganda battalions into North China to smooth the way for the Nationalist Army. In his own mind there was no question about the success of his movement. The Communists, he felt, were definitely defeated and he had no fear that they would give him any further trouble. He saw as his only remaining obstacles the isolated war lords who still controlled outlying provinces. He impressed me as a determined but patient man, one who would take advice from those he respected. He was completely dominated by one main idea—the national unity of China. When our interview was over Chiang Kai-shek told us he had set aside the morning to ride with us to visit a nearby mountain waterfall that was praised as one of the most beautiful sights in all China. When we replied that we had to return to Shanghai at once to cable his comments to the world he was both surprised and disappointed. He could not understand how we could travel so far and miss seeing what to him appeared as a great scenic marvel, for China has few waterfalls. A Chinese general seems to retain an enduring appreciation for beauty. Perhaps the hard-boiled Western reporter who does not have it misses something.

On our steamer journey back to Shanghai we had a panic on board when the Woosung forts mistook us for a hostile vessel from the North and sent a dozen shots in our direction before recognizing their error. The shots all missed and we picked up the Chinese who had jumped overboard when they saw the gun flashes and the shell splashes near our ship.

A few days later I reached Peking where I interviewed Chiang's hated enemy, Chang Tso-lin. This Northern warlord leader of the old school presented an interesting contrast in personality and ideals. Chang Tso-lin lived in constant fear of assassination. During the interview, which took place in a picturesque old palace of the Forbidden City, I noticed armed guards peering at me from behind curtains and drapes. His appearance belied his reputation. He looked small, sallow, and altogether insignificant as he shuffled into the room. He wore a beautifully embroidered Chinese costume. By way of handshake he limply touched the tips of my fingers as though any physical contact with a foreigner was distasteful. I sensed a deep antagonism to foreigners. He never smiled nor showed the slightest sign of cordiality. It made me realize the wide gulf that separates Occident and Orient. There was something almost feline about this man and I caught the sweet fragrance of the opium of which he was the victim. When I asked him about the possibility of union between North and South China he said that the first prerequisite was a more decisive break by Chiang Kai-shek away from the Communists. He did not feel that Chiang had sufficiently purged his government of Russian influence.

I naturally was skeptical about the sincerity of these remarks since they came from a military dictator who was resisting the first important Chinese movement for national unity. He called his own administration "democratic." It was democratic, he insisted because he was trying to help the people over whom he ruled. He resented the presence of American troops in Tientsin as a reflection on his own ability to keep order and suggested sarcastically that we economize by sending them back to the United States. The point he wanted to emphasize most was that China and the United States had a common enemy in Russia. He said that Communist Russia would like nothing better than to crush the United States, the most powerful capitalist nation in the world. But he was sure that China would go her own way. "Here in Peking," he said, "you see young Chinese who have been in your country run around in American clothes and ape your ways. They are foolish. They may look like Americans but they are Chinese, and they will remain Chinese. With us change comes very slowly and it is foolish to try and hurry it. We must and will remain Chinese."

In Peking there were many Russian agents affiliated with the Soviet Consulate. They were boring from within in the north as they had in the south of China. When I asked an American-trained Chinese student what he thought about communism he replied thoughtfully, "Communism is not all bad. The Chinese will welcome any movement that seems to raise their standard of living."

On my 1927 tour of the Far East I stopped briefly in the Philippine Islands. I had always been a strong advocate of prompt independence for the Philippines. I was anxious to visit the Philippines to gather fresh ammunition for the independence campaign. Instead I gathered information that convinced me that, in the interest of the Filipinos' independence should be postponed. Neither the people nor the islands were ready for it. There were still too many practical obstacles in the way of that economic independence, which is the only sound basis for success in political independence. Only a handful of American-educated leaders seemed ready for independence and they wanted it so that they might run the island in their own way. The mass of the people had little interest in independence and less understanding of what it involved. Independence was a potent political slogan and it was exploited to the limit by all Philippine politicians.

In Manila, where I attended sessions of the Philippine legislature I heard colorful oratory but little common sense. The speeches had more to say about America's successful revolt against Britain than about the economic problems of the islands. It is true that man does not live by bread alone but he must have food to live at all. When I visited a small country school the English teacher called on one of the pupils for a recitation. With much dramatic flourish the boy declaimed Patrick Henry's famous "Give me liberty, or give me death" speech. His accent was terrible but his enthusiasm was infectious. Many of the leading politicians who daily proclaimed their devotion to the ideal of independence confessed to me privately that something short of complete political separation would be much more practical and from their personal point of view quite acceptable. I was interested to hear this from Emilio Aguinaldo, the leader of the Philippine insurrection movement of 1900-01.

"We are not ready for independence," he said, "and I am not sure when we will be." Hastily he added that I must not quote him since to say this publicly would at once make his political position in the islands impossible. He was head of the Veterans Association which naturally made much political capital out of the independence cause. From various political leaders including Manuel Quezon I received such suggestions as territorial or dominion status or complete autonomy within the American tariff system and with a guarantee of American protection. This would have meant responsibility without authority, a situation which individuals and governments should always avoid.

One of the underlying reasons for tension between Filipino leaders and the American authorities was race discrimination. The test of social equality is admission to club life. No Filipino was eligible for admission to the Manila Elks Club or the Army and Navy Club. This was a sore point, particularly with those Filipinos who were graduates of American universities. This policy of racialism had unfortunate effects. It militated against good relations between Americans and Filipinos. Efforts of individual Americans like Acting-Governor Gilmore to develop friendly social intercourse with Filipino leaders and their families did much good but could not offset the harm done by others.

I left the Philippines impressed with the fine work that had been done by American authorities in improving health and education. But real political or economic independence seemed a long way off. Most Filipinos favored complete and immediate independence but the leaders such as Quezon, Rojas, Osmeña, and Aguinaldo with all of whom I talked were realistic enough to admit that if the islands were to prosper they would need American tariffs, American subsidies, and American protection for some years to come.

My necessary about-face on the Philippine independence question taught me an important lesson. It is dangerous to form opinions at secondhand. A responsible publicist should always try to check his opinions by firsthand contacts and observations. For many years I have done my best to do this as much as possible by seeking personal contact with the men, places, and events that dominate the news. But the truth remains elusive no matter how hard we strive to find it and recognize it.

16

My first visit to the Soviet Union left me open-minded about this Russian experiment. I was not in sympathy with most of what they had done. Life under the new regime seemed drab and regimented but I was willing to concede that for the average Russian life might be a little better than the life most Russians had known under the Czars. I was inclined to think that the Russians, given a chance, might work out a form of government and way of life for themselves that could be accepted by the world at large without further attempts at armed intervention.

I returned to Russia in 1929 with a group of American bankers, industrialists, and newspapermen. The trip was organized by the American-Russian Chamber of Commerce with the co-operation of the Soviet authorities to show these men opportunities for two-way trade between Russia and the United States. Several important American industrial and engineering firms were active in Russia setting up automobile plants and helping to build some of the construction projects called for in the Five Year Plan. This tour represented a cementing of established relationships and the development of new contacts. Among the ninety members of the tour were a vice-president of the Westinghouse Corporation, a representative of the Chase National Bank, and officials of International Business Machines and Remington Rand. Among the newspapermen who joined the party were William Henry Chamberlain, H. R. Knickerbocker, Eugene Lyons, Walter Duranty, Ernest K. Lindley, and Oswald Garrison Villard.

We had an excellent chance to study Russia's problems at first hand. It was particularly valuable to meet and talk with Americans who had worked in Russia for some time, such as J. K. Calder, an outstanding engineer. He was the construction engineer in charge of putting up a giant tractor plant in Stalingrad. He cited the small number of foremen used in Russia, about one to a hundred and fifty workers (in America about one to twenty). Supervision was virtually impossible. In comparing the efficiency of Russian and American workers he said that the Russians were about one fourth as efficient. With the introduction of American methods of supervision he said they got work done in four days that had been done in twelve. Mr. Calder also told us about the waste of time that results from the system of perpetual conferences. When he first began working in Russia he found that most of his time was devoted to an enormous number of conferences and meetings that concerned themselves with the most minor problems. He soon decided to send his Russian assistant to these meetings, so that he could be free to do more important work.

The Russians were drawing upon foreign experts for help in the development of their oil production. An American expert from the University of Oklahoma had been hired to give special technical courses to the workers in the Grosny oil fields. Skilled technicians represented the greatest shortage in the oil fields. Under the Five Year Plan Russia's technical schools were supposed to increase their quota of specialists for work in the oil fields. But the constant emphasis on Marxism left too little time for attention to special skills. Many of the men turned out were, by our standards, woefully unprepared.

We also met Colonel Hughes Cooper who had helped design and was now building the great Dniepestroy Dam. We spent a day going over the project with him and his engineers. Colonel Cooper pointed out that the Russians always planned far more grandiose schemes than they could possibly execute. He was convinced that the Five Year Plan could not work out on schedule. By setting impossible targets in the first Five Year Plan, Stalin stimulated the Russian people to a degree of accomplishment that would not have been attained had the goals been more modest. Stalin himself had little firsthand knowledge of economics. He simply applied to the industrial field the same ruthless determination he had used to consolidate his political control. He pressed forward with industrialization at a terrific pace. All things considered, the Russians were doing extremely well.

Colonel Cooper was convinced there were great opportunities in Russia for American investors. He was impressed by the extent of the country's undeveloped resources. In discussing various aspects of the Five Year Plan he said the idea of lighting every peasant home with electricity was just a dream. "The trouble with the Russians," he said, "is that they ignore the immediate practical problems and dream about future accomplishments. They should sit on some of their theorists and talk about practical things. They talk to me about a five hundred million dollar electrification plan and I tell them they would do better to begin by fixing the electric elevator in the Savoy Hotel in Moscow, so that just for once the darned thing would work."

"The men governing this country aren't normal," he said. "There is scarcely a man in the government who hasn't spent years of his life in jail." When we asked about the strength of the regime, he said there was no chance that the Soviets could be ousted from power. "I feel that we should give these people a chance to try out their theories. You cannot make them change. Any changes that come in Russia will have to come from within."

It was men like Commissar Lunacharski whom Colonel Cooper had in mind when he said "the men governing Russia aren't normal." Lunarcharski was a veteran Bolshevik and the first Commissar of Education in the Soviet Union. He had been active for a long time in the revolutionary movement before 1917, and had suffered imprisonment at the hands of the Czarist police. He spoke French during our interview with him and I served as translator. His remarks caused more misgivings among us than any other interview we had during this 1929 visit. We found Lunacharski a fascinating individual. He had the head of an intellectual, the eyes of a tired cynic, and the lips of one who loves the good things of life. He was completely frank and ruthless in his enunciation of Communist revolutionary doctrine. The world he said was suffering from the disease of capitalism and the Communists, like surgeons called to cure a disease by a major operation, inevitably would have to shed some blood. "The very existence of capitalist society," he said, "constitutes a war without end against humanity. This situation must be changed radically. . . . We oppose all wars between peoples, but we are for the war of the peoples against their oppressors. . . . We are convinced that there must be further suffering before our Communist ideas can be put into effect. . . . Our task is to organize the people of the world for this struggle. . . . When the proletariat is organized we propose to present our ultimatum to the possessing classes. They will not surrender their possessions peacefully. We must take them by force."

On hearing this exposition of the inevitability of violent world revolution, Sam Lewisohn, who among other things is an important copper company executive and who had hoped to try to promote American-Russian trade, exclaimed, "Good Heavens! The beggars want to cut our throats! They are barbarians masquerading as social workers!" The Lunacharski interview ended for him and several others any ideas they had of doing business with the confirmed Marxists of the Soviet Union.

On another occasion when I sat next to one of the key Communist officials I recalled Colonel Cooper's comment on the character of the Russian leaders. This was at one of those elaborate banquets which began at seven and ran until midnight. There were all sorts of dishes and a great profusion of vodka and sweet Georgian champagne. When I asked this Communist official why he ate and drank so sparingly, he told me that as the result of his many years in czarist jails he had lost all taste for food. It is these past experiences that have hardened the Soviet leaders. Instead of making them more compassionate and responsive to human suffering, they have become indifferent to the sufferings of others. Most leaders of the Russian Revolution were political refugees, lived under terribly difficult conditions, spent years in jail, years in Siberia, always fighting for their beliefs. When men like these gain autocratic power they cannot exercise it with tolerance and human sympathy.

In the midst of most housing developments in Russian cities there are large communal buildings devoted to recreational and education activities. These are known as palaces of culture and rest. In one of these palaces at Nishni-Novgorod on the Volga we discovered a group of young boys being taught the art of war. All parts of shells, rifles, gas masks, and machine guns were on display. There was an illuminated wall map that traced the history of the Russian Revolution. Special colored electric lights traced the routes of the different foreign invasions of Russia from 1917 to 1922. They showed where the White Russian Armies, headed by Generals Kolchak, Denikin, Yudenich and Wrangel, invaded and also where the French, British, Japanese, Czechoslovakian, and American forces had sought to defeat the Communist Revolution. We have forgotten these invasions but the Kremlin has not. For our particular benefit colored blue lights were flashed on at Vladivostok and Archangel, the two ports where American troops were stationed. When I asked the instructor in charge of the military training for young boys, how he could reconcile this emphasis on militarism with the much-advertised Communist love of peace, he said, "Our country is surrounded by enemies. We must be prepared to defend ourselves. For this reason it is necessary for us to give our population military knowledge.

Twelve-year-old Hans poses for a formal portrait in Milwaukee.

At twenty, young Hans as a volunteer in the Spanish American War.

At Harvard, thespian H.V.K. in a Molière play (1906).

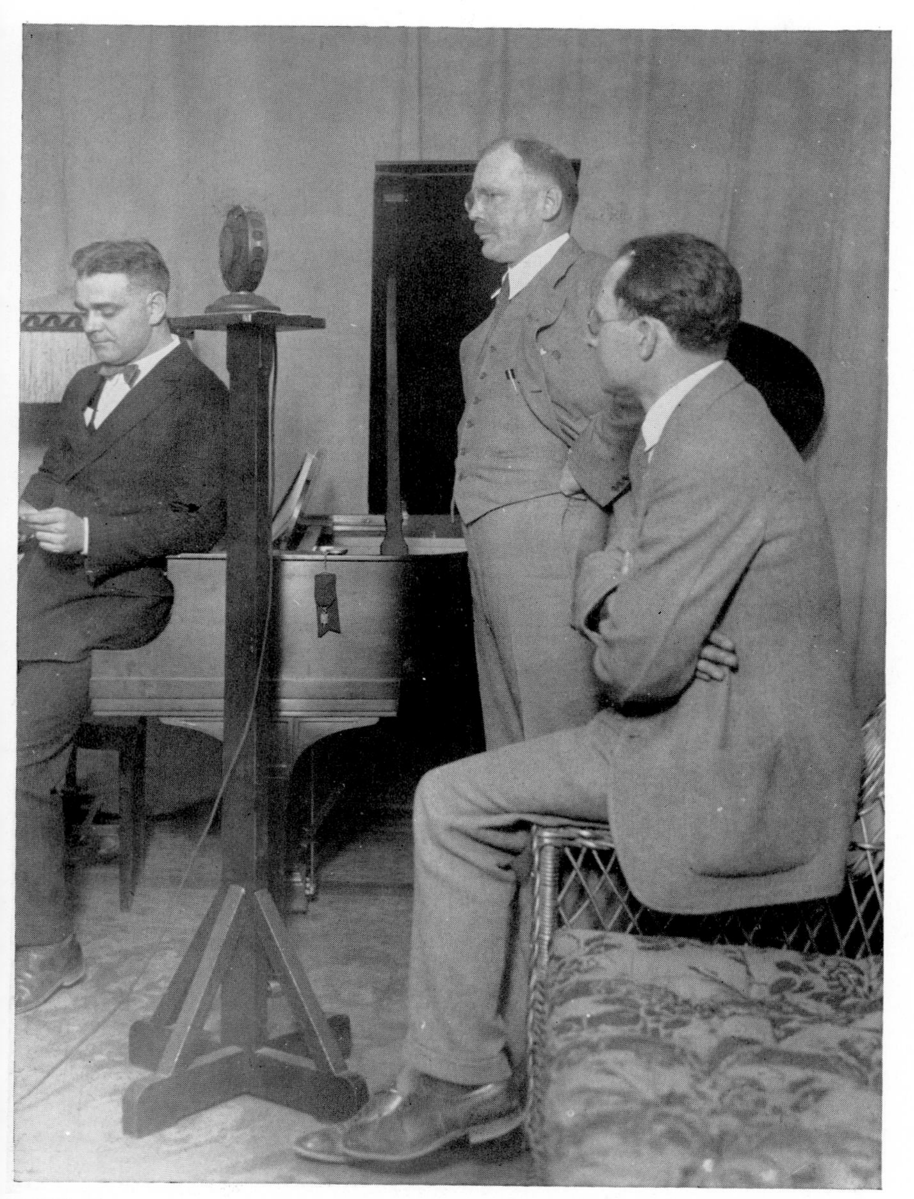

H.V.K. faces one of the early carbon microphones (1924).

During one of his early trips to Soviet Russia, H.V.K. and correspondent Ernest K. Lindley (center) interview Commissar of Education Lunacharski (1929).

H.V.K. interviews Adolf Hitler in Berchtesgaden shortly before he took over power (1932).

H.V.K. and his wife, Olga, chat informally with King Alfonso XIII at a polo match in Spain (1926).

H.V.K. and engineers on hotel roof in Hendaye, France, on the Spanish frontier, from which H.V.K. made one of his famous 1936 battle broadcasts.

H.V.K. and wife Olga celebrate the completion of fifteen years o
the air (1936).

"Let me congratulate you on your campaign, General. You've got H. V. Kaltenborn in a swivet." COURTESY OF COLLIER'S

At Guadalcanal in 1943. The first network broadcast from this island, arranged by H.V.K., was cut off because an Army sergeant happened to sing one line from a popular song chorus not previously cleared with N.B.C.'s New York office.

H.V.K. chatting with the late Wendell Willkie (1940).

H.V.K. and his son Rolf interviewing Secretary of the Treasury John W. Snyder. COURTESY OF RENI PHOTOS

H.V.K. photographed by Mrs. K. with General Douglas MacArthur and Mrs. MacArthur after a luncheon in Tokyo, Japan.

H.V.K. in Korea during his round-the-world flight, with Syngman Rhee, President of South Korea.

H.V.K. with Ernest Bevin, British Foreign Secretary.

I.V.K. on a rickshaw ride in Durban, South Africa, being pulled by Zulu chief.

H.V.K. with Louis Lochner, former Associated Press chief in Berlin and Marlene Dietrich, favorite movie star of the Kaltenborn family

H.V.K., still an enthusiastic tennis player, shown with two of hi favorite partners—his wife, Olga, and tennis star Alice Marble.

ere is H.V.K. with his favorite dachshund, Emil.

H.V.K. engages a formidable chess opponent in his granddaughte[r] Karen while his son Rolf looks on.

The Russian people must always be ready for defense against invasion but Communist Russia will never engage in a war of aggression."

This stress on military training was a deep disappointment to Oswald Garrison Villard who shook his head sadly as the young instructor talked. Villard always despised militarism and was shocked to find the Soviet Union preparing for war. This did much to sour him on the Russian Revolution which he had always followed with sympathetic interest.

One significant change between 1926 and 1929 was the increasing display of Stalin pictures. His picture always appeared beside that of Lenin and more frequently alone. It was evident that Stalin had consolidated his power. Cities were being named after him. The history of the Revolution was being rewritten to give him a more important role and to deprecate the part played by Trotsky. Stalin's fiftieth birthday in 1929 was celebrated with great pomp. All the newspapers carried lyrical tributes. A slogan was coined, "Stalin is the LENIN of today." Stalin worship had begun.

During this trip we had a group interview with Ian Rudzutak, who was then Peoples' Commissar for Transport and a member of the all-important Politburo. Like Molotov, Voroshilov, and Stalin, he was a "home-grown" Bolshevik leader. Rudzutak had supported Stalin in the struggles against Trotsky. Some years later he turned against Stalin and was liquidated in the course of the 1937 trials. American recognition of Russia was a sore point and by mutual agreement we did not discuss it. One of the chief problems was the question of the Czarist and Kerenski debts to the United States. The Communists refused to accept responsibility for these debts, claiming that they were made by a hostile government. In talking with Rudzutak, we were informed the Soviets might accept responsibility for the Kerenski debts but not for those incurred by the Czars.

Rudzutak's frankness amazed the Russian correspondents who were with us. They had never experienced any such frank exchange of question and answer with a Politburo member. Those American correspondents, who sent back regular dispatches about the interview, experienced considerable difficulties with the censor. No full text was permitted to leave the country. I escaped censorship by mailing a letter to the *Brooklyn Eagle*.

My most interesting social gathering on this trip was a reception for the American press by the Russian press. The Russian League of the Press arranged a special entertainment in the building known as the House of the Press in Moscow. This corresponded to the Washington Press Club in this country. The occasion was heralded as an entertainment but the program featured speeches to be delivered by Oswald Garrison Villard and myself. Mr. Villard was introduced as a long-time friend of the Soviet Union. He was brief, courteous, and noncommittal. His enthusiasm for Soviet achievement had cooled considerably since he entered the country. Then I was introduced as the man who had told millions of Americans that Russia was the world's most interesting country for a visitor. I decided to be frank and told my listeners that Russia's progress would not be determined by the number of factories she could build but by the extent to which she honored freedom of the press. There was little applause for my remarks.

The Russian journalists had arranged a special performance by the theatrical troupe known as the Blue Blouses. These amateur actors presented excellent satirical sketches lampooning various aspects of life under the Soviets. I believe we saw one of the last performances by the Blue Blouses. They were a loosely federated semiamateur group with branches in most major cities but their lampooning was too effective for the authorities. They were disbanded soon after 1929. There was no place for critical humor in a dictator state.

Following the Blue Blouses, a dance orchestra played. The daughter of a Russian official told me that at first the authorities had banned the fox trot on the ground that it was erotic and bourgeois. But the same young lady admitted she enjoyed dancing the fox trot. We danced and I discovered something about Communist individualism. She was determined not to let me lead and insisted on going her own way while I tried to go mine. The result was a vigorous but uncoordinated hopping which illustrated the difficulty of smooth co-operation between communism and capitalism.

The Soviet Union did everything possible to make our trip comfortable and to impress the foreign visitors. We had a special train that included their best sleepers. A shower bath had been installed at one end of each car which, like most Russian plumbing functioned in hit or miss fashion. The two dining cars provided excellent meal service. Our baggage was passed with practically no inspection, a most unusual courtesy when entering or leaving the Soviet Union. As a rule every scrap of paper is carefully looked over.

Moscow seemed less drab than three years before. Street traffic still consisted largely of horse-drawn vehicles but there were an increasing number of automobiles. We ourselves went about in a fleet of Lincoln cars. The Russians who directed the industrial plants we visited were all optimistic about the economic future of the Soviet Union. The Five Year Plan was discussed as though it had already been fully realized. The Communist officials set their industrial targets at incredible heights. One predicted that inside of a few years every one of the fifty million Russian farmers would have his own automobile. Yet decades will pass before the Russian farmers get even what we would call backwoods roads. Russians have a habit of discussing future goals and industrial targets as accomplished facts.

It was in 1929 that Stalin began the forcible transformation of Russia. The first Five Year Plan had been officially launched in October, 1928. At the same time the ruthless collectivization of agriculture was begun. Stalin had issued orders to liquidate the private farmers, the kulaks as they were called, and a virtual civil war was waged against them. Millions were deported to work camps and many villages were leveled because they resisted collectivization. In the process large quantities of horses, cattle, and sheep were destroyed. Much land lay idle. Along with the industrial and agricultural transformation came all sorts of new restrictions on personal liberty. Yet on the whole the Russian peasants profited from the revolution. Under the Soviet regime the farmer achieved a more important position. He has retained some of his individualism even when he is a member of a collective farm. It was the peasants' resistance to forced collectivization that shook the stability of the Stalin regime.

For some time the peasants have been unable to withhold grain from the Communist authorities. Machine Tractor Stations have multiplied and the important farms are now under close centralized control. The mechanization of Soviet agriculture makes it possible for the Communists to check what each farm produces. But on many collective farms the peasant has retained his own little house and his own small plot of ground, which he cultivates with complete devotion. What he raises there is his own and he can sell it on the private market. He works for the collective because he must but his heart interest centers on the tiny piece of land that he farms for himself.

Before the Russian-American Chamber of Commerce party returned to America we took a poll on whether or not we should at once recognize the Soviet Union. It may be significant that this intelligent group divided evenly on this issue. I advocated recognition. It was my feeling that the Soviet Union should be recognized for what it was—the established government of Russia. I believed the time had come to admit that for better or worse the Communists were in complete control of Russia and would remain so. On balance I believed that recognition would be more helpful than harmful to the United States and the democratic cause. The sooner we dissociate from the legal form of diplomatic recognition the idea that it implies any kind of approval the better we can serve ourselves and the democratic cause we champion.

17

THE STOCK-MARKET CRASH OF 1929 DID MORE THAN bring financial disaster to millions of Americans—it sparked the world-wide depression of the 1930's. It showed up in bold relief that the world's postwar recovery rested on an insecure foundation. The shadow of fascism already loomed over parts of Europe as a counterthreat to communism but the conditions brought about by the economic collapse finally provided the most suitable climate in which both fascism and communism could flourish.

In looking back to the 1929 crash, it is interesting to speculate whether if Al Smith and a Democratic administration had been elected in 1928 instead of Republican Herbert Hoover the course of history would have been different. My answer would be no, for while the personalities of the two presidential candidates were dissimilar, the political platforms on which they ran simply used different words to express similar ideas. Both parties looked upon business as the backbone of the nation and promised not to interfere with the prosperity boom. Even over the tariff issue which had formerly divided the two parties there was no longer a wide divergence. It is probable that after the depression was well underway Al Smith might have been more ready to sponsor far-reaching federal relief measures than were offered by the more conservative President Hoover.

I had many opportunities to see Al Smith in action and followed his political career with affectionate interest. For many years I spoke from the same platform with him at an annual Washington's Birthday Luncheon given by the Guggenheimer family for the newsboys of New York. Al Smith was the featured speaker and I was a filler-in before he came. In those days newspapers still had a large newsboy street sale. This was before radio ended the sale of extras, and before newsstands monopolized street business. After the newsboys' party I sometimes rode over to Brooklyn with Al Smith who would join in with the Washington Day Parade of the Volunteer Fireman's Brigade and the dinner that followed.

Smith's easy humor and human touch were at their best in these newsboy talks. He told amusing stories of his own experiences as a "newsie" and showed a warm and sympathetic understanding of the problems faced by New York's underprivileged boys. During all the years in which I covered Smith's speeches I never heard him give a dull talk. He was always lively and entertaining and invariably provided easy listening even when he talked about budget problems. What I particularly admired was his rare gift for explaining problems of government in simple terms and in homely language. As Governor of New York he used this technique most effectively over the radio when, on occasion, he appealed to the voters for support against a hostile legislature. Although we did not think of this son of Tammany as a "reform" governor, he certainly accomplished more long-needed reforms than almost any predecessor. He was imbued with a sense of social responsibility. This grew out of his belief that the first obligation of those who are elected by the people is to do something for the people, not for a group or clique or even a boss, but for those who put you into public office. I am proud to remember that I voted for Al Smith every time he ran for office, including his bid for the presidency. He was wise enough to be aware of his limitations. He had the humility of the truly wise man who can accept advice. Had he become president I believe he would have appointed a first-class cabinet and would have relied upon it for guidance. Perhaps the man who picks a good cabinet and then seeks the constant counsel of its members is a better president in the long run than the brilliant man who picks a cabinet made up of devoted followers and then runs things himself. Much of the Soviet Union's power is due to the fact that the Politburo and not Stalin alone directs Russian policy.

Herbert Hoover was unfairly made to shoulder the responsibility for the Great Depression. Few people remember now that before the Wall Street crash, as President, he issued repeated and unheeded warnings about the dangers of an overexpanding stock market. He was also aware that even in boomtime America there was poverty and unemployment. He promoted studies of these problems and helped organize citizens' commissions to see what could be done to mitigate human suffering. In newspaper circles he was known as the hardest working president that Washington had seen in some time. In this he stood in marked contrast to his immediate predecessor.

Herbert Hoover always worked better with individuals than with large groups. He preferred dealing with the members of his cabinet on a man to man basis rather than in more formal cabinet meetings. This aversion to group discussion was carried over to his dealings with the press. He never enjoyed large press conferences and they did not reveal him at his best. These gatherings were stiff and formal. There were no jokes or offhand casual remarks. Hoover stood throughout the proceedings and during most of his administration insisted on written questions submitted in advance. He had no liking for the informal give-and-take and the spontaneous comment at which Franklin D. Roosevelt proved himself so adept.

While he was President, Herbert Hoover showed himself in a much better light during quiet personal interviews. He liked such interviews for the opportunity they gave him to express his own ideas.

His apparent inability to conciliate or persuade groups of people and his unwillingness to try hampered his effectiveness as President. He was unwilling to make minor concessions to achieve major results. He was not like the willow tree in La Fontaine's fable that bends with the wind and later snaps back. He was more like the sturdy oak that would rather break than yield. On one occasion after he had explained to me a particular policy so lucidly and effectively as to win my admiration I blurted out, "Mr. President, why don't you say that to Congress?"

"Oh, I have said just that and they paid no attention," he replied in a tone of irritation. He felt that once he had explained something people should understand and act on this understanding. He would not repeat or persist or continue patient persuasion. He had none of the wiles of the politician. He was never a party man before he came into the presidency and he refused to act as one. Before he was nominated by the Republican party there was some doubt as to whether he was a Democrat or a Republican.

It is my conviction that the arts of the politician are essential to a president. He needs them to win election and to make a success of his administration. Under our form of government the president must secure and hold the cooperation of Congress as well as the support of many different groups and individuals. He must have certain well-ingrained political instincts to succeed. He may be a perfect administrator but unless he can command continued support from those persons whose help is essential to a good administration he will be rated as an unsuccessful president. Which means that with all else that he needs the president of the United States should also be a good salesman.

Herbert Hoover was above all a man of character. He exemplified the finest tenets of the Quaker faith by the way in which he lived and served. It is a happy thing for both Herbert Hoover and the American people that he has lived long enough to render his greatest service after retiring from the highest office in the land. Once unjustly scorned, he has won the admiration of his fellow citizens and of the whole world.

The stock-market crash of 1929 and the Great Depression that followed made this half-century's biggest single impact on the thinking of the American people. Many people still remember it purely as an American business phenomenon of domestic origin and of concern only to the United States. But this financial crash had far-reaching consequences throughout the world. It was another proof that even then we were living in an integrated world. It did not take World War II, as some still think, to show us that we were part of One World. Anyone who examines what happened after the Wall Street crash can find ample proof that any major crisis here was already bound to affect the world at large.

I was traveling with a group of American business leaders in Russia just before the crash came. The only man who expressed apprehension was the vice-president of the Electric Bond and Share Company, a big holding corporation, who received daily cablegrams telling him that the stock of his corporation was selling at constantly higher prices which, he said openly, were bound to collapse. Throughout Europe, everyone seemed pleased with the business boom in the United States. For one thing it meant the continuation of large-scale American loans to Europe. New York had replaced London as the financial center of the world. In 1928 we loaned abroad some one and a quarter-billion dollars to prop up the economies of Europe, particularly in Germany. When the news of Black Thursday (October 24, 1929) caught the world by surprise Europeans as well as Americans were alarmed. Everywhere men expressed the hope that it was only a momentary setback that would soon readjust itself. As things worsened Europeans became panicky. The flow of money from the United States dwindled to a trickle. Financial difficulties developed as our loans dropped from one and a quarter billion in 1928 to only two hundred and twenty-five million dollars in 1929 and subsequently to nothing.

Europe could no longer look to America for support. Economic nationalism received a great stimulus. The goal of free trade was abandoned. With high and still higher tariff walls and rigidly controlled economies each country began to fight for its economic life. In September, 1929, Aristide Briand had proposed a United States of Europe, which represented his dream of making Europe into a political and economic unit. In the changed atmosphere following the crash Briand's idealistic proposals were soon set aside.

Nowhere was this more evident than in Germany. From 1924 to 1929 Germany had made remarkable progress toward stability. These were the years when Gustav Stresemann was at the helm. Thanks to his diplomatic skill Germany returned to the family of nations. The vexing problem of reparations was resolved by compromise—and American dollars. In 1927 the Allied Control Commission which had supervised German disarmament was withdrawn as a gesture of good will. Moderation and good feeling characterized Germany's domestic politics. In the *Reichstag* elections of May 1928, the moderate Social Democrats were at the pinnacle of their power with 152 seats. The Communists had fifty-four and the Nazis twelve. The great tragedy of the German republican experiment is that, except for Gustav Stresemann, the Germans were unable to produce any outstanding democratic leader. Most of the members of the twenty Republican cabinets were competent enough, but few were outstanding.

Yet what doomed the German Republic was not so much lack of leadership as the disastrous economic depression inaugurated by the Wall Street crash. Germany was almost totally dependent for credit and financial support on the United States and was not yet self-supporting when American aid was withdrawn.

The death of Gustav Stresemann coincided with the Wall Street crash. Both events marked a turning point in German history. The world economic crisis had immediate repercussions in Germany. Exports dropped off, unemployment rose drastically—and the Nazi party gained seats in the *Reichstag*. In the 1930 election the Nazis increased their representation from twelve to 137. The Communists also gained and joined with the Nazis to destroy the Weimar Republic. Following the Comintern line the German Communists singled out the Weimar Republic and the Social

Democrats as their chief enemies. They did not fear the Nazis because they reasoned that if the Nazi party did come to power this would only pave the way for a soviet Germany. Conditions would become so bad that the German workers would revolt.

Dr. Heinrich Brüning was Chancellor of Germany from March, 1930 until May, 1932. As a member of the Catholic Center party he had been closely associated with the leading generals of the small but powerful German Army. He was a soft-spoken intellectual and in appearance reminded me of the Roman cardinals immortalized by the painters of the Italian Renaissance. There was something ascetic in his face and manner. He talked like a man who had unlimited patience and was determined to achieve his ends. One of his first acts on coming to office had been to invoke Article 48 of the Weimar Constitution which granted him dictatorial emergency powers. By using Article 48 and dissolving the *Reichstag* he was able to put his first budget into effect. From then on the German Republic was ruled on an emergency basis by decrees. The influence of the *Reichstag* declined and precedents for dictatorial rule were established.

In the troubled times when the French invaded the Ruhr and postwar inflation was at its height there had appeared on the German scene the figure of Adolf Hitler. Now, like an ominous bird of prey, this figure again hovered over Germany.

Back in 1923 two months before the famed Beer Hall *Putsch* in which Adolf Hitler had attempted to seize the government of Bavaria, I visited Nazi headquarters in Munich. Even then Hitler was recognized as the leader of a powerful political movement. At that time he was called the uncrowned King of Bavaria. In actuality the Hitler government even then rivaled the regular government of Bavaria. Their closely knit autocratic organization radiated strength and efficiency. In response to my questions on party policy the Nazis presented me with a copy of the *Twenty Five Points of the National Socialist Party Program.* This party platform which remained unchanged in theory, though modified in practice, was a strange mixture of arrogant nationalism, theoretical nonsense, and sound social reform. It called for the union of all German-speaking peoples, renunciation of the Versailles Treaty, and colonies for Germany. The program also called for the government operation of all trusts, for profit sharing, and for the elimination of land speculation. There were also declarations against speculators and war profiteers. Crucial to the entire Nazi program were the anti-Semitic points that attributed all of Germany's misfortunes to the Jewish people. The Jews became the scapegoats for the personal and national frustrations of the Nazi party members and sympathizers.

There were two headquarters of the Nazi party in Munich at that time. One was devoted to military matters and to the creation of a new army of storm troopers. The other was concerned with administrative matters and propaganda. The toleration of this private army within Germany proved fatal to the Republic. The Brüning government never took wholehearted or effective steps to check the growing power of the S.S. Their headquarters had a most effective recruiting division which issued literature, held meetings and drills, and provided its members with uniforms and equipment. This had great appeal for many Germans, especially for those who were unemployed. Here was food, shelter, clothing, and soul-satisfying occupation. Here was compensation for the humiliating demilitarization of the once powerful Germany. All of the wealthier members of the party were obligated to make substantial money contributions and to provide jobs for less fortunate party members. Each party member was required to make some contribution. By exacting sacrifice the party stimulated loyalty.

I asked Adjutant-General Hoffmann, then Hitler's chief of staff, about the sources of the party's funds. He gave two answers, "I don't know," and "I can't say." When I asked him about the relation between the Hitler movement and the local Bavarian government he smiled and answered, "They don't bother us." This answer was significant since it was the same answer I heard later, in 1932, when I asked another Nazi leader about relations between the Hitler party and the government of the Weimar Republic. Without the tacit connivance of at least some leaders of the Weimar Republic the Nazi party could not have come to power when it did.

I was surprised to learn that very early in the Nazi party's history in addition to the storm-troop headquarters the Hitlerites had already formed a "shadow government," located in the administrative headquarters. Hitler knew just what posts in the Bavarian government would be occupied by different Nazi leaders. His entire staff was organized on the basis of heading certain civilian departments. Each department had its files and was operated so as to be ready to take over at a moment's notice. They told me that if they came to power the next day their government would function automatically and would pursue policies already worked out. Even a decade before the Nazi party came to power its plan of action was carefully prepared.

To learn more about the attitude of the local Bavarian government toward the Hitler movement I interviewed the *dejure* head of the government Eugen von Knilling. He was a jolly, optimistic, south German who proved surprisingly frank. Asked how he could permit Hitler's rival government to exist alongside of his own he replied, "You talk as though Hitler were opposed to the things that I believe in. You must remember that Hitler has a nationalist orientation. His concern for Germany's future is justified. The Bavarian government is in sympathy with many of the Hitler doctrines."

Economic difficulties multiplied at a rapid rate throughout Europe in the months and years that followed the Wall Street crash. Financial insecurity spread, international trade dropped off, prices fell. The only economic index that rose was unemployment. Each country reacted in much the same way to the developing crisis. More and tighter government controls and regulations were imposed. Laissez-faire economics disappeared. Each country, beginning with our own, retired behind high and higher tariff walls.

In Italy, where economic troubles were chronic, Benito Mussolini began to consolidate his power and to impose greater controls over the country's political and economic life. It was not until then that Italian fascism began to show its revolutionary nature. Benito Mussolini had come to power with the march on Rome in 1923, a result of the disorders and disillusion that followed the war. Only gradually did he begin to assume total power and it was not until after 1929 that he transformed Italy into a truly Fascist state.

France vainly sought to isolate herself from the worst effects of the depression. The country turned to national self-sufficiency, raised tariffs and stubbornly held the franc to the gold standard. However when Great Britain went off the gold standard in 1931, France's financial structure also began to crack. Britain's abandonment of the gold standard was sparked by a brief mutiny in the British fleet, but even earlier faith in the British pound was declining. Britain's foreign trade was dropping off, unemployment was rising. Her currency was weakened by the default of German and Austrian loans and the failure of the biggest bank in Austria. Her Labor government under Ramsay MacDonald seemed unable to take bold measures to deal with the crisis and soon resigned. The National coalition government that took over made the momentous decision to go off the gold standard. Britain then turned its back on its traditional policy of free trade and also embarked on a course of economic nationalism.

The economic depression thus had political repercussions in every country of the world. Governments changed hands. New leaders arose. In America, where elections are regulated by the calendar and not by events, the political change did not come until 1932. The Republicans under Herbert Hoover went out of office and the nation installed a new Democratic administration headed by that great innovator Franklin Delano Roosevelt.

18

I FIRST MET FRANKLIN DELANO ROOSEVELT IN 1920, during the Harding-Cox campaign. As vice-presidential candidate he presented a vital and attractive picture. Few people gave the Cox-Roosevelt Democratic ticket much of a chance to win. Young Roosevelt, however, refused to be discouraged about his chances. Once after he made a particularly eloquent speech expressing his complete confidence in Democratic victory, I asked him what vote he was counting on to win. With great seriousness he answered, "I am counting on the great silent vote." Roosevelt was to learn a great deal more about politics in the ensuing years. By 1932 he had become a master at the game and his new mastery showed itself.

By the time the Democratic convention met it was abundantly clear that broadcasting was an important political weapon. Radio was firmly established as a mass medium. Its growth had been phenomenal. The Columbia Broadcasting System assigned Ted Husing and me to cover the 1932 political conventions for the network. Ted Husing was to do the running commentary and descriptions, while it was my task to analyze events and political developments.

By this time, radio had become for me a full-time occupation. Writing and lecturing were sidelines. The *Brooklyn Eagle,* like everything else, had been hit by the depression. It had changed hands, and, when Frank Gannett felt obliged to turn it back to some of the former owners in 1930, I was asked to take a large salary cut. Instead, I quit. It was hard to leave the *Eagle* after some twenty-eight years of pleasant association but the paper had changed and I was willing to face the risks involved in making a change myself. Those were dark and difficult days for many men who had lost their savings as well as their jobs and who were forced to begin again. For me, the picture was brighter. I had not lost my savings and had considerable experience in the new business of broadcasting, one of the few industries that grew to prosperity during the depression period.

Soon after resigning from the *Eagle* I signed a contract with the newly organized Columbia Broadcasting System for a regular weekly news commentary. I was also assigned to special events of national or international significance. And so it was that I found myself in Chicago in 1932, in the sweltering Chicago Stadium, helping to broadcast the Democratic convention which was to nominate Franklin D. Roosevelt for president.

The greatest problem in the radio coverage of this convention was to keep the radio audience interested during some of the long dull speeches. Politicians had not yet learned the value of radio time. The delegates themselves took little interest in most of the speeches, and we felt sure that most of the radio audience would tune us out if we kept these speeches on the air. So we had to develop interviews and other special features. Commercial programs did not fill as many daytime spots as they did later on, so it was up to us to fill time. That is one reason why the 1932 convention is one of the few that have had almost complete coverage. Such a broadcasting marathon has not often been repeated.

We soon learned that if we cut out any part of the convention proceedings some people would feel offended. Whenever we faded down a long speech which we considered dull or unimportant and substituted something of more general interest telegrams and angry telephone calls accused us of censorship or partisanship. They demanded we stop interfering with convention proceedings. The "home folks" were insistent on hearing what their own delegate had to say, no matter how uninteresting his speech might be to others. Then if we gave in and switched back to the convention proceedings other listeners would complain that dull speeches were no proper substitute for their favorite entertainment programs.

Despite the best efforts of the convention managers and radio officials it was impossible to persuade most politicians to shorten their speeches. Those who addressed the convention considered it as their greatest oratorical opportunity. Not only their friends but the whole nation would be listening. Every speaker had heard that Bryan's Cross of Gold speech won him the presidential nomination. So the flood of oratory continued.

Three songs played on the bellowing convention organ still ring in my ears. "How Dry I Am," the cry of the anti-prohibitionists; "Sidewalks of New York," which pleased the Al Smith forces; and "Happy Days Are Here Again," the Roosevelt theme song, were heard every hour of every day.

Competition between the different networks was very keen. There was great rivalry to see who could first report new developments or even rumors. There was also rivalry to see who could first get the most prominent politicians in exclusive interviews. There was even the most tricky kind of rivalry to secure display of network initials—CBS, NBC, or MBS—in photographs of the convention proceedings. Announcers were instructed to hold our CBS microphones before politicians' faces so that when the photographers took their pictures the important initials were sure to show up prominently. Unfortunately for us the newspapers soon caught up on this free publicity effort by their upstart rivals and they simply blocked out radio initials on all negatives.

The first real issue to come before this convention was the seating of the Huey Long delegation from Louisiana. This was the first national appearance of the Kingfish, who was then an ardent Roosevelt supporter. It was also my first opportunity to meet this unique American phenomenon. He was a curious mixture of appealing and repulsive traits. He was coarse in his personal habits, vulgar, crude, and ostentatious. However, I came to respect his skill as a manipulator, as a politician, and as a speaker. He was not an orator but his speeches were simple, direct, and they overflowed with pertinent Biblical allusions. He had a gift for homely analogies. His voice had good color. It was well under control and he used it effectively.

Huey Long presents a neat problem in ends and means. There is no question that he furthered important public improvements in his state of Louisiana. The roads, schools, and hospitals built under his regime helped to modernize this rather backward state. But the cost was high and corruption flourished. He was an absolute dictator and never hesitated to use violence. He capitalized on the lethargy of previous state administrations but he degraded democracy in the process. Yet the blame for Huey Long lay as much with the voters who ignored or supported him and the followers who obeyed him as with the man himself. The worst damage done by Huey Long was that he made a mockery of democratic government. He persuaded many good people that only a ruthless dictator can bring them the benefits to which they are entitled. By flaunting some laws he reduced respect for all laws. It was not pleasant to see the apparent respect with which he was treated by important Democratic party leaders.

The nomination for the presidency stimulated a hard-fought, bitter battle at this convention. A Democratic victory seemed inevitable. The chief struggle was between the Smith and Roosevelt forces. Despite Al Smith's defeat in 1928, he was most anxious to have the nomination in a year in which he knew that victory would be in his grasp. He had been the nominee when the odds were against him in 1928, and he had increased the Democratic vote considerably over 1924. Now he wanted another chance when the odds were on his side.

Few preconvention nomination campaigns have been as carefully organized as that of Franklin D. Roosevelt. James Farley's now famous trip throughout the United States to corral convention votes was unique in American political history. No man had ever made a more thorough canvas of state and district leaders. He slighted no one. He was always genial and talked against no other candidate. But constantly and persuasively he sold Roosevelt. As a result of this intensive cultivation he came to the convention with a majority of the delegates securely pledged. Because of the Democratic convention rule requiring a two-thirds vote important work remained to be done to clinch the nomination. It was an exciting week filled with intrigues until the Roosevelt forces finally had it "in the bag."

F. D. R. planned to fly to the convention if nominated and make the acceptance speech in person. There is little doubt that he was well aware of the dramatic effect such an action would create. I wonder whether even he realized just how powerful that effect would be. His entrance was carefully prepared and the convention was in a perfect mood to receive him. His appearance before the crowd evoked an unparalleled demonstration. He exuded confidence and well-being. He was totally assured and certain of victory. Everyone felt that this supreme self-confidence presaged victory in November.

I also participated in the radio coverage of the famous Inaugural Day speech of March, 1933. I will never forget the electrifying effect of the phrase: "We have nothing to fear but fear itself." It excited me to the point where I delivered a ten minute extemporized editorial before getting back to my real job of describing the drive back to the White House as I followed the presidential automobile in my short-wave radio car. Here was a speech that seemed to lift a nation's spirit and to change its mood. We all realized that F. D. R. had begun well.

There was an amazing difference in atmosphere between the Hoover regime and the Roosevelt New Deal. During the first few months of the new administration almost everyone who surrounded Roosevelt was jolly and good humored. There was a new, fresh, informal attitude. Visitors were welcomed. Even the secret service men seemed to have relaxed their restrictions. Steve Early, the President's press secretary, gave me permission to observe a typical day in the White House and I was free to walk in and out of rooms and talk to anyone I pleased.

Marvin McIntyre who handled appointments for the President showed me F. D. R.'s memo technique. On a small sheet of memo paper the President would pencil a brief direction on a letter or document. "Mac ack," one of the most common, meant that McIntyre should acknowledge receipt. "Mac act" meant that the President wanted McIntyre to take whatever action was necessary. "Mac ref" meant that McIntyre was to refer the matter to the department or person whom it concerned. Roosevelt liked to see as much correspondence as possible. He did not want to be left out of things.

Perhaps the strangest human being in the buoyant atmosphere of the early New Deal was Louis Howe, "the Gnome" as he was called. He would walk about from office to office dropping a comment here and a word there, keeping track of what was going on. His asthmatic attacks hampered his activity but his influence was potent. Everyone knew that he was one of the few men who could say no to the President and get away with it.

I asked him just how he would describe his White House job. He smiled a bit wearily and said that he served as an oil can. Wherever there "was a squeak" he would drop a "bit of oil" in order to make things run more smoothly and quietly. He also said that another of his important tasks was to keep "the Boss" apprised of current opinion throughout the country. For this purpose he prepared a daily digest of nationwide clippings of editorials and signed columns. Howe himself selected what the President should see. He sent a similar digest to the key men in the administration. The President relied heavily on this service which enabled him to keep in close touch with press comment.

The White House secretariat of that day was dominated

by a spirit of good feeling and wholehearted co-operation. F. D. R.'s buoyant spirits were infectious. Everyone who could participated in the White House press conferences. The President's personal secretary, Miss LeHand, once said to me, "I never miss a press conference unless I've jut got to keep on working, and even then I always wonder what it is they are laughing about. They always have such a good time." For there rarely was a press conference without a good laugh for everybody, often at somebody's expense.

This press conference was an important weapon in Roosevelt's political armor. He quickly won the loyalty of the working pressmen at the start of his term and this helped counteract the antipathy of many publishers. He was always ready to help make the newspaperman's job easier. He prepared news for those conferences and sometimes saved it for release at the conference. This stimulated interest and attendance. Thus it assured good coverage for whatever story Roosevelt wished to emphasize.

Nearly always at the end of the conference one or two "visiting firemen" would be brought up to the President's desk to be personally introduced to the President. It was amusing to note the skill with which F. D. R. would instantly seize control of the conversation. He would follow up something said at the press conference or pick up something from his desk such as new stamps that had come in for his collection. Always genial and charming, he would direct a few words personally to the visitors but rarely gave them a chance to ask serious questions of their own. Because of the length of his term, I saw F. D. R. more often than any other President but I rarely went away feeling that I knew what he really thought or felt.

Roosevelt even prepared special jokes and stories with which to regale the White House correspondents. He loved to tell jokes on members of his cabinet or more often on a member of the secretariat. Roosevelt had the actor's tradition that "the show must go on" and was a good enough actor not to give an impression of worry or concern. His own attitude had much to do with changing the psychology and mood of the nation.

On one occasion I expressed myself enthusiastically to Supreme Court Justice Felix Frankfurter about a press conference I had just attended and the masterful way in which Roosevelt had handled it. Frankfurter agreed but said he was fearful that Roosevelt had established a dangerous precedent. He said, "Roosevelt happens to be one man who has the quick incisive mind, the self-control, and the gift for repartee, which these catch-as-can sessions require, but what about his successors? The President of the United States should not answer questions extemporaneously. He should not be subjected to that kind of interrogation. It is too risky. There are too many people listening to what he says. His remarks are followed attentively throughout the world. They are subject to all kinds of interpretations. It is a constant risk and mistakes are inevitable. The negative aspects of these press conferences offset the positive gains."

For my own part I hail these exchanges as a supreme example of the democratic process. They take the place of the question period in the British House of Commons. The President always can and often does dismiss an indiscreet or unfair question. Even a mistake can be revealing. And good questions at the right time bring forth answers that add greatly to public information.

The pronounced difference between President Roosevelt and Vice-President Jack Garner was apparent from the beginning of the New Deal. The two men were quite unlike in background, political views, personality, and general outlook. Roosevelt, with his characteristic shrewdness, recognized Garner's real worth and the value of his advice. A self-educated and self-made man, "Texas Jack" had played the good old game of politics for some forty-four years with unbroken success. One of the stories current in Washington in 1933, during the time of the unrest in Cuba, was that Roosevelt called up Garner and asked him what should be done in Cuba. "Let's keep out of Cuba," Garner replied.

"But what if an American citizen is killed?" Roosevelt asked.

"Well," said Garner, "I'd wait around a bit and see *which* American it is."

In the course of one rather long talk I had with Garner he refused to say one word of approval or disapproval about New Deal policies, although he was very frank about himself. When I persisted in trying to draw out comments on the New Deal he said, "Kaltenborn, you might as well quit. Lots of people would like to know the answers to those questions you've put. But whatever I'd say would be misconstrued. It is easy to create the appearance of a difference in opinion between Roosevelt and me. The man I should talk to about such a difference is the President. If he consults me he will get my frank reply. And let me tell you that it will be frank! But that's a matter between us. There is not going to be any friction between us and I am not going to say anything that might create it."

This was one reason Garner sidestepped all social invitations. He said, "There is too darned much stiffness at those dinners. There is a good deal of hypocrisy too. And what a lot of gossip! When I go out I want to enjoy myself and to be free and easy. I don't want to be obliged to hang a barndoor lock on my tongue."

Harold Ickes was an unusual specimen as a cabinet officer. Although he was a shrewd politician he never seemed to be at all "political." Certainly he was no party man since his loyalties crossed party lines throughout his career. Above his desk in Washington hung a picture of Albert Fall, the Secretary of the Interior who had been convicted in the Teapot Dome Scandal that followed the Harding administration. Ickes said he kept the portrait there so that it might always remind him and his associates of the potential troubles and temptation implicit in his office. He was meticulous to a fault in checking over the public works' contracts for the vast projects authorized in New Deal days. He was often high handed and arbitrary, but the kind of watchdog over spending of which there are never enough in a free-spending administration.

Henry Morgenthau never struck me as an impressive figure in his job as Secretary of the Treasury. F. D. R. gave him an apt name when he called him "Henry the Morgue." In the Roosevelt administration he was primarily a "yesman." Yet he pursued some ideas such as the pastoralization of Germany with rare persistence. In personal interviews he was rather hesitant and unsure. This resulted from modesty as well as ignorance. The feeling in Washington was that Roosevelt was his own Secretary of the Treasury on all important matters.

At my first meeting with Henry Wallace, Secretary of Agriculture, I was impressed with his global concept of the farm problem. When he talked about agriculture he had the entire world in mind and he knew a great deal about farm experiments in the far corners of the globe. He felt that not only could he regulate crop production in this country but that he could persuade other countries to do likewise. He envisioned a world-wide normal granary—where just enough, and not too much, would be stored. He wanted a free exchange of commodities across frontiers in such a way as to avoid too much feast or famine anywhere. The first note that I made on coming from my first visit with him was "a flexible international mind."

But the practical difficulties involved in regulating agriculture on the Wallace terms were impressed on me when I wandered through some of the offices of the Wallace Department and saw the size and scope of the bureaucratic machinery set up under the new Agricultural Adjustment Act. The amount of regulatory machinery essential to administer A.A.A. was a fearsome thing to behold for anyone who believed in the American farmer as master of his own domain. Thousands of inspectors had to be sent into the fields. Thousands of accountants had to keep track of what each inspector reported about, what each farmer was growing, and what benefits every grower or nongrower was entitled to receive. As soon as the A.A.A. helped one group of farmers, other groups were affected and called for similar benefits and protective regulations. If one particular crop was controlled, the farmer would plant excessively in other crops. If acreage was controlled he would use only his best acres. That produced a new surplus, which also had to be controlled. Farmers were paid millions of dollars *not* to produce crops while President Roosevelt was telling us that one third of our people were ill fed.

For every problem that was solved two or three new problems were created. Fortunately for Wallace and the New Deal, the Supreme Court ruled the A.A.A. unconstitutional. I am convinced that this saved the program from complete collapse and gave the administration a chance for a fresh start on our still unsolved farm problem.

I never completed my estimate of the late Harry Hopkins but I liked him personally, admired his loyalty and devotion to his work and his President, and thoroughly distrusted some of his ideas. He always had a hard job although it seemed easy to most people. Giving away somebody else's money is not so simple as many think. In one talk I had with him he told me that it was far cheaper to give relief than to create jobs for the unemployed. "Two and one-half times as cheap," he said. But he was more concerned with the morale of his relief clients than with what it cost to take care of them.

Jesse Jones was the complete opposite of most of the New Dealers. As the representative of big business he was a unique figure in the Roosevelt administration. He surrounded himself with hard-headed, competent businessmen. He was a shrewd bargainer, an ideal choice to head the government's biggest lending agency. Not only did he have the confidence of Congress but he also brought to the New Deal the support of many businessmen whom Roosevelt would never have been able to win over.

The presence of Jesse Jones among the New Dealers illustrates one of F.D.R.'s special abilities. He was able to secure the loyalty of the most diverse individuals who brought to his administration the support of widely scattered and divergent groups. Yet when you consider the different types of the men around Roosevelt there was a surprisingly small amount of bickering and feuding in the early days. Later, of course, it was inevitable that clashes had to develop between men like Jesse Jones and Henry Wallace. Roosevelt dominated his own cabinet much more than most American presidents. His personality controlled both the administration and public opinion to an extent which was probably unparalleled in time of peace.

During the winter of 1933-34 I received many letters

from radio listeners criticizing Mrs. Franklin D. Roosevelt and her manifold activities. Such complaints became even more common as the years wore on. But back then they were something new. I was anxious to find out how Mrs. Roosevelt felt about the uproar she was creating. I mentioned this to her good friend Senator Robert Wagner on one of my frequent visits to Washington. He suggested right away that I talk directly to Mrs. Roosevelt about these criticisms and arranged a meeting.

She received me in a small room at the top of the White House and immediately apologized for the small and cramped quarters. The White House was full, she explained, since members of her large family were visiting and the Vincent Astors among others were to be house guests. I explained that I wanted her reaction to the constant criticism of my radio audience of her activities. She responded in her usual friendly fashion and immediately asked me to put my questions as bluntly as I chose.

I responded by telling her that many people felt that her lecture tours and other outside activities forced her to neglect her duties as the White House hostess. She explained that it was all a question of organization. She had solved the problem by working out her official schedule of White House functions far in advance and then fitting her other activities into the time that remained. "I have always been a good organizer," she said. "But," I said, "is it dignified for the First Lady of the land to pursue outside activities to this extent? My radio listeners say you gad about too much." Here is her reply, "A woman does not sacrifice her dignity by leading her own life. Dignity is a matter of personal conduct. Dignity is after all a matter of how we do the work we can do and the work we are called upon to do."

She went on to justify her frequent travels on the ground that they helped her gather invaluable information for the President. She put it this way, "I get about much more easily than the President, and I have contacts much more easily than he can have them. I learn many things that it may be helpful for him to know. People will say things to me they would not or could not say to him. They may not always be important but they can be helpful. I am eager to help Franklin in every way possible but I also have my own life to live. I must also be mindful of the fact that in a few years I am going back to that life. This is, after all, only an interlude." It proved to be a far longer interlude than she could have possibly anticipated at that time.

She did not enjoy political life as much as her husband. "Franklin," she said, "is peculiarly well suited to do the job he is now doing."

19

SHORTLY AFTER FRANKLIN D. ROOSEVELT CAME TO power, the United States followed England's example and went off the gold standard. The abandonment of the gold standard marked the end of an era. The co-operation of the major powers in maintaining it had been a powerful stabilizing force. By supporting this established yardstick to measure the value of local currency, each power was surrendering a bit of monetary sovereignty to promote the general aim of international economic stability. When the major powers went off gold they embarked on restrictive policies of economic nationalism.

The London Economic Conference which met in June, 1933 was called by President Roosevelt in co-operation with the British Government. I was sent to London by the Columbia Broadcasting System to cover the conference in co-operation with Cesar Saerchinger, European manager for CBS. I particularly remember the good time we had doing one particular broadcast. To get the British public's reaction to the conference we scheduled one of the man-in-the-street broadcasts which were an everyday affair in the United States.

Our first problem was to get the permission of Scotland Yard. We explained that we wished to set up a microphone in Piccadilly Circus and ask passers-by to answer questions about the conference. Scotland Yard was most apprehensive since because of time differential we preferred to do our interviewing late at night. They not only feared international complications if some careless Briton spoke unguarded words but pointed out that in Piccadilly Circus we might suddenly find ourselves interviewing a "lady of the evening." This, they said, might give Americans an unfortunate impression of London street life. The broadcast went off without a hitch and an interview with a young woman who said she was a hairdresser by day and an "amusement girl" at night provided some of the best moments on the show. A slightly intoxicated *bon vivant* in evening dress insisted that the Economic Conference was "marvelous, simply marvelous" but was unable to explain why.

Yet there was little gaiety at that conference. It was a solemn futile kind of business as soon as it became apparent that the United States was not prepared to help stabilize European currencies. Actually the conference represented a final effort by the major world powers to cope with the world economic crisis by joint action. Of the many speeches during the opening days I remember only one, that of a little man from a small country. Chancellor Dollfuss of Austria had the courage to speak out against Hitler and tell the truth about the man who was soon to have him murdered. He ended his talk with a prophetic quotation from Schiller's *Wilhelm Tell,* "No man of peace can live his days in peace when wicked neighbors choose the way of war."

The United States delegation was headed by Cordell Hull, Secretary of State in the new Democratic administration. One basic idea dominated his mind while he held this office. He believed that peace could be maintained through world economic co-operation, that economic peace provided a sound foundation for political peace. He was, of course, absolutely right, but world peace through economic co-operation is a long-range goal and there are many difficulties in the way. The greatest obstacle Hull faced in trying to put through his pet idea, the reciprocal trade treaty program, was the traditional pressure in this country for high tariffs. He could not guarantee that his own country would go along with tariff reduction. In 1933 United States tariffs were at their highest peak.

I had met Cordell Hull in Washington during the early days of the New Deal. The first time I saw him he impressed me as a man who was safe, sane, and slow like Jack Garner. When I asked him whether the reciprocal trade treaties might not injure weaker industries within the United States he said, "I don't think I would give that first consideration. You have to take the broader view. The first thing we have to do is to restore trade by reciprocal agreements. In the course of the general economic improvement that will follow there are bound to be certain dislocations. The general overall gains will more than overcome the little damage that will be done here and there. The overall gains will offset a few minor disadvantages. The test lies in whether the country at large is benefited.

He went on, "Some people think I am crying in the wilderness by calling for better political relations through better trade relations. I tell them, no. I tell them that I am convinced I am on the right track and I shall keep pounding away at my idea. I remember that back in the Dark Ages it was the work of the few pious monks who painstakingly copied manuscripts that preserved for all time the learning of the Middle Ages and before. We simply have to keep alive the fundamental ideas of sound international economic policy."

Cordell Hull was placed in an unfortunate position in London. He had not been given full authority and had not even been allowed to help select the members of his own delegation. The members were appointed by Roosevelt without consultation with Hull. Some believed in tariff reduction, others did not. Some believed in the restoration of the gold standard, others violently opposed it. The late Senator Key Pittman of Nevada confided to me that the only reason he was at the conference was to do something for silver. Senator Couzens, Michigan conservative, sensed the basic conflicts within the American delegation. The day before the conference opened he told me frankly that America would soon have to decide between two courses of action: (1) to follow a program of international co-operation abroad, or (2) to pursue a policy of economic nationalism at home.

Cordell Hull had no control over the delegation. Publicly he issued statements that suggested unity of opinion among the American representatives. Privately he confessed that they were hopelessly split. President Roosevelt had drastically censored the speech Hull was going to deliver at the opening of the conference in which he planned to condemn economic nationalism. In addition Hull feared that his reciprocal trade treaty program was being ignored by Congress in the welter of other New Deal legislation. At one point he frankly admitted that he was the head of a delegation that did not agree with him, and Secretary of State under a President who did not agree with him.

With the American delegation divided and a great diversity of views among the other nations the conference was on the verge of collapse. At that point President Roosevelt sent in a fresh team, consisting of Raymond Moley and Herbert Bayard Swope. Moley, one of the original members of the Brain Trust, was sent with the power to negotiate an agreement on currency stabilization. When he arrived Hull quite naturally felt that he was being rudely superseded by Moley. He became indignant and isolated himself in his hotel room. When newsmen asked Moley what was his dominant impression of the conference after being there a few days he answered, "My dominant impression is that everybody here is very mad."

Moley finally succeeded in working out a limited agreement on currency stabilization that he submitted to Roosevelt for approval. After a few days of thinking the whole thing over on a yacht off the coast of Maine, President Roosevelt flatly rejected the proposal and sent the bombshell message that ended the conference. The message dramatically condemned wicked "international financiers" and stated that the United States would not subject itself to the "vagaries of European currencies." In brief it was a complete negation of everything the conference had set out to accomplish.

A few days later the meeting broke up in utter futility. Raymond Moley summed up his feelings to me in one unprintable word. The London *Telegraph* concluded an editorial on the death of the conference with this truthful sentence, "The fact which it is useless any longer to cloak is that the American delegation was throughout hopelessly divided within itself and completely out of touch with the rapid changes of the Presidential mind."

It was a thankless task that the leading statesmen and economists of the world had set for themselves. As the conference proved it was impossible to reverse the strong world-wide trend toward economic nationalism. The delegates were unable to take any effective action to mitigate that trend. The statesmen who attended disregarded the pleadings of some of their more far-sighted economic advisors because of domestic political pressures. Long-range economic considerations had to give way before immediate political requirements.

Roosevelt's expression of economic isolationism which broke up the conference was symptomatic of a world trend. President Roosevelt had just begun his experiments in currency manipulation and was unwilling to limit his domestic program by international currency commitments. Stabilization conflicted with his inflationary efforts to restore economic prosperity in the United States. The London conference caught Roosevelt at a bad time. He had just assumed office and was immersed in a domestic crisis. Thereafter, history was to show Roosevelt ready to participate in the international conferences that followed.

20

IN 1936 GERMAN TROOPS MARCHED INTO THE RHINE-land in violation of both the Versailles Treaty and the Locarno Pact. Here, if ever, was a time for vigorous Franco-British action to check Hitler before he became strong. We know now that his troops had orders to retreat if they encountered the opposition predicted by the German General Staff. But the military experts were wrong and Hitler was right. There was no opposition. Bold aggression succeeded and continued to succeed. The forces that were to lead to World War II were unleashed and they moved on to the inevitable end.

Most people who met Adolf Hitler before he came to power in January, 1933 were apt to underestimate him. I was no exception. We underestimated the fanatical drive and the magnetic power of the man. We overestimated the desire and ability of the German people to resist. Hitler could never have become Chancellor without the assistance of the German right-wing business leaders and politicians who financed his movement and negotiated the deals which made him Germany's political leader. Nor could he have come to power without the co-operation of the Moscow-directed German Communists who helped destroy and discourage the democratic elements that tried to maintain parliamentary government. Once in power Hitler was supported by millions of Germans who gladly submerged their individual desires to his all-embracing leadership and who hoped that even without war Hitler might retrieve some of the losses resulting from World War I.

After meeting Hitler I myself felt almost reassured. I could not see how a man of his type, a plebeian Austrian of limited mentality, could ever gain the allegiance of a majority of Germans. This was in the fall of 1932. Hitler had flatly rejected the terms under which the aging President Hindenburg had proffered him the chancellorship. The Nazi party had also suffered an electoral setback which reduced their representation in the *Reichstag* from 230 to 196. Louis Lochner, then Associated Press correspondent in Germany, and I had both asked for an interview with der Führer. Quite unexpectedly my Harvard classmate Ernst Hanfstaengl, then Hitler's liaison officer for the foreign press, telephoned me that the Führer would see us the next day in his Berchtesgaden home. We knew about his tendency to orate at newspapermen and we came prepared with a series of questions to which we were determined to get answers.

Hitler had no love for foreign newsmen. He greeted us in a perfunctory and hostile manner. The interview took place on the porch of his charming chalet in the Bavarian Alps near the Austrian frontier. It was a lovely spot and we sat on the porch that dominated a beautiful view of the mountains. It was a warm summer morning and canary birds were chirping merrily in cages that hung all over the porch. In these surroundings Adolf Hitler began to talk with frowning face as if he were haranguing a crowd. I purposely irritated him with my first question: "Why does your anti-Semitism make no distinction between the Jews that flooded into Germany during the postwar period and the many fine Jewish families that have been German for generations?"

"All Jews are foreigners," he shouted back. "Who are you

to ask me how I deal with foreigners. You Americans admit no foreigner unless he has good money, good physique, and good morals. Who are you to talk about who should be allowed in Germany?" That got us off on the tone which dominated the entire interview.

His intense hostility to France came out in his response to a question about a possible understanding between France and Germany. "There can be no good relations between Germany and the outside world, not while France continues to act as a bully!" he shouted at the mountains behind us. "France is holding us down. We are helpless. She is choking us to death. I know how to deal with France. They will learn to reckon with us!"

On Russia he was equally vehement. "You can't have good relations with Russia if you have many Communists in your own country. We have too many Communists in Germany to make good relations with the Soviet Union possible."

Asked if he felt that Nazism was an article of export he replied, "I don't have to export national socialism. People are coming to me from all over the world. They see many excellent traits in our doctrine which they would like to develop in their own countries. Many points in the Nazi party program could be used by other nations.

"One thing is certain," he went on, "democracy is not for Europe. Europe must have authoritarian government. We have always had it through church, king, and kaiser. Parliamentarism is not native to us and does not belong to the German tradition."

It was his belief that once a majority of the German people expressed confidence in him he could then proceed to govern them as their Führer, without tolerating any interference. But he never pretended that he could rule without popular consent. As he put it, "I don't expect to take power until I get the approval of the German people. I must have the support of the broad masses. A government cannot sit on bayonets. It must derive its strength from the people. Once the people give their approval to an individual it means that they want that individual to take over and govern. They don't want him to be hampered by parliamentary debates. They expect the leader in whom they have placed their confidence to be a real leader.

"A dictatorship is justified once the people declare their confidence in one man and ask him to rule. That is the basis on which I expect to establish my government in Germany."

After this meeting with Hitler I judged him to be too much of a fanatic, too vehement in expressing his beliefs to appeal to sober judgment. Those of us who met him before 1933 could not imagine that such a person would ever be able to translate into action the plans he had sketched in *Mein Kampf*. He did not appear to have his own mental and physical processes under sufficient control to be able to harness them to the achievement of a specific goal. He suggested embittered failure more than future success. His inflexibility and apparent inability to compromise would make it difficult for him to come to power in the normal way of political procedure. Most successful political leaders of the past have been adept at adjusting to change. They were willing to bargain to achieve their ends. The substance of Hitler's speeches and his party platform were often either self-contradictory or absurd.

What we underestimated was the appeal of the irrational and the impact of cleverly manipulated and constantly hammered propaganda on the minds and emotions of the German people. Hitler once told me that there are three rules for successful propaganda: "Make it simple—say it often—make it burn!" Hitler knew better than most outsiders the strength of his own party. He told me, "I have the biggest single party in Germany. Moreover, any unit in my following is worth two of the units in anybody else's following. Within the ranks of the Nazi party I have the bravest, the best, the most energetic human material in Germany. What is even more important our ranks are disciplined. My men obey."

When I asked him before he came to power whether he would use his disciplined forces for a march on Berlin he said, "I do not have to march on Berlin. I am already *in* Berlin. My fifteen million voters in and out of Berlin are already worth thirty million. These fifteen million can be put to work on the word of one man—and I am that man!"

On January 30, 1933 President Hindenburg appointed Adolf Hitler Chancellor of the German Reich. On February 27 the *Reichstag* building was gutted by a fire, clearly set by the Nazis. On March 5 the German people went to the polls. The National Socialists received the largest number of votes of any single party—seventeen million out of thirty-nine million votes cast. It was still a minority party but the *Reichstag* voted dictatorial powers to Adolf Hitler and his reign of terror began.

The brownshirted Nazi storm troopers were systematically encouraged in their brutality and hooliganism. There were all sorts of violence and cruelty, burning of books, smashing of store windows, beating of non-Nazis. These government-sanctioned outbursts ranged from sadistic attacks on helpless Jews to assaults on foreigners who did not give the Nazi salute. In the summer of 1933 my son Rolf was struck by a Nazi storm trooper for failing to salute one of the endless passing parades of Nazi banners. When the German Propaganda Ministry heard of the incident they sent me a formal written apology in the hope that I would not feature my son's misadventure in a broadcast. I had, of course, no intention of exploiting a personal experience.

There was an uncomfortable and almost hysterical atmosphere in Germany during the first year of the Nazi regime. Later Nazi violence was more quietly and systematically organized and less apparent on the surface.

I never felt at ease in Nazi Germany. The atmosphere was always tense and strained. The visitor who lacked sympathy with Nazi policies and purposes was uncomfortable and isolated. Free speech was no more. Friends talked in whispers. Press and radio were completely controlled.

For many Germans this made things easier. No more of the uncomfortable task of making up their own minds. No more doubts and hesitations. A newsdealer, whom I asked for a particular paper, said he did not have a copy. "Why worry about that one. Take your pick of these," he said. "They're all alike anyway."

The Nazis followed the Soviet plan of using every instrument of thought control to put over their ideas and to suppress criticism. You had to become an isolated outcast or an enthusiastic believer. There was no middle ground. Many Germans whom I knew well were hostile to much that Hitler represented yet they found it expedient to pay lip service and to go along with the regime. I learned long ago that the bulk of mankind is not born for martyrdom. We are foolish to expect many men to die or suffer for their beliefs when a bit of dissembling will enable them to protect not only themselves but also those they love. Many Germans sincerely believed that Hitler would temper his extremism once he was firmly established in office. Others felt that, bad as Hitler was, Nazi rule would certainly prove better than Communist rule.

I asked Dr. Kessler, who was one of Hitler's chief economic advisors, how the socialism of the National Socialist party was to be put into practice. He answered directly, "There is no socialism under Hitler and there never will be." He explained that Hitler's original program did contain elements of socialism but that they had all been wiped out. He maintained, as Hitler had repeatedly pointed out, that you could have a party program and yet pay no attention to it. That it was better to leave the original program intact and ignore it rather than change or amend it. Any change would be a confession of weakness. There must never be an admission of error—that is one of the important elements of totalitarian philosophy. Dr. Kessler made one interesting admission, "Hitler was never the world's greatest economist," he told me. "He learned long ago that certain economic points in his program were wrong. But if he had changed them it would have opened him to attack all the way down the line."

Once the Nazi party was in power its economic policies became practical and direct. Trade unions were smashed, strikes were prohibited, national self-sufficiency was encouraged, and the entire business structure of Germany was harnessed to the totalitarian war machine.

Although I was in Berlin at the time of the famous Blood Purge in the summer of 1934 I learned little about it until after it was virtually over. This was the purge of Ernst Röhm, head of the storm troopers, ex-Chancellor Kurt von Schleicher, and hundreds of other key figures within the Nazi party. The storm troopers included many unemployed adventurers. They had been drawn into the movement in good part by the appeal of the Socialist planks in the Hitler program. They performed an invaluable function for the movement during the long rise to power and then the consolidation of power in the first year of the Third Reich. Once force had triumphed, their usefulness was coming to an end as the regime settled down to the serious business of governing Germany.

Many of the storm troop leaders felt that Hitler was betraying the Nazi revolution by his concessions to the large industrialists and his neglect of the Socialistic aspects of his program. The storm troop organization had grown in size by 1934 to a restless two and a half million. Its leader, Captain Ernst Röhm, was a close personal friend of Hitler, who had helped build up the storm troopers since the early twenties. Captain Röhm wanted to amalgamate the storm troopers with the regular army, the *Reichswehr*. But the aristocratic General Staff of this highly trained military elite had no intention of having their army inundated with less disciplined storm troop rowdies. Hitler realized that since he now had close to absolute power the *Reichswehr* was more valuable for his purposes than the storm troopers.

Claiming the existence of a plot against the life of Adolf Hitler, the elite Nazi guards, the *Schutz Staffel,* most of whom were storm troop graduates, moved swiftly and relentlessly on the nights of June 30 and July 1. During the blood bath of those two days about a thousand Nazi leaders were shot on direct orders from Hitler. Victims of this purge included Röhm, Gregor Strasser, General Kurt von Schleicher and his wife, key Nazi leaders, and several Germans who had been high in the Catholic political party.

This purge broke the power of the storm troopers and gave Hitler ultimate control over the *Reichswehr*. The left-wing leaders of the Nazi party were liquidated or intimidated. This reassured the important business leaders of Germany who were supporting the Nazis. The purge of 1934 made Hitler's power in Germany supreme. Possible rivals were eliminated. Former Chancellor Brüning fled the country in disguise a few days before the purge and later found a refuge in Cambridge at Harvard University.

In August, 1934 President Hindenburg died at the age of eighty-seven. By decree Hitler assumed all powers of the presidency and thus confirmed officially what had already become fact. In the plebiscite held to ratify this action thirty-eight million Germans voted *Ja*. Seven million still dared to vote *Nein* or invalidate their ballots.

I watched the ferment of adulation that surrounded the person of Hitler when I attended the giant Nazi party festivals in Nürnberg. The atmosphere in the Nürnberg City Hall where I found myself the only foreigner was most disturbing. It revealed so completely the irrational willingness of these Germans to worship a mediocre human being. I never felt more alone in my life than when I refused to join this crowded hall of intoxicated idolaters in raising my arm in salute to Hitler. I kept my arm rigidly at my side and fortunately no one noticed me. All eyes were riveted on the platform, on der Führer as he spoke in acceptance of the city of Nürnberg's prophetic gift—one of Dürer's famous etchings, "The Knight Who Rides with Death."

In the summer of 1934 Adolf Hitler experienced the first real check that followed his rise to power. It came from the man who would one day be his ally, Benito Mussolini. Hitler had long been agitating for the incorporation of Austria into the Third Reich. In July, 1934 a small band of Nazis seized the Vienna radio station and assassinated Chancellor Engelbert Dollfuss. Before they could consolidate their coup, Mussolini mobilized his troops along the Brenner Pass and said that he would defend the independence of Austria. This decided the Nazis to back down. Kurt von Schuschnigg succeeded Dollfuss as the Chancellor of an uneasy and restless Austria. Not until four years later did Hitler decide that the time was ripe for annexation.

I saw the Italian troops on the Brenner Pass in that summer of 1934 and got the impression that they were no match for German soldiers. Yet I was convinced at the time that Mussolini would go to war had the Germans tried to annex Austria by force in 1934. In the years that followed Europe missed the valuable lesson which Mussolini's successful intervention should have taught.

Whatever Benito Mussolini might feel about German aggression in 1934, two years later he saw nothing wrong in sending his own Fascist troops to finish the conquest of Ethiopia. More skillful diplomatic handling of Mussolini by the democratic powers during the crucial years 1932-34 might well have met some of his legitimate claims and kept him on the Allied side as Italy's real interests demanded. The first time Mussolini met Hitler in Venice he did not like him. Democratic statesmen knew this but failed to take advantage of Mussolini's pride and vanity to play one dictator against the other.

Hitler and Mussolini were opposite personalities. Several times I interviewed them both during the same summer and was impressed with the contrast. Hitler was something of an introvert, Mussolini the complete extrovert. The one was a provincial, the other a cosmopolitan. The one was a narrow nationalist, the other a son of the Roman Empire. Mussolini was more flexible, more susceptible to flattery. Because of Italy's basic weakness he could have been won over by relatively unimportant concessions. Mussolini had all the faults of a dictator. He was indifferent to moral laws, he loved to swagger and he was a complete egotist. But he had a sense of humor and he remained a realist. When his vanity or his ambition did not get in the way his shrewd intelligence dictated sound decisions.

The first time I met Mussolini was in 1931. He had invited a group of foreign journalists to the Palazzo Venezia to show us his new plans for the remodeling of Rome. He had developed a great scheme for new wide roadways through the heart of Rome to the Colosseum. He planned to tear down many buildings and widen the streets. His idea was to transform Rome into a modern city while retaining and re-creating some of its ancient glory. It was also a public works project to help take care of rising unemployment.

Mussolini outlined his plans with great enthusiasm. He stood before a giant map of Rome and with a dramatic sweep of his arm eliminated whole areas. He was clearly the actor in this public performance. He enjoyed playing a part before an attentive audience and was completely at his ease with the gentlemen of the press. Not so long ago he had been one of them. In this respect he was far different from Hitler, who always disliked personal contact with those who were not in complete agreement with him. One reason why Hitler orated in personal conversation was to prevent a listener from disagreeing with him. Mussolini on the other hand seemed to enjoy interruption. He welcomed intellectual challenge as a good fencer welcomes a clever thrust. He liked debate and the give-and-take of lively conversation because he was good at it.

Mussolini was talking peace when he saw foreigners in 1931. He denied that Italy had any imperial ambitions. He spoke of the great need for internal developments such as the reclamation of the Pontine Marshes, the development of hydroelectric power, and the expansion of agriculture. He had great plans for Italy's colonies.

He was a changed man when I talked with him in 1935, just before he embarked on his conquest of Ethiopia. He was then surrounded by a great number of guards and there were all sorts of checks and double checks when I came to the Palazzo Venezia for my interview. Mussolini had become much more inaccessible to newsmen and a good deal of negotiation was needed to secure an interview. On this occasion I was surprised to find that Mussolini's press secretary had scheduled a small-town newspaperwoman from Alabama to share my interview. As we waited to be called I could not refrain from asking her how she had secured the appointment. She showed me a most impressive document. It was a formal letter of introduction to the Duce inscribed by the

Governor of Alabama in flowery language and bearing the large gold seal of the sovereign state of Alabama. I don't wonder that the Office of Press and Propaganda were impressed.

Possibly in deference to the Alabama lady Mussolini was gaily decked out with a white suit, blue shirt, and a brightly checkered tie. He even treated us as important guests by rising from his chair and advancing to the front of his desk while we covered the interminable distance from the door all the way across the immense room. He conducted the interview in English which he spoke slowly and precisely. As he hesitated for a word I would tentatively suggest one. Several times he accepted it but more often he rejected it and chose one of his own. He had a keen sense of word value and in addition to English spoke French and German with considerable fluency. I have tried him in all three languages and found him most familiar with French.

Our talk naturally centered about Italian plans for Ethiopia. I told him I had just come from Geneva and was sure that the League of Nations would take action against him if he pressed on with his Ethiopian campaign. At this his dark, penetrating eyes flashed. "The League!" he exclaimed. "The League, the League! What did the League do in Manchuria? The League will do nothing!" He was almost right, the League voted economic sanctions and then did nothing to enforce them.

In 1928 Mussolini had signed a treaty of friendship with Haile Selassie, Emperor of Ethiopia, which gave him primary economic rights in the country. Mussolini claimed that France and Britain who were also interested in that part of Africa had interfered with the execution of this treaty because, as he put it, "They are jealous of Italian aspirations. They have never treated us fairly in Africa."

The Ethiopian campaign wedded Mussolini firmly to Hitler and proved the success of dictator aggression. France and Britain pursued an indeterminate policy that undermined the League, antagonized Mussolini, and failed to check Italian aggression. After first ignoring the issue, the League of Nations finally overcame French and British reluctance to take any kind of action. When sanctions were voted oil, one of the most crucial of modern war materials, was exempted from the prohibition against imports to Italy. The United States joined the other democracies in supplying Mussolini with the fuel of conquest.

By March 1936 Mussolini's Ethiopian campaign was carried to a successful conclusion and the impotence of the League of Nations was apparent to all. Emperor Haile Selassie made a last tragic and futile plea in Geneva, "God and history will remember your judgment . . ."

21

THE TRAGIC SPANISH CIVIL WAR THAT BEGAN IN 1936 took a human toll of more than one million lives out of a population of twenty-seven million. No family escaped loss. When the Civil War began the statesmen in Britain and France correctly sensed that this struggle might well become the spark for another world war. Reflecting the dominant pacifist spirit, which prevailed in their countries as it did in ours, they were determined to preserve peace at all cost. Appeasement had prevented the Ethiopian conflict from spreading and they planned to follow the same hands-off policy in the case of Spain. Although the Popular Front government of Leon Blum in France was sympathetic to the Loyalist (Popular Front) government in Spain there was too much concern with France's internal problems to permit any vigorous course in foreign affairs. It was the French who first proposed that all the Great Powers should refrain from sending any war materials to Spain. A Non-Intervention Committee made up of fifteen countries, including France,

Germany, Italy, Britain, and the Soviet Union was established to carry out this policy.

In the United States a strict neutrality policy was adopted. This maintained our traditional policy of isolation. President Roosevelt expressed general United States opinion when he said, "We shun political commitments which might entangle us in foreign wars."

Though Germany and Italy joined the Non-Intervention Committee they paid no attention to the obligations they assumed. Both Hitler and Mussolini openly declared they intended to bring about a Franco victory. They recognized Franco's government as the legal government of Spain. They defined as illegal intervention anything that helped the Loyalists.

Stalin and his agents in Spain favored the Loyalist cause, and they worked hard to transform it into a Communist cause. The Moscow line was one of "moderation" in Spanish domestic politics. Stalin was pursuing the United Front policy. He was wooing the democracies in an effort to gain allies against Nazi Germany. The full story of Stalin's intrigues in the Spanish Civil War has yet to be told—and may never be told since most of his secret agents in Spain were liquidated on their return to Moscow.

In France there was a strong movement in favor of intervention on the side of the Loyalists despite the official French line of nonintervention. The movement gained in strength as Italian and German intervention on behalf of Franco became more apparent. In Britain too there was considerable popular sympathy for the Loyalists but the Foreign Office was trying to woo Mussolini away from Hitler and there was fear that involvement in the Spanish struggle might endanger the vital British Mediterranean life line through the Suez Canal.

The cruel and bloody character of the Spanish struggle was apparent from the first. There was little difference between the two sides as regards the blood lust, the cruelty, the torture, and the vindictiveness. In 1936 I was on the front with both armies. It had not been easy to get accreditation to both sides. My lecture circular, a photograph of myself with

Adolf Hitler, proved to be my passport to the Franco side after more formal documents and testimonials proved useless. However, that same Hitler picture nearly proved to be my undoing a week later when I sought to get to the front lines of the Loyalists. The Loyalist commander at Irún took one look at the Hitler picture, sputtered a stream of angry Spanish and summoned an immediate conference of his staff. It looked dark for my chance of getting through when I suddenly remembered that the same lecture circular also contained a small picture of myself taken with a Soviet commissar. I pointed this out to the commander and explained that I had visited the Soviet Union many times and that as an American radio commentator I had to interview anyone and everyone. This saved the day. From then on I made my headquarters in Hendaye on the French side of the Spanish border and spent alternate weeks with the rival armies, coming back to France to do my broadcasts.

My personal sympathies were with the Loyalists because that was the liberal, democratic side. Franco, the Church, and the Army stood for the old Spain with many fine traditions but blocking political progress. On Franco's side were some of the best elements in the country, but he was also backed by the forces of reaction, a corrupt military clique, an outmoded monarchy, and a political-minded Church hierarchy. The Carlist soldiers on the Franco side were ardent monarchists and devout Catholics. They insisted on wearing their traditional red berets in defiance of all laws of self-protection at the front. When I was on the Loyalist side in the front lines I saw what magnificent targets these red berets made. When a group of Carlists gathered together to pray before going into battle their berets made a large red blotch of color and became a perfect target for artillery and machine-gun fire. When I told this to the Carlists they said that the red beret had always been a Carlist tradition and they refused to give it up.

Not once while I was in Spain did I hear an impartial or dispassionate analysis of the Civil War. There was always bitterness, prejudice, and hatred. Calm analysis was impossible for any Spaniard. While the atrocities were bad enough, each side emphasized and exaggerated those committed by their opponents. In all my experience with large and small conflicts I have never felt the curse of war more keenly than while reporting the Spanish Civil War.

During the early months of conflict I visited a number of prison camps and found hundreds of Spanish prisoners who had accepted the first chance to surrender. Wherever a Spaniard happened to be when the struggle began, that is where he was forced to go into the Army. If a young man was in Franco-occupied territory he had to serve Franco. If the war's beginning found him in a Loyalist area he had to join the Republican Army. There was hardly a family in Spain that did not have representatives on both sides of the conflict. German prisoners told me that they regarded the war in Spain as a rehearsal for a larger conflict. Italian prisoners complained that they had volunteered for service in Africa but were sent to Spain instead.

Every time I came to the front lines on either side soldiers offered me their rifles and suggested I take a pot shot at the enemy. They thought I was squeamish to refuse. On one occasion I was foolish enough to accept an invitation to be a target. I was visiting a shattered building in University City which served as a Loyalist outpost during the siege of Madrid. The Franco front-line sharpshooters were entrenched only a hundred feet away. There was a peep hole where the Loyalist guard kept watch. Only the day before a Franco sharpshooter had sent a bullet into the Loyalist guard's eye. After telling me this, the Loyalist soldiers challenged me to take a look through the peep hole. To maintain prestige with the soldiers—such is human vanity—I looked long enough to see the Franco sharpshooter bring his gun up toward his shoulder. That was all I needed to see and I ducked before he pulled the trigger. The bullet missed the hole and the Loyalist soldiers had a good laugh. Then one of them sought to shame me by peering out of the hole until the very second the sharpshooter pulled the trigger. That kind of game delighted the daredevil Spaniards. They took many unnecessary chances. To draw fire they would stick out a hand, or wiggle a finger, and always roared with laughter when I refused to accept some kind of a dare. In besieged Madrid my wife and I took a considerable risk without realizing it. When the manager of our hotel apologized for putting us on the top floor we expressed our delight with the beautiful view of the city. Only later we learned that everyone with sense avoided the top floor of any big building because it was always the top floor that was wrecked by the shells that continued to pour into the city.

In the early months of the Civil War some of the battles seemed more like war games than war itself. On the Franco-Spanish frontier near Hendaye there was a narrow river with a snakelike course. A French farm jutted right into the midst of the battle for the Spanish city of Irún but both sides took care not to violate French soil. As the battle for Irún began and shells and bullets whizzed over this French farm I conceived the idea of broadcasting a battle description punctuated by battlesounds. A French radio engineer, who was keen on the idea, located a telephone line in the abandoned farmhouse that stood between the two battle lines. To get the best sound effects we ran a long cable from the house to a small haystack located at an ideal vantage point to both see and hear the artillery shells. Both shells and bullets were flying fairly high so the danger was not great. But I was not thinking of danger. I was determined to make the first actual battlefield broadcast in radio history. When I finally got communications through to New York and told them I could give them a description of a battle in progress with the actual sounds of rifle and artillery fire, I received back this answer, "Stand by. Too many commercial programs just now. Will call you later."

So I stuck to my haystack hoping that the scene of battle would not shift. Twice while I was waiting our transmission lines broke or were cut by bullets. My intrepid French engineer crawled out and made the necessary repairs. Late in the afternoon New York sent us the go-ahead but we found that the Bordeaux relay engineer had gone out for an *apéritif*. Finally at nine o'clock in the evening we got through and for fifteen minutes described the burning cars, the maneuvers of a small armored train, the shell explosions, and the burning buildings, stopping occasionally to let the listeners hear the peculiar whine of flying bullets and the dull explosion of artillery shells. For this broadcast I received an award from the Headliners Club of Atlantic City. But when I returned to Spain in 1937 my wife went with me into besieged Madrid and into the front lines to keep me, as she put it, "from doing foolish things."

For days before Irún fell to the Franco forces the correspondents reporting the war had an easy time following the battle. There was a charming small French café on a hillside just above the river boundary where we were able to lunch and sip good French wine while observing the battle through field glasses. Occasionally a stray shot or a shell from a plane landed on French territory. I began to suspect that some were aimed at us but none landed close enough to spoil our digestion.

Of all the groups within the Loyalist Popular Front the most unusual and typically Spanish were the Anarchists. Anarchism seems to appeal to the Spaniard's fatalistic and individualistic streak. The Anarchists refused to make common cause with the other parties. They fought fascism and General Franco with the utmost bravery but insisted on fighting by themselves and in their own way. They rejected incorporation with other army units. Yet they gladly accepted the most dangerous assignments and threw their lives away recklessly. Prompted by curiosity about their way of life and thought I spent a week end with a small Anarchist detachment assigned to a front-line mountain artillery position.

The Loyalist military leaders had told me that while the Anarchists were indifferent to discipline they could always be counted on to defend their positions with great bravery. They were known as *dynamiteros* because their favorite weapon was a dynamite stick which they used as a hand grenade. This dynamite made my week end with them one of the most nerve-racking of my life. They loved to juggle their homemade weapons as a boy loves to play with fire crackers. They were exhibitionists and made a great show of their indifference to the possibility that if a stick of dynamite should drop to the ground the juggler and at least part of his audience would be no more. Once the art of juggling had helped save my life. I thought it would be a strange twist of fate if someone else's failure to juggle successfully should end it.

My Anarchist group included a young girl dressed just like the young men. She shared their unconcern about death or danger. She was accepted as an equal and had her turn in serving as the leader for the day. There were no officers but since someone had to issue orders the members of the group took turns. When I asked whether the girl had a sweetheart among the group they looked at me with astonishment. "Anyone who touched her," I was told, "would be killed on the spot."

When I tried to discuss politics with these youngsters I soon discovered that it is difficult to pursue a logical line of thought with an Anarchist. "What kind of a government do you want here in Spain?" I asked.

"No government!" was the answer. "We want to live our own lives." And that was the best answer I could get. They were likable, vital young people. But they delighted in describing their ruthless exploits. One of them told me in sickening detail how he had cut the heart out of an enemy prisoner and rifled his Catholic emblems. One young Anarchist said to me, "I hope I get a chance to kill my uncle because I am going to cut his heart out."

Civil wars throughout history have always been particularly cruel wars but the Spaniards outdid themselves. No other European people seems to take such diabolic joy in cruel deeds. Along with this cruelty went a complete indifference to death. I have never met a braver or more fatalistic people. They made me feel very uncomfortable for I was constantly afraid to take the chances that to them were a daily commonplace. I asked Miguel de Unamuno, the aging Spanish philosopher, about this quality of fatalism in the Spanish people. "The Spaniard's spirit of desperation," he said, "represents something of the fundamental tragedy of Man. The truth is that we Spaniards are a sick people. Don't forget that we have in our veins a combination of Moorish blood, Castilian blood, and Jewish blood. That is a unique amalgam. It is these racial strains that fight within us."

The talk I had with Unamuno took place in Salamanca, which was in the hands of the Franco forces. Unamuno was teaching at the Salamanca University and had accepted without protest the Franco occupation. This was surprising to me because he was one of the spiritual founders of the Spanish Republic and had always believed in liberal democratic ideas. He explained that he had remained on the Franco side because he truly believed that the Franco forces were fighting on the side of civilization. "Does this mean you want to see a Fascist government in Spain?" I asked.

"Certainly not," he said. "I am going to be against whatever side wins this war because the victorious side will need restraint."

I asked him how the students at Salamanca University felt about the Civil War. "Many young people in Spain have gone to the front without caring on which side they fought," he replied. "Their aim seems to be to have a good time and to enjoy life while they can."

Unamuno never spoke out openly in support of the Franco side. He was living in Franco territory and simply accepted it philosophically. The Franco leaders were none too sure about his support. During our talk a Franco captain stood at my elbow and listened carefully. But the old Spanish philosopher seemed unconscious of his presence as he voiced his thoughts on unhappy Spain.

22

Hitler and Mussolini began their working partnership during the Spanish Civil War. This co-operation of Berlin with Rome—it was never friendship—made it unlikely that Mussolini would try to check a second attempt by Hitler to take over Austria. So the way was clear for Hitler to try again—and he did.

In March, 1938 Adolf Hitler summoned the Austrian Chancellor Kurt Schuschnigg to visit him at his country home in Berchtesgaden, which had been transformed into a mountain fortress. He presented the Austrian leader with a series of peremptory demands—units of the German Army were to be incorporated into the Austrian army, the Austrian Nazi party was to be given free rein, imprisoned Nazis who participated in the Dollfuss assassination were to be released, and, most crucial of all, a Nazi was to be appointed Minister of Public Security.

Schuschnigg, himself a minor milder dictator, was not prepared to accept such a complete surrender. He ordered a plebiscite to prove to the world that most Austrians did not approve surrender to Hitler. But the German Führer had no intention of letting a free election jeopardize his plans. He ordered the plebiscite canceled on threat of invasion. Only the month before, following a purge of the *Reichswehr,* Hitler had taken over supreme command of the German Army. These motorized troops stood ready on the Austrian frontier to move at his command.

Schuschnigg then made a last-minute effort to get support from Mussolini. Four years before Mussolini had mobilized his troops on the Brenner to prevent what was now about to happen. But the newly formed Rome-Berlin Axis had tied the hands of the Italian dictator. Schuschnigg next looked toward England and France. They too had guaranteed Austrian independence. France was in the midst of one of her interminable cabinet crises and Anthony Eden, the last champion of collective security in the Chamberlain government, was on the verge of resigning. Both France and England took one mild step. The British and French ambassadors informed Hitler that they would "look with disfavor" upon the Nazi acquisition of Austria. Hitler rightly judged that this mild form of protest meant that he would have a free hand. He continued his pressure.

The Austrian cabinet was indecisive. Certain members favored *Anschluss* with Germany, although a majority still hoped to keep Austria independent. Ultimatum followed ultimatum. The final one was telephoned by Göring in the most insulting terms. The Austrian government yielded. German troops crossed the border without opposition and occupied Vienna on March 12, 1938. The next day Hitler rode in triumph through the streets of Vienna and on the same day sent a telegram to Mussolini, "I shall never forget you for this . . ."

Czechoslovakia was next. From now on it was never so much a question of what Hitler would do as what England and France would do when Hitler continued his course of aggression.

Czechoslovakia held a special place in the hearts of democratic peoples the world over. More than any other country in

Central Europe this little nation had earnestly tried to live up to democratic ideals. If Czechoslovakia, like Austria, were to disappear as an independent country it would mean the end of the Versailles Treaty and Hitler's supremacy in Europe would be assured. France had a formal mutual defense treaty requiring her to defend Czechoslovakia against all aggression.

The world looked on in fascinated horror as Hitler began the series of moves that was to result in the capitulation of Czechoslovakia without the firing of a single shot. In the settlement at Munich in September, 1938, the Czechs were not even represented. France and England were pursuing a policy of complete appeasement and they made abject concessions to the dictator's demands.

Yes, Hitler could have Czechoslovakia's Sudetenland if he would only agree that this would really "appease" him and that he would ask for nothing more. After all, there were many Germans in Czechoslovakia and they did present a vexatious minority problem.

Hitler agreed that he would stay appeased. He got the Sudetenland and said he wanted nothing more. Millions of Europeans foolishly believed that now we would have "peace in our time." Had not Neville Chamberlain, the Prime Minister of Great Britain, proudly displayed a piece of paper signed by Adolf Hitler that said so?

The events of the last three weeks of September, 1938 are intimately familiar to me. I probably know more about them than about any other similar period of the last fifty years. During the twenty days and nights of the Czechoslovak crisis that culminated in the Munich Agreement I made 102 radiobroadcasts, each ranging from two minutes to two hours in length. This was the first great international crisis in which radiobroadcasting participated intensively every step of the way. After the *Anschluss* of Austria the radio networks realized the importance of having a competent staff of newsmen stationed in the key capitals of Europe to cover what seemed to be the increasing number of diplomatic crises. The Columbia Broadcasting System was fortunate to have at the head of its news department an alert and experienced newspaperman, Paul White. He sensed the tremendous interest the American people had developed in foreign affairs and saw that CBS had good men in all important capitals. Columbia was also fortunate in having as its capable European manager Edward R. Murrow with headquarters in London.

He made all the necessary advance preparations to cover the next international crisis. Columbia signed up first-class reporters like William Shirer in Berlin and Maurice Hindus in Prague. When the Czechoslovak crisis began CBS was prepared to cover the progress of events thoroughly and completely. The mechanical setup to tie up and untie the entire network in a matter of seconds or to bring together New York and five European capitals for a round-robin discussion involved the most ingenious devices, some of them developed on the spot by inventive radio engineers who loved to meet a new challenge. Largely because of this advance preparation CBS managed to capture and hold the bulk of the listening audience throughout the duration of the crisis.

The intensity with which America listened to the radio reports of the Munich crisis was without parallel in radio history. Portable radio sets which had just been developed had a tremendous sale. People carried them to wherever they went, to restaurants, offices, and on the streets. That was the day of taxicab radios and every standing cab was surrounded by crowds as on World Series days. Here was a world series with a vengeance! Never before had so many listened so long to so much. Millions of Americans concentrated intently as they heard the words: "America calling Prague. . . . London. . . . Come in Paris. . . . Berlin. . . . Munich. . . ." The CBS network of 115 stations constantly cut into its regular broadcast schedule to bring bulletins and analyses of important developments as they occurred. By means of international broadcasting the American people heard in person every leading figure in the crisis —Hitler, Chamberlain, Mussolini, Daladier, Benes, Eden, Masaryk. In 1938 all this was still a novelty and much of it was unprecedented.

Two-way transmissions and hookups enabled me to talk back and forth with newsmen in the different foreign capitals via transatlantic telephone while all America listened in. On several occasions I was able to transmit to a man stationed in a foreign capital news of which he was entirely unaware because of censorship.

It was my job during this crisis to broadcast and comment on the news as it occurred. As a result, none of my 102 talks was prepared in advance. They were all extemporized under a pressure I had never before experienced in seventeen years of broadcasting. News bulletins were handed to me as I talked. Speeches of foreign leaders had to be analyzed and sometimes translated while they were being delivered. In addition, split-second timing, always essential, became one of the physical requirements of network operation. I had to keep a constant eye on the control room for signs telling me when I was on or off the air. Sometimes when I had just launched into an analysis of some foreign leader's speech I was given a signal to wind up my talk in exactly one minute. This meant that I had to conclude my remarks in some sort of orderly and logical fashion as I watched the seconds tick away on the studio clock. On other occasions I was told to comment on a new development for exactly three minutes before the network switched to a foreign capital. Then suddenly they would discover that connections with Europe could not be made at that time and the engineer would signal me to continue my comments and expand them until further notice.

During routine broadcasting the networks used to keep a staff of musicians or at least a pianist standing by, ready to fill any odd seconds or minutes that might develop in the broadcasting schedule due to technical failure or the nonappearance of a performer. During this crisis period, CBS dispensed with musicians and free moments were filled with Kaltenborn instead of the usual brief musical interlude. I had little sleep during those days and not much in the way of substantial food. I napped occasionally on an army cot in one of the offices and my wife brought up from the drugstore below an occasional container of coffee and a sandwich. Sometimes she brought a thermos bottle of my favorite soup from the home kitchen.

Many people have asked me how I was able to deliver those extemporized comments during the Munich crisis. My only answer is that those broadcasts were really not much different from the radio talks, platform lectures, and newspaper editorials I had been doing ever since 1900. I had always talked and written current history and so I was prepared. It was just a good deal more of the same, only under pressure. In the course of those broadcasts I drew on everything I had learned during my entire lifetime, my travels, my interviews, my knowledge of languages, my close association with current events. My knowledge of German proved particularly important. There was one time when the professional translators, several of whom were refugees from Nazi Germany, became so nervous and excited by Hitler's oratory that they threw up their hands and could not continue translating. As a result, I had to take over this extra job of spot translation and at the same time make mental notes of the crucial points in the speech so that I could comment on its significance immediately after it had ended.

All of the CBS stations were linked together in such a fashion that by pressing a single button I could read a news bulletin and make a comment that would be heard throughout the country. Programs of all sorts were periodically interrupted by these news flashes. I remember when a running account of an important horse race was cut off the air just before it got under way. The Archbishop of Canterbury was making a prayer for peace and the network officials thought it was more important than the horse race. The sports announcer describing the race did not know he had been cut off. So when the Archbishop finished his prayer and the network returned to the racetrack the announcer was in the midst of a lyrical description about what a wonderful and exciting race it *had* been. After several minutes of his excited anticlimactic comment word was passed to him to tell his audience at least which horse had won the race.

One of the most destructive storms in New England history occurred at the most exciting point of the Munich crisis. As a result Columbia received thousands of telegrams from infuriated listeners. When we turned to the crisis New England protested, when we turned to the storm the rest of the country protested. People were emotional and irrational and the deluge of letters, telegrams, and long-distance calls broke all records. Never before or since have I had a chance to refuse to talk on the telephone to so many prominent people.

When the crisis was over we in America sighed with relief. Along with most Europeans we wanted to believe that the Munich agreement meant "peace in our time." But it was more of an uneasy hope than a real belief. Here is the way I put it in my final comment as the crisis ended with the signing of the Munich pact:

> Hitler always says after each of his conquests, "Now, no more. All is well." But there has always been more and there may be more still. On one occasion Sir Robert Walpole, who was Prime Minister of England two centuries ago, said when the British people rejoiced because he had kept them out of war: Today they ring the bells. Tomorrow they will wring their hands!
>
> We can only hope that this prediction will not again come true.

As everyone now knows, Munich was a beginning, not an end. In his book *Mein Kampf* Hitler had said,

> Every nation that once submits to a foreign demand has lost part of its power to resist. Each time it makes a concession it is less able and less willing to resist the next demand. That is why the shrewd victor will always ask for what he wants by degrees. Once a nation has begun to give rather than fight back, it will keep on giving and giving, provided only that the victor nation does not ask for too much.

The next year, in the summer of 1939, I made my first transatlantic plane trip to Europe. Twenty-five years before my wife and I had also left America to visit a Europe on the eve of war. That crossing took twelve days—this one less than a day. On this plane trip the airplane officials as a special favor assigned to us what they called the bridal suite in the rear of the passenger compartment of a four motored Pan American Clipper. It was luxurious as well as speedy travel.

In London the British people felt that war was probably inevitable but they dreaded the moment when it would break out. The Munich appeasement failed. It had not stopped Hitler from absorbing the rest of Czechoslovakia in March. Now he was beginning new pressure on Poland. Mussolini was encouraged to take over the little state of Albania. There was a stiffening in the British attitude but the British leaders realized that their country was hopelessly unprepared for modern war. Most of the preparations I saw in England during that summer were clumsy and inadequate. The blackouts and other defense measures seemed inefficient. The picturesque balloon barrage, looking for all the world like a herd of floating baby elephants, was supposed to intercept enemy planes. It probably cost many times what it was worth, which is undoubtedly true of most efforts at civilian defense.

Britain was stumbling along the road toward war preparation with the popular slogan, "Business as usual." There was a shortage of technicians and of the skilled labor needed in the organization of defense. The Royal Air Force was printing large advertisements and posters pleading for any and every kind of skilled help. The armed forces didn't even have enough motorists, cooks, and butchers. There were many appeals for men to be trained for such diverse tasks as balloon operators and medical orderlies. Despite the good pay and generous annual leaves the response was apathetic.

I found the mood of the British people more pacific and less assertive than I had ever known it before. They accepted war as a terrible, inevitable, and depressing prospect. There was a curiously unrealistic atmosphere. At a luncheon meeting in London at which I met a group of outstanding British publicists, the talk centered on such topics as, "Should peace terms be announced before the war begins?" "How can we best reach the Germans by propaganda?"

There followed a long discussion about beaming a short-wave radiobroadcast into Germany to explain the British point of view. The dropping of leaflets from airplanes all over Germany was enthusiastically recommended by a member of Parliament. There was real confidence that it would be possible to reach the minds of the German people and turn them against Hitler. The postwar treatment of Germany was also debated in great detail. The meeting adjourned with everyone joining in the hope that all problems would be solved with Hitler's death. There was a general agreement that this was the best way to ensure a peaceful world. But since Hitler did not seem ready to oblige, the British went on unenthusiastically with the gloomy business of digging trenches in Hyde Park.

I had occasion to discuss the Munich settlement with the peace-loving Lord Halifax, who had succeeded Anthony Eden as Foreign Secretary the year before. He gave me many plausible reasons why the British had acceded to Hitler's demands. The most urgent of these was the fact that France and England were simply not prepared for modern warfare. For years the British had disregarded the warning voice of Winston Churchill who told of Germany's increasing strength, particularly in the air. Only reluctantly had the British finally introduced conscription in 1939. But Lord Halifax indicated the new and stronger attitude of the British.

"We will have to act if Hitler invades Poland," he told me. When I asked him why he felt Poland was worth fighting for more than Austria or Czechoslovakia he said, "If Hitler takes Poland that means he is reaching toward the Mediterranean, toward the Balkans, down the Danube. He is reaching into the area where we have major responsibilities and where we are concerned with the life line of the British Empire. If he attacks Poland we must respond. First, because we have undertaken a definite obligation to come to Poland's aid, and in the second place because when Hitler strikes at Poland he strikes at the vital interests of the British Empire."

By this time the British Foreign Office had come to the reluctant conclusion that in view of Hitler's demands on Poland a strong military alliance with the Soviet Union was definitely desirable. British diplomats were in Moscow to see what could be arranged. "We have to make arrows with whatever wood we can find," Lord Vansittart declared.

One of the fatal prewar blunders of the Western powers was the exclusion of the Soviet Union from the crisis discussions in 1938. Russia up to that time was definitely wooing the democracies. Those were the days of the United Front policy. Communists throughout the world on orders from Moscow soft-pedaled talk of revolution and instead preached cooperation with the democracies against fascism. The exclusion of Russia from the negotiations in 1938 prompted Stalin a few months later to say, "One might think that the districts of Czechoslovakia were yielded to Germany as the price for her undertaking to launch a war on the Soviet Union."

The happy prospect of throwing the dictatorships against one another had certainly crossed the minds of British and French statesmen. In 1939, in view of the impending Polish crisis, the British made a belated attempt to make up to Russia. But by then it was too late. The Russians were convinced that collective security would not work. From September, 1938 Stalin gradually reverted to a policy of isolation. From then on Stalin viewed the Fascist powers and the democracies both as "wicked imperialists." He saw no visible grounds for hostility between Russia and Germany, and at the same time conveniently kept the door open to negotiations with Britain and France. Stalin played a shrewd diplomatic game. It is not too far-fetched to suppose that any time after Munich he would have welcomed war between the democracies and the Fascists. Such a conflict would enable Russia to take a neutral position and intervene on whichever side her interests seemed to lie.

In April, 1939 Stalin continued negotiations in Moscow with the British for an alliance against possible Nazi aggression. The price of this alliance was to be the absorption of the Baltic countries into the Soviet Union. This was more than the British and the French felt they could pay. The Poles too were reluctant to sign any agreement that might bring Russian troops on Polish soil even "for the good of Poland." When Stalin could not get what he wanted from the democracies he began overtures to Nazi Germany. In May, 1939 he dismissed Maxim Litvinov who had been the great protagonist of collective security and who knew how to get along with Western powers. I had seen Litvinov at Geneva warning the members of the League against the dangers of appeasement and he had impressed me with his seemingly sincere devotion to the cause of joint action against aggression. Litvinov was replaced by the more isolationist and Russian-oriented V. M. Molotov. Stalin may also have felt that Molotov would be better able to deal with Hitler since unlike Litvinov he was of "Aryan" descent.

I was in Paris when the news came in August that Hitler and Stalin had signed a nonaggression pact of friendship. This news stunned Paris as it did the rest of the world. Everywhere the French asked, "What does this mean?" Everyone was reluctant to draw the frightening conclusion that it opened Hitler's way to war. The pact freed Hitler from danger in the East. The meaning of the pact was war.

On this trip I met for the first time our Ambassador to Great Britain, Joseph E. Kennedy. As I entered his private office he was pacing the room in his shirtsleeves in a dramatic mood. He raised his hand and said, "You have come to me in one of the most important moments in world history! We are engaged in a fight for time!"

He talked as though he was convinced of American involvement in the impending conflict. He was pessimistic about the possibility of working out any lasting settlement with Hitler. "We might," he said, "get an agreement that would last for a short time. There is no longer any confidence in Hitler's word. Even if a compromise settlement were now worked out, people would say, 'This is only another Munich.' Yet I think anything that keeps Britain at peace is in the interest of the United States. I stand for peace, but if war comes I believe we should help all we can in a financial way, but not in a military way. We are close to the danger line. Chamberlain feels he cannot make too many concessions. Yet gaining time is the most important thing we can do at this point." Ambassador Kennedy also told me that the concessions Prime Minister Chamberlain made at Munich were absolutely necessary because Britain was totally unprepared for war.

In 1939 France had complete confidence in the high quality of her military preparations. The French felt secure behind their Maginot Line and placed great faith in their Army. When I talked to the American Ambassador, William C. Bullitt, about this attitude he said, "The French have now digested the idea of war. They don't want it. But if it comes they are ready for it. The emotional crisis in France is past. They do not worry any more. A year ago the situation was different. Today they take the bombing of Paris for granted. There can be no question of selling out Poland either by the British or the French.

"France has said," Bullitt went on, "that if Britain fights, France will fight too. A year ago that was not true because at that time the British Ambassador to France informed the French that the British would stay out even if France went to war to defend Czechoslovakia."

France's overconfidence was shared by many outside observers. An American military staff officer in Paris told me the French Army was the best in the world and the Maginot Line was impregnable to ordinary military attack. "To crack it would require an artillery concentration the Germans will never be able to provide." As for the airplane, "Most people overestimate the effect of air raids. What air raids did not do in Madrid and Barcelona is far more important than what little they did accomplish."

On August 19, 1939, two weeks before war came, I talked with Georges Bonnet who had been a firm champion of appeasement. He was then France's Minister for Foreign Affairs. My first question was, "Do you agree that war is imminent?" His answer, "No one can predict. The situation rests with one man. It depends on what Hitler has in mind . . . and perhaps he has not made up his mind. The situation here is clear. We have a definite commitment to go to war on the side of Poland whenever Poland becomes involved. . . . Of course, we hope war can be avoided. We certainly don't want it. But today we are infinitely stronger and better able to meet it."

The storm center of Europe in those days was of course Germany. As I flew into Germany from London I could see the white streak of the new *Auto Bahn,* the super automobile highway running from Cologne to Berlin. The road ran straight across the country as far as the eye could reach. Actually it stretched from the French to the Polish frontier. Our plane was flying low and I could distinguish the traffic that flowed along the highway. There were few passenger cars. Most of the traffic consisted of what the Germans called "truck trains." A lead truck towed three or four others. They looked like military vehicles.

My visit to Germany proved unexpectedly brief. After I alighted from the plane at the Tempelhof Airport in Berlin the Nazi secret police checked my passport. After a few routine questions I was asked to wait briefly. This "brief wait" lasted more than an hour. Suspecting it might last longer when I could get no response to my questions, I asked permission to continue my wait in the airport restaurant. There I spent another hour chatting pleasantly with Bill Shirer the CBS correspondent, with my wife, and some of her German relatives. After a total wait of over two hours I was summoned to the secret police office. "Your presence in Germany is not desired," I was told. "You must return to London."

"May I ask why?" I responded.

"You delivered a lecture in the United States in which you referred in uncomplimentary terms to der Führer," said the officer in charge.

"When and where was this lecture delivered?" I asked in an effort to learn what particular reference had been reported to Berlin. "We cannot give you any further information" was the reply.

Since I had attacked Hitler in a hundred lectures and broadcasts there was little use in trying to argue. The secret police officer in charge reiterated firmly, "You must return to London at once."

"But I don't want to go back to London. If I must leave I'd like to go to Poland. Can't you put me on a train?" The answer was negative. "What about Denmark?" Still negative. The officer insisted I had to leave immediately for London. I had new hope when I learned that the next plane for London was completely filled. But this did not daunt the Nazis. I saw them hustle out some unhappy passenger and I was given his seat.

Just before I boarded the plane I remembered that I had brought with me some pipe tobacco for Bill Shirer. I quickly opened my suitcase and was about to hand it to him when a secret police officer rushed up and confiscated the tobacco. When I remonstrated he said that it was against the rules for any expellee to give anything to anybody in Germany.

I learned later that the Nazi secret police had a special black list. It included the names of those who were to be held at the airport until someone in Berlin decided whether they were to be jailed or expelled. I was lucky to be in the latter class.

My wife took the next plane out of Berlin and reached London just in time to have me interview her on the air in a broadcast from the British capital. My classic greeting to her as taken from the recording was, "Gee, Olga, I'm glad you're out. Now come here and tell us what you saw in Berlin."

23

When I arrived back in the United States on August 30, 1939 I was asked by reporters at the airport if I thought war would break out immediately in Europe. I replied that the odds were still seven to five in favor of more appeasement. Two days later Hitler's blitzkrieg roared across the Polish frontier. On September 3 England and France declared war on Germany. World War II was underway.

How do I account for my wrong guess? After visiting England and seeing for myself how utterly unprepared the British were for war, I could not see how the British would dare at that point to challenge Hitler's military might if they could find some formula that would postpone the evil day. I therefore felt that another Munich might well result from the desperate diplomatic maneuvers that were then underway. I failed to allow for the determination and the courage of the British people once they looked squarely at the issues involved. I have never since underestimated the British.

Directly after I returned to this country I went on another lecture tour and did my regular broadcasts from various cities throughout the United States. As I traveled about America I was conscious of the overwhelming desire that we keep out of the war. At the same time I learned how much the American people continued to hate and despise Adolf Hitler and the Nazi party.

The debate between the isolationists and the interventionists became more intense as the war continued. Controversy over America's foreign policy was not confined to those in high places. From September 1939, until Pearl Harbor over two years later brought an end to the debate, the battle of words went on. Should we participate in the struggle? Americans, God bless 'em, have many and varied opinions on everything and everybody and they are never averse to saying what they think in no uncertain terms. The mail I received during these two years provides ample testimony. A glance at some of this mail serves two purposes—one, it shows the variety of communications that come to a radio commentator, and two, it reveals something of the spirit of those times.

Americans were faced with the crucial question, what should we do about the war in Europe?

> This country must do everything within its power, except send men, to aid the Allies at once!

In the same mail came this:

> Let no one think America is going to pull England's chestnuts out of the fire.

Who was distributing the most propaganda in this country, the British or the Germans?

> For every word of German propaganda coming into this country a million words of British propaganda are spilt.

Were the British people honest?

> So the British people are very honest people, eh? What ever happened to all that dough they have been owing us since the last war?

Were all Americans interested in this war?

Only highly paid propagandists like yourself and those who are profiting by it are interested in this European war of greed.

Who was sponsoring my radio program at this time?

I know that George VI is your king and sponsor.

Why had the King and Queen of England made a visit to America before the war?

The king and queen did not come over here to view Niagara Falls. Nor was it a desire to afford us uncouth Americans a glimpse of real royalty. There was something else on the agenda at that famous wiener roast at Hyde Park beside the initiation of Their Majesties into the mysteries of hot dogs with mustard. There were promises made during that visit which are prime movers behind Roosevelt's actions in steering us into another war.

Were Americans neutral in 1940?

After listening to your broadcast this afternoon I most vehemently disagree with your statement that the majority of Americans are neutral as far as the European war is concerned. I, for one, and all of my friends are definitely on the side of England.

Were Americans anti-Hitler?

People are anti-Hitler, but this doesn't mean that they are pro-British or pro-French. I've heard hundreds of people denounce Hitler, who denounced Britain in the same breath. I might add that anti-Hitlerism doesn't mean anti-Germanism.

My memory of Britain is that of a snobbish ungrateful people who threw it in the teeth of our soldiers that we came only after they had won the war and who, with the contemptible French handed us out the worst of everything and treated us more like enemies than men who had saved their national existence. And my memory of Germany—which had every reason to hate us—is a picture of a motherly old German woman who took sick American boys into her home and took care of them while they had the flu and pneumonia. A number of us wouldn't have come back if it hadn't been for these German "barbarians." I'm not going to fight people like that again.

Were all mothers isolationists?

In a visit with a mother yesterday who said about her only son, a recent high school graduate, "His father told him he was just an American and if he must fight, to fight with all his Love of Liberty." Then she said, "Only those who are willing to make sacrifices are fit to live in a Democracy."

Were our young poeple as patriotic as they should be?

Have you realized how little patriotism this present generation of young people have had brought to their minds and attention? From the time these young people have been old enough to understand, they have heard their parents crab about the state this country is in, depression, useless spending, politics, and graft, etc. What can you expect these kids to do for their country without proper training at home and in school?

Can't you in your broadcasts, give them ideals and stir up a little patriotism among the younger men and women whom we are going to have to rely upon to fight our war for us should it be necessary? You can't blame them for not being loyal, when so much has been done to undermine their love of country and little to stimulate and build all that we hold precious.

Were Americans aware of the dangers to civilization if Hitler won?

The man on the street does not appear to realize that civilization has not been so threatened since the time of Genghis Khan.

You can do more than any one man, except the President of the United States, to convince the public that it is cheaper in men and treasure to help do now what we might have to do later alone.

How could Hitler and Mussolini be overthrown?

I'll be as brief as possible. Every time Hitler or Mussolini's picture comes on the movie screen, everybody laughs in derision. That news will spread to the German people in time, namely America is laughing at their idol. I note the psychological effect it had on me when recently several people gave me a big "horse laugh." Nothing discourages like ridicule.

What should women do?

A group of women here in North Carolina seem "bound and determined" to organize a "preparedness club." They started out by saying everyone should be armed and taught in marksmanship, Boy Scout trained, etc. I suggested that before they plunged into such activities they should find out whether the government wished it or not. It is rather hard to hold them down, but they agreed to write to the Dies Committee and to the Governor of the state to make inquiries. I said I would write you and get your advice and suggestions.

What is wrong with the world today?

What is wrong with the entire world today is that women have taken all the jobs away from the men, and now there is nothing to do with the jobless men but to send them to war to be slaughtered. I am a woman and I don't think it is right the way the women have taken over all the jobs.

What should be done about "this fellow Kaltenborn?" I received one letter from the Ghosts of 1776 who said my name had been placed on a special list for "liquidation by a firing squad."

Another angry listener wrote:

> I have put on you the curse of the thirteen lice, twelve black and one white. Three weeks from this date it will take effect.

Many people, even during the busy days when we were launching our defense program, were not too busy to write and berate me for the way I pronounced "iron"—"i-run." Others did not like anything about my radio comments and wrote directly to the Pure Oil Company, my sponsor.

> Your gas can't be any better than Kaltenborn's so I'll get both some place else.

Some letters however were more flattering, as witness this one received on May 9, 1940:

> No one is more capable to answer the question, will DEMOCRACY LAST? than one who is an eminent authority on current events; one who is active in world affairs and who understands the situations that exist behind the headlines. Thus I appeal to you, Mr. Kaltenborn, with the hope that it will not cause you the slightest inconvenience to answer this important question, Will Democracy Last? We, the members of the Ninth Grade English class are required to write an original essay concerning democracy and if you know what a low mark in English means to a student whose ambition is to be a foreign correspondent, please be kind enough to answer promptly, frankly, and briefly.

The fact that this letter was dated May 8 and the assignment was due on May 10 prevented me from doing full justice to the subject.

Such letters alternated with others that had the forceful eloquence of brevity and merely said: "You skunk"—"You stink"—or "Nuts to you."

As the "phony war" period ended in the spring of 1940

the tenor of the letters changed. They became more serious, more passionate.

> While enemy bombs have been pulverizing the great British Empire, Yankee Blowhards like you shout your heads off about nothing at all. Why don't you old fellows use the air to encourage the Yankee boys to join the Army or Navy and help Britain. No, you have left the British to fight and die.

The fall of Norway sent a chill through many citizens.

> Well, Norway is being mopped up—after being gobbled up, and we are wondering where the madman will strike next. That defeat was hard to take and I fear there will be many more if Britain keeps old Chamberlain at the helm.

The surrender of King Leopold in Belgium brought forth this tirade against England:

> Three cheers for Leopold the III for refusing to fight and have his men starved and butchered for dear old England while her High All Mighty Command sits at home pulling their puppet strings across their maps and watching out for their own hides and interest regardless of who gets hurt or killed.

From Ohio came this note.

> At the height of my intellectual stupidity I am never able to understand why all the small democratic nations did not combine and gang up on Germany in time to save themselves. Why did they wait to be picked off one by one?

The fall of France brought this letter from Chicago.

> After hearing your analysis of the French war news I do so want to thank you for your consoling words. How very kind of you indeed. . . . It is needless to say just how sad we all feel. Such a terrible tragedy to befall the world . . . what I

> cannot understand is how Germany was ever permitted to become so powerful—I pray God the murderous brutal Germans will pay dearly for all the suffering they are inflicting on the world today. . . . Kindly forgive me for expressing myself in such a manner but I feel no kindness toward the Nazi Germans. They have caused so much sadness and sorrow in the world.

Regarding the new Vichy Government in France a man in San Francisco wrote:

> We should be the last nation in the world to criticize them. France today is absolutely helpless under Hitler. God knows they are paying bitterly for their mistakes, every one of which we are duplicating at this late date. In September, 1938 we called them cowards because they did not declare war on Hitler. In June, 1939 when we knew war was inevitable we refused to repeal our so-called neutrality law. In September, 1939 we slapped an embargo on all war materials. (Which embargo has never been extended to Hitler's Asiatic accomplice.) After three months of wrangling we allowed France to buy war materials provided they paid cash before delivery. (In some cases they also paid for the factories.) Since July, 1940 we have given them something called moral support. Do you think there is anything in the record to give them reason to love us or in which we can take any pride? In other words our ostrich eggs are hatching and coming home to roost.

Should we condemn Marshal Pétain for surrendering to the Nazis?

> Why, Pétain is much greater and nobler of character than Winston Churchill could ever be. Pétain did the best he could for a conquered country, he deserves respect and honor. Winston Churchill is just a big loud blusterer. What does he do? Just brags about England and tries to get the boys of the United States to do England's fighting. There is no democracy about Churchill. He is 100% bluff.

But in the same mail came many other letters praising Winston Churchill.

As the possibility of our involvement became more likely I received thousands of letters condemning my attitude on Britain, on Charles Lindbergh, on labor, on Lend Lease—and an equal number praising my stand. Both the isolationists and interventionists were highly emotional and poured out their feelings:

> Now that the Lend-Lease bill is passed I hope you are satisfied and will please stop putting out so much British propaganda. Maybe you won't stop until our boys are killed in another foreign war. I hope only that when you are on your way to the other world the ghost of our dead boys will not haunt you.

From Montana came another letter:

> The people of the state of Montana, contrary to what Senator Wheeler says, are in favor of extraordinary power for the President so that prompt action can be taken in the preservation of our first line of defense, the British Navy. The consensus of opinion is however that a definite time limit should be placed on that power.

On Labor:

> When you defend the CIO I am afraid you are defending the Hitler-Stalin Army. . . .

And the same mail brought this:

> You have hit an all-time low for dirty digs at Labor.

There were hundreds of pro and con letters on President Roosevelt and his policies. There were also a good many dealing with the Roosevelt family. From Washington, D.C.:

> The other day I saw Mrs. Roosevelt walking on the street coming from her job. She was walking home around lunch

time. She was about fifteen blocks to her domicile and here she was unescorted going down Connecticut Avenue. Now I ask you what other country where the Executive's wife, be it a queen, or a Russian ruler, or monarch's wife would one find walking in the open in such days as these without a bodyguard or some protection. That is freedom and democracy, but then there are no other Mrs. Roosevelts—none like her.

The plight of the Finns after the Russian invasion in 1940 stirred one American to make this suggestion:

> How about opening up parts of Alaska to the dispossessed Finns? I know our own people have failed to colonize it successfully and it seemed to me it might become a refuge for those poor people.

But there were those who had little sympathy with the beleaguered Finns:

> Don't you think you in company with other commentators overdo the Finnish thing just a trifle? After all, the republic of Finland with Butcher Mannerheim in control isn't much of a democracy. Ex-czarist officers don't go a long way toward democracy according to my way of thinking. . . . Bleeding Finland, like bleeding Belgium may be used to get us into the mess.

Even after Germany invaded Russia in June, 1941 some Americans continued to be very suspicious of Russia:

> Are Germany and Russia really at war? Who has seen proof? Could it be the dictators are telling the greatest lie the world has ever known? Anything is possible!

Yet there were many who would tolerate no criticism of the Russian war effort:

> Your comments on the Russian situation are very unfair. What are you trying to do? Lower the morale and help Hitler

win the war? There is a people of 170,000,000 human beings fighting for their very life against a monster who if he sets his gorilla foot on that soil, it will take centuries before they would see the light of day again. . . . England didn't do so well in the beginning either, did she?

In the light of later history it seems significant that so little attention was paid to matters in the Far East. I received about a thousand letters regarding the situation in Europe for every one on Japan. Many Americans seemed to agree with this correspondent:

In regard to the Orient this one woman's opinion would be that we should put first things first and deal with Japan later through the League of Nations—or whatever takes its place. We have our hands full and let's not divide our attention. We have a big job to do and the sooner we get at it the better.

However, there were others who kept harping on the menace of Japan and in 1940 I received many cards like this one from Florida:

This family is very grateful to you because you are pounding away trying to have the sale of war materials to Japan stopped.

This one came from Oklahoma:

You recently said you had seen drums of gasoline in Texas ready to go to Japan. It was just under the aviation qualification. I talked with an engineer for one of the larger oil companies in Fort Worth and he said that with the gasoline goes tetraethyl lead and instructions on how to mix it so that it can be raised above the "aviation" qualifications. That means our "aviation gasoline" embargo means nothing! We should cease all trade with Japan now!

For suggesting that Japan was pursuing its own "Monroe Doctrine" I was quickly taken to task by this writer:

Our Monroe Doctrine while existing primarily for our own protection also affords protection to our sister American republics and also respects their rights. On the other hand the Japanese scheme of things exists and has long existed as a definite plan solely for the aggrandizement of the Japanese and does not hesitate to trample on the rights of their Far Eastern neighbor countries.

The attack on Pearl Harbor stimulated a flood of poetry. On December 10, I received this which represents average quality:

'Twas the seventh of December in forty one
Pearl Harbor attacked by the rising sun.
We'll never forget this month or year
For it's five in two seconds, one if all clear.
We're all awakened, united as one
Ready for the Jap and his pal the Hun. . . .

Two days after Pearl Harbor this came from a man, who though no poet, at least had his heart in the right place:

We are sending you a dollar to be sent on to Mr. Roosevelt, President of the United States, to "keep 'em flying for liberty."

One writer saw a parallel between the attack on Pearl Harbor and the new Russian counterattack against Germany:

Maybe the Russians were able to draw heavy reserves from their Eastern front to throw at the Germans through an understanding that removed the Jap's fear of bombers from Siberian bases.

At the time of the Russ-Jap pact Stalin impressed the Japs that he too is an Asiatic. . . . Don't you think that after the Axis is beaten every country will have to deal with Communism?

Many others continued suspicious of Russia:

I do think the Japanese affair is terrible. You know ever since Joseph Stalin sat on the fence this past year and nodded to Hitler I can't place much faith in him. And I do believe we should be a little careful. Seems like old Joseph Stalin sat like a cat licking his chops and the curl in the corner of his mouth. I still say to my thoughts, beware of him.

But others were confident Russia would prove a faithful ally:

Assuming Russia is not ready to assist the Allies by letting them use Siberian bases at present, I feel sure when Russia is a little more free later she will do the right thing. She has an old score to settle with Japan.

One letter was signed "Joe Stalin Himself":

Ye Gods, what a nasty way of talking you have—those peculiar inflections and that jerky, nervous, ugly manner of speaking are so horribly annoying. And then your pronunciation! That is really something! The word Russia has only two syllables. Please don't pronounce the *i*.

How could we have been so surprised by the attack on Pearl Harbor? This question was frequently asked.

Tokyo made no bones of its Pacific plans as disclosed in a book published over a year ago entitled, *The Triple Alliance and the Japanese American War*. This book was distributed among trusted Japanese agents in America. It was written by Kinoaki Matsuo and embodied a complete manual of strategy in the western Pacific. This book included the complete Axis plan of attack from the bombing of Hawaii to the final elimination of the American threat to world peace. It would appear that here is another *Mein Kampf* that was not seriously considered while we planned our strategy in the Pacific.

Even in the days following Pearl Harbor there were many who felt like this man:

> . . . despite all that has actually taken place far too few of our people yet realize what now confronts us. It is probably no exaggeration to say that business still is pretty much "as usual" in a great majority of cases. Too many people seem to believe that someone else, somewhere else, is going to do the thinking, the working, and the fighting.

Maybe this man was right. We were stunned for a little while by what happened at Pearl Harbor, especially since most of us had been watching Europe. Perhaps, we, as a nation, had given the impression we were expecting someone else to do our fighting for us. But this impression did not last long. America, united as never before in our history, soon rolled up the greatest fighting force the world has ever seen —outfitted and equipped by the greatest production drive in history.

24

During the war years I visited the important war fronts and also made many visits in this country to military camps and stations and war production plants. In 1943, after a bit of negotiating in Washington, I secured permission to make a comprehensive tour of the Pacific war front. The Navy, which was running things in the Pacific, was not keen about visiting firemen. So, after accumulating five separate inoculations and a variety of documents, including one that told the Japanese to treat me like an army captain, if captured, I was set to go. When I was about to take off on a Navy patrol plane to fly from San Francisco to Hawaii, I was suddenly asked if I had been given a release for this trip from my local draft board. I checked all my innumerable papers but soon realized that this was one document I had not troubled to get. Being sixty-five years old at the time, I did not expect the draft to catch up with me. However, the regulation stated clearly that a release from the draft board was necessary before any civilian aged sixty-five or under could leave the country. After a good bit of persuasion, the military officials finally agreed to let me proceed with the flight on the ground that I was close enough to sixty-six to justify an exception, and they were impressed with my argument that, as a Spanish War veteran, I was more entitled to a pension than a draft call.

Our first stop was Pearl Harbor. As we circled the island before coming down for a landing, I saw the hulks of our fleet that had been bombed on December 7, 1941. The damage actually inflicted came as a shock when I saw it with my own eyes. At that time, few Americans realized what had actually happened.

This flight made me appreciate the tremendous distances involved in the Pacific war and the logistic problems that we faced. Unbelievably long supply lines and a most elaborate defense system were required. "Island hopping" was being discarded in favor of "by-passing" but this only served to speed up the supply problem. The difficult task of keeping long supply lines open also faced the Japanese. By our control of the sea secured after the occupation of Guadalcanal, we were able to cut off many Japanese garrisons on islands scattered through the southwest Pacific. The Japanese were simply unable to supply these isolated garrisons and, as a result, had to let them "wither on the vine," a process that continued for years after the end of the fighting.

The whole naval war in the Pacific was primarily a problem in logistics. It was always a question of supplies. That was the beginning, the middle, and the end of every operation. How much could be delivered to a given place in a given time determined how and when an operation could be carried out. As I looked over my navy war map of the Pacific, it seemed to me that the logical place from which to strike at the home islands of Japan was the Aleutian Islands. But I soon learned that while this would be most logical from the viewpoint of geography it was impossible because of the hopeless weather conditions. Some years later when I was on an Aleutian airstrip during a howling windstorm with low visibility, I saw the point. In war so much that is logical is not practical.

As I stopped along the bases scattered through the Pacific, I heard one regular complaint. Barely was a supply base well established and the personnel comfortable when the base had to be moved further north and west. It was an exasperating experience for these men to make a lonely base seem a little homelike through long and laborious efforts and then have to pull up and out. Theirs was the monotonous job of building and moving one base after another throughout the entire war.

Some of the commanders on these isolated islands told me that the men actually welcomed an occasional air raid because it broke the monotony. I was told that a raid stimulated morale because it gave the supply and guard units a feeling that they were actually engaged in an important fighting operation. As in most wars since the beginning of time the most exasperating feature is the inevitable tedium and boredom that most participants experience. The supply and maintenance work in the Pacific made an outstanding contribution to victory.

During my stay in the war zone the principal military operation was taking place on the island of Bougainville. I arrived there a few days after our first landing while we still occupied little more than a beachhead and the Japs were still trying to push us off. To get to the front lines where the fighting was under way I had to make what was called a short, one mile walk through tropical mud and jungle to a forward base. This walk, in tropic heat, was the most exhausting physical experience I have ever undergone. When I finally dragged myself to the final destination, I was completely worn out. Reluctantly I admitted to myself that even a healthy man of sixty-five is not quite as spry as he likes to think.

To make the Bougainville operation possible, we had a close-linked chain of bases extending over a distance of some six thousand miles. I hope our political leaders realize the importance of some of these Pacific bases for the future defense of the United States.

Another Pacific war lesson was the need for continued close co-operation among the three armed services. Even on some small islands I visited, the Army was on one end of the island and the Navy at the other, with little contact or co-operation.

They had worked out a few problems of joint supply but often the Navy had a surplus of what the Army lacked. Everywhere the Navy was better situated and far better supplied than the Army. The Navy always had its ice cream, its soft drinks, its laundry facilities, its varied diet no matter where ships were stationed. The Army was rarely so fortunate. Navy fliers, on their days off, would supply their forward bases with cases of beer flown from Australia. Naturally the Army men felt jealous. For weeks at a time a naval vessel is a self-contained, self-supplying unit even on patrol in enemy waters. Not so the advanced Army unit. It cannot encumber itself with luxuries. I was the more delighted to find a fully equipped, competently manned Red Cross unit ministering to the needs and comfort of our front-line fighting men on Bougainville.

In building airstrips on some of these islands in record time, our Seabees did a remarkable job. Whenever we took over an airstrip from the Japanese, our men would improve it and lengthen it. When there was no airstrip, they would wipe out a piece of jungle and in less than a few weeks lay down the steel matting that provided the temporary runways.

While on Bougainville, I had the doubtful pleasure of experiencing regular Japanese bombing raids at night. The island of Bougainville is dominated by a picturesque volcano that, when it flared up at night, provided an admirable guiding beacon for the Japanese bombers. The bombs dropped by the Japanese were not very large and caused surprisingly few casualties. I was quartered in the canvas-covered trench occupied by the commanding general of the island. When the air-raid alarm was sounded, I looked toward the general to see whether he had any suggestions about an air-raid shelter. I was ready and eager to follow wherever he might lead. To my dismay he only swore briefly, rolled over and went back to sleep. I heard the whistle of the bombs and could see and hear the explosions not far away. However, everybody seemed to accept this as a routine thing. Next morning the general explained that only a direct hit in a trench was dangerous and that direct hits were few.

On Bougainville, I saw at firsthand the remarkable adaptability, courage, and ingenuity of American soldiers in action. On the fronts in Africa, Italy, and Germany which I visited later, things were stabilized. On Bougainville, everything was fluid and extemporized. I was surprised to see how well American National Guardsmen had adapted themselves to the difficult new techniques of jungle fighting. I saw men who, only three months earlier had been civilians, doing a remarkable, veteran job of jungle fighting under the most difficult conditions. The Japanese were always much more familiar with this type of fighting, yet it did not take our men long to equal and excel them. What our men never could learn was to keep going on the very small amount of food on which a Japanese soldier lived and fought.

One thing that pleased me mightily was to see a tent full of soldiers just back from their nearby front-line duty watching one of the latest American moving pictures. Film equipment and even entertainers came right up to the front lines. In this particular front-line location, the men also got two hot meals a day. This feat was accomplished with new types of motor transport which could travel through the mud and sludge of the jungle.

I had several uneasy hours on the plane flight to Bougainville from Guadalcanal. I was traveling with a marine general and his aides. We began this flight with fighter escort which was reassuring since much of the distance was over Jap-controlled waters and Jap-held islands which had been by-passed in our push to Bougainville. The Japanese still had a few fighter planes operating from these islands.

Everything went smoothly until we lost our way as well as our fighter escort during one of the torrential rainstorms that frequently occur in the Solomon Islands area. Our pilot decided it was safer to try and find our way back to Guadalcanal than to hunt for Bougainville. Soon the young pilot sent back word to the marine general that he was completely lost and asked him what to do. This request produced a violent and picturesque stream of profanity.

"How in ———, ———, ——— should I know which of these ———, ——— islands are held by the Japs?" he asked the pilot.

"Use your compass, use your map, use your head. Land somewhere. But don't ask me what to do! I can't fly a plane!"

Considerably chastened, the pilot carried on. Fortunately for us, a few minutes later the clouds suddenly lifted. We could see land below. The pilot took one careful look and shouted with relief, "We're over an American island!" If the clouds had lifted and we had found ourselves over a Japanese island, this book might never have been written.

Anyone who meets General Douglas MacArthur for the first time is bound to be impressed by his gift of language, his dramatic personality, his sense of history, and the spiritual and religious overtones in his conversation. The first time I met him was in Australia in 1943 when he was in a particularly resentful and belligerent mood. He felt that he had been unfairly deprived of the war materials which he urgently needed for the Pacific campaign. The Washington decision to regard Hitler as Enemy Number One did not appeal to him. "If only I had the right kind of support," he said, "we could make much more rapid progress against Japan." The Pacific campaign was still going slowly after almost two years of fighting. Only scant reinforcements were reaching Australia. Both his training and combat programs were hampered by lack of adequate supplies. He made no effort to conceal his bitterness and disappointment. He had a feeling that politics was responsible for what he called the "neglect of the Pacific war." I had the impression he believed President Roosevelt feared him as a potential presidential candidate. Yet it was evident to me that he had no real intentions of becoming a candidate in the 1944 elections. He was too completely devoted to the task at hand. It may be that he believed the threat of his candidacy might persuade the administration to give him more support in the Pacific war.

MacArthur, in my opinion, does not have the qualities required by a politician. He is a great leader of men, a most competent administrator and completely selfless in his devotion to duty. As an army commander he takes high rank. He gets along best with those over whom he has authority. He inspires both loyalty and affection. He is not adept at the art of persuasion, nor is he always tactful. I came away from my first meeting with MacArthur with the feeling that I had been talking to a great man.

General MacArthur will always be a controversial figure because he creates enemies. He is the type of man who generates strong loyalties and strong hatred. Every navy man in the Pacific was bitter about MacArthur which, to my mind, only shows the need for service unification. It is true, of course, that MacArthur's distinctive, unyielding personality contributed to the tragic division of authority that plagued us both before and after Pearl Harbor. His own personal conduct and occasional vindictiveness brought down upon his head a great deal of bitter criticism—some of it justified, most of it undeserved.

Feuds and rivalries between the Army and the Navy persisted throughout the entire Pacific campaign. Admiral "Bull" Halsey made a conscientious effort to better these relations. At his headquarters he ordered all officers to discard their neckties, since the army men wore tan and the navy men black ties. No one wore coats, and once the ties were off you couldn't tell the two services apart. Admiral Halsey deliberately encouraged this uniformity to emphasize the need for co-operation. Halsey, with his own distinctive, colorful personality inevitably clashed with MacArthur, although differences diminished after their first personal conference.

Everywhere I traveled during the war I was conscious of Army-Navy friction. Quantities of navy material, which could have served the Army, were allowed to deteriorate instead of being turned over. Each service jealously protected its own supplies. Fortunately, for the successful prosecution of the war, this friction decreased as the war continued and some co-operation developed.

Admiral Nimitz was a quiet and scholarly type of man, a marked contrast to "Bull" Halsey. As I talked with him at Pearl Harbor, I had the feeling that I was in the presence of a man who had worked out a real philosophy of life. He was modest, quiet, and thoughtful. He told me that our main task in the Pacific was to get our forces to the Chinese mainland. He felt that until that was accomplished, Pacific operations were primarily the task of the Navy and the Air Force. He anticipated that the main effort of the American Army in the Pacific would be to drive all the way up through China and push the Japanese back to their homeland. Nimitz emphasized the impregnable character of some of the Japanese defenses in the Pacific Islands. Later I saw with my own eyes with what great care and painful hand labor the Japanese had built up their dugouts and pillboxes so that we were only able to take them with a high rate of casualties. It took us a long time to learn how to conquer these strong points by the use of flame throwers and explosives instead of by direct man-to-man assault.

It was fascinating to learn how we got the most out of the few Japanese prisoners we were able to take during the early stages of the war. The successes of military intelligence and the methods used to achieve them are among the top secret aspects of warfare. If the enemy learns where, when, and how we succeed, they take steps to close up those sources of information. The way in which we handled Japanese prisoners and the methods we used to secure information from them were at once humane and successful. Patience played a large part and as far as I know, torture played no part in our approach. The American officer who was in charge of this work in one Pacific area happened to be one of my enthusiastic radio listeners. After I had agreed to all sorts of secrecy pledges, he allowed me to visit the prisoner compound and to talk with some of them.

The process of interrogation of a particular prisoner might last for weeks. Men were questioned separately and together, and we often recorded what they said among themselves. Once a Japanese decided to co-operate, perhaps as the result of a little applied psychology, he would be most eager to be helpful. The appeal to vanity proved much more productive than the appeal to fear. The methods used by the psychologist to get at the truth were most effective. By these elaborate and careful methods, and by the translation and evaluation of diaries taken from dead soldiers, we were able to get invaluable information, even though the number of prisoners was always small. Nisei (Japanese-Americans from Hawaii) were particularly helpful in translating these diaries. This was just one of the many ways in which these loyal American citizens helped our prosecution of the war. One of them was always in the front line to interrogate at once every prisoner that might be taken. Yet every Nisei knew that if he should be captured it meant torture and death.

When I made this tour of the Pacific front, we had finally regained the offensive. Strategy was still based on the decision that Hitler was Enemy Number One—but the Navy had recovered from the Pearl Harbor disaster and had regained mastery over a large part of the southwest Pacific.

My first trip to Europe after we entered the war took place in 1942. It was brief and limited in scope. I had really planned a week-end round trip to London both to get a glimpse of Britain at war and to call public attention to the wartime development of high-speed plane service across the Atlantic. Fog kept me in Scotland for the better part of a week, so I made nightly broadcasts from Glasgow and did not interrupt my regular broadcast series.

In those days bombing planes were taking off from Gander, Newfoundland, bound for Europe at the rate of one every five minutes during certain hours of the day and night. The trip to the Prestwick, Scotland, airfield took thirteen hours. As our plane flew over Ireland, I could not help but reflect on the serious blunder made by Chamberlain when he relinquished the remaining British naval bases on Irish soil just before the outbreak of war. Many Allied merchant ships that were sent to the bottom by U-boats could have been saved if the British fleet had been able to operate from Irish bases. Patrolling aircraft could have controlled thousands of additional square miles of ocean if they could have taken off from the west coast of Ireland.

I had heard so much about wartime austerity in the British Isles that I was frankly surprised to find so few surface evidences of it. Cows were grazing in the fields among the cement posts that were supposed to prevent the landing of hostile aircraft. In Glasgow, sporting matches and other forms of entertainment were going on as in peacetime. When I asked about this, I was told that Winston Churchill had said, "Recreation is an essential factor in keeping up wartime morale." The people I saw on the streets appeared well dressed, since British clothing is generally of good material and lasts for years.

It was on this trip that I heard for the first time the often repeated quip about our doughboys, "The trouble with the American soldier is that he is overpaid, overdecorated, overfed, oversexed—and over here." There was occasional friction between British and American troops. The Tommies didn't like to see the GI's so popular with British girls. They could not afford to compete in providing treats and entertainment. British introverted reserve and American extroverted heartiness clashed, particularly in the first years of the American "invasion." We made mistakes in dealing with the British and they made mistakes in dealing with us. Isolated quarrels were frequently exaggerated.

The Glasgow radio headquarters, from which I made my broadcasts to the United States, was carefully guarded. The British anticipated that any German landing party would first make for the radio station to use broadcasting facilities. Commando raids were feared either from the air or by sea.

One thing that impressed me during this visit to Scotland and on a later visit to the Panama Canal was the uselessness of most defense preparations. When these go beyond the necessary minimum they are apt to be wasteful. Blackouts were wasteful in the last war. Experts tell me that in cities like London, the use of more light would not have resulted in more damage from bombs. Searchlights, antiaircraft firing, the reflection from a water surface, inevitably indicate the location of a city. Walking or driving during a blackout was a frightening and hazardous experience. In Scotland, I had to make a forty-mile automobile trip from the radio station back to Glasgow after my midnight broadcasts. This trip was always an unpleasant experience. The drive was made in total darkness yet the driver, anxious to get home, bore down hard on the accelerator. Again and again he would sweep by another car, which I had not seen until it was just about on top of us. How the driver could see at all was beyond my understanding. He seemed to sense turns in the road through experience or some uncanny intuition. I admired his skill but deplored his reckless courage.

I spent an interesting two hours with a Canadian bombing unit that had made several trips over Germany. After much persuasion I received permission to sit down with the members of the crew to talk with them about their activities. In the United States we did not know much about these boys—and most of them were boys who were making the nightly raids over Germany that were then just getting under way. The thousand plane raids had not begun but several hundred planes would go out on the same raid. These were all young men and the average age seemed around twenty. The particular group I met had returned safely from seven raids over Germany in eleven days. This indicated the intensity of their work. They agreed that the worst moments on any assignment were the two hours before they took off. The tension of waiting was always worse than the actual experience. Every time they took off they went prepared not to return. They had all allocated their few possessions and had left instructions for their disposition. They all knew that not all planes would return but each crew member carried a charm or good luck piece in which he came to believe more fervently after each safe return.

What troubled them most during these raids was not so much the flak but the deadly efficiency of the German night-fighter planes. The bombardier told me that his happiest moment on each raid was just after he got rid of his bomb load. Every bomber carried a camera which brought back a fairly accurate record of the success or failure of the mission. We know now that successes were greatly overestimated. Most of the trips were made by dead reckoning since following a radio beam helped enemy fighters locate their approach. Bomb crews were not allowed to take notes during the briefing sessions that preceded each flight lest these notes fall into the hands of the enemy. One thing most of them disliked, though they knew it had to be done, was the careful detailed interrogation of each member of the crew, no matter how tired, on just what he observed during the raid. The idea was to check every crew member's observations against those of others to get the best composite picture possible of just what happened. There is an inevitable tendency to indulge in wishful thinking. One of the men told me that after several raids you became familiar with the enemy "hot spots" and learned how to avoid them. Unfortunately, in avoiding the hot spots, a bomber might also avoid the targets where his bombs are supposed to land.

The morale of these men was most impressive. They were, of course, carefully picked and apparently possessed iron nerves. They seemed almost totally indifferent to danger.

I was to remember these brave boys and the many others I saw on the fighting fronts when I heard civilians back home bemoaning their difficulties or when I had to report wartime strikes.

25

I DID NOT GET BACK TO THE EUROPEAN WAR FRONTS again until the winter of 1944-45. Then I flew over to cover our fighting fronts which, by that time, extended from Africa to Germany. After a brief stop at our great African airbases at Casablanca and Tunis I went on to Italy.

There I followed the route taken by the valiant Fifth Army in fighting its way step by step to Rome, to Florence, and still farther to the north. What a desperately difficult and costly operation that was! Mountain range after mountain range. Our men inched their way up one slope after another only to discover that still another mountain lay ahead. To me the Italian campaign was just about the most futile and wasteful operation we have ever undertaken. The Germans had plenty of time to arrange each defense position so as to make us pay a high price for every mile we advanced. We showed little imagination in that campaign. Our men just slugged ahead with small costly gains. Numerous machine-gun nests harassed our troops and made progress painfully slow and costly. Both General Mark Clark and General Alexander indicated in their talks with me a lack of enthusiasm for the task they faced. The best they could say about their efforts was that they were keeping a few German divisions from going to France. The troops fighting on the Allied side in Italy came from the far corners of the earth. Within a few hours I encountered Brazilians, South Africans, Japanese-Americans, Australians, British, Poles, French, Italians, and of course Americans including Negro troops.

To counteract discouragement and boredom with the Italian campaign great efforts were made to give the men a good time when they came to Rome for a rest between their grueling sessions at the front. Some of the largest hotels were turned over to our soldiers. There were plenty of hot baths, good meals, and comfortable beds. There were tours of Rome, American film shows, concerts, and dances. Conditions in Rome were far from ideal. For the Romans there was little food, no heat, no electric current. The Germans had done a good job of sabotage as they retreated through Italy. Water supply systems were crippled, and all repairs were slow and costly.

Air travel gives a sense of a country's physical geography. I had frequently traveled through Italy and France by train, but only as I flew over both countries seated in the plexiglass nose of an American bomber in December, 1944 did I take in the marked contrast between the natural poverty of much of Italy's area and the great fertility of France.

My entrance into Paris that year gave me a tremendous feeling of elation. Because of many happy personal associations with Paris I had come to love it as tradition says we must. The fall of beautiful Paris to the Nazis in 1940 was for me the low moment of the war. So when I drove into liberated Paris in the winter of 1944 it was one of my most happy experiences. I was overjoyed as I recognized the unharmed familiar landmarks. There they stood beautiful as ever, intact and undamaged. It was a bright winter afternoon that showed Paris at its magical best. Crossing the Seine I encountered a happy omen. I actually saw a fisherman on the bank catch a tiny silvery fish. Through the years I have watched those patient fishermen many times ever since my first visit to Paris in 1900, but never before or since have I seen anyone catch a fish.

Paris had already recovered from the German occupation. At the Ritz Hotel where I was quartered thanks to the friendly intervention of Army Air Transport I learned what gastronomical wonders a French chef can accomplish with plain American GI rations. With their wonderful gift for sauces and flavorings, the Ritz chefs beatified our familiar canned goods.

In France I found more psychological than physical damage. The French seemed to be trying to make up for their defeat at the hands of the Germans by punishing with extreme severity all those French, men and women, who were more or less involved with the Germans during the occupation. The crime of collaboration was defined as doing business with the Germans or working for the Germans. Little attention was paid to what would have happened to anyone who refused to do as he was told. The leaders of the Resistance who were now in control had risked their lives. They felt they had the right to expect high standards of conduct from their fellow countrymen. Ordinary human weakness and compromise was called collaboration and was being punished with a vehement vindictive spirit. Some sixty thousand Frenchmen had already been jailed as collaborators. Many had been arrested unfairly and on flimsy evidence, frequently invented by Communists who saw an opportunity to liquidate their enemies.

General de Gaulle was the key figure in France. His was the most important personal role in the early phases of the liberation. He was hailed as a great hero and symbol of French resistance. I saw him receive an ovation as he entered a meeting of the National Assembly in Paris. He was a striking figure, unusually tall for a Frenchman and carried himself with fine military bearing. He was the ideal "man on horseback" whom the French have both followed and feared. Like most men of this type De Gaulle had certain qualities which proved to be a handicap in persuading other men to work with him. He was obstinate, inflexible, and unco-operative. He lacked political sense and seemed overbearing and proud. Nevertheless his competence as a soldier, his rugged honesty, and his devoted patriotism made him the best figure to unify France during this first critical period of the liberation.

From Paris I visited the fighting front now close to or beyond the German frontier. There I became aware of the continuing debate on whether small bombers should be used to support our troops in the close-in fighting in which they were then engaged. In many localities the front lines were only a few hundred yards apart. As a result our own bombers sometimes attacked our own men. The nearness of the enemy lines to our own and the frequent bad weather made it almost impossible for our bombers to "soften up" the enemy without dropping an occasional bomb behind our lines. The question was whether we could afford to sacrifice a few of our own men to our own bombs in order to weaken the enemy for a later attack. Here you have one of the many difficult wartime problems faced by every general. The infantry commanders to whom I talked cited the disastrous effects upon the morale of our men when even a few American soldiers were killed by American bombs. They preferred to do without the air preparation. Yet they acknowledged that such preparation reduced their casualties when they attacked.

There were many other difficulties associated with the war in the air. Near the front lines it was not always easy for our planes to differentiate between German and American road traffic. We worked out elaborate identification markings which the Germans soon imitated. We changed these markings at intervals according to a secret code. But even this was discovered, and it was a constant game of hide-and-seek on the ground and in the air. Lots of mistakes were made by both sides.

The extent of intelligence information was remarkable. Through all sorts of different methods our troop commanders were frequently well informed about the location and plans of the enemy. The Germans were equally well informed about our situation. I sometimes wonder whether we do not overdo the secrecy business. So much time and effort are wasted in useless secrecy precautions that become more of a hindrance than a help. The military mind is constantly making regulations but often forgets to unmake them when they have served their purpose.

Seeing the American soldier in action again gave me a tremendous respect for his courage and fighting capacities. Our men were competent, resourceful, and well trained. Without doubt they were the best-equipped fighting men in the world. The need to economize ammunition in the midst of battle is a desperate handicap and one we were nearly always able to avoid. We strove to be so well equipped that we could substitute machines for men, artillery preparation for infantry assault. We kept sufficient manpower in reserve so that it was possible to alternate personnel. Of course, as our advance began to gather in tempo, our men sometimes outran their supplies. But our Army was so organized and equipped that supplies soon caught up with the advance forces. Supplying front-line troops by air was a significant innovation that has now become routine. Here is one of the most important revolutions in warfare developed during World War II.

In Aachen, the first German town of any size we had occupied, I learned something about the nature and policies of our occupation army. We were using Germans to a far larger extent than had been anticipated in the work of occupation. Only a few Americans supervised the German administrators. The American troops were all needed at the front so we used German personnel to carry out civilian tasks. Germans even constituted the Aachen police force which maintained order and rounded up the growing number of German army deserters.

Our Army had a rule against fraternization but oddly enough not against what we called "contact." This was a subtle semantic distinction that our military personnel worked out on an individual basis. American officers were certainly not fraternizing with their rather good-looking German secretaries. They were simply having business contacts with mutually satisfactory results. Since most of our officers spoke no German the secretaries often played an important role.

In Aachen we found that the Germans responded to our

leadership and direction just as readily as they had responded to orders issued by the Nazis. There was practically no sabotage or guerrilla activity. The people of Aachen were happy that for them the war was over. Most Germans co-operated much more enthusiastically than we had anticipated.

I made a few broadcasts from the front lines back to the United States. Getting by jeep to the broadcasting headquarters in the dead of night was always a harrowing experience. There were no signposts, and several times we just missed driving into enemy lines. On one occasion we were halted by a front-line sentry who fired a warning shot. He told us that in another two minutes we would have been in enemy territory. These drives always took place around midnight due to the time differential with America. Hunting for a mobile broadcasting unit in a foggy winter night in wartime Belgium is an experience I don't want to repeat.

On one occasion my jeep broke down just half an hour before broadcast time while I was en route to broadcasting headquarters. I was lucky enough to persuade the driver of a British mail truck to take me to my destination, where I arrived just three minutes before air time. How that driver could see where his big truck was going was beyond me. He told me that he did it from the feel of the road as he neared one side or the other. He remembered all turns on any road he had covered during the day. Meeting vehicles he said was the most risky part of driving through the nighttime fog. Experienced drivers could stay on their side of the road by the feel. The danger was caused by less skillful drivers. When I thanked the British Tommy at the end of our ride for having saved my broadcast he waved away my thanks with the philosophic remark: "This is a war in which we've all got our jobs to do." I've always been sorry that I was in too much of a hurry to get his name.

This kind of a night drive was not the best preparation for a coherent, calm and dispassionate analysis of the war. Nevertheless, I managed to struggle through and New York reported excellent reception. Merrill Muller, my NBC radio colleague who was the regular NBC man assigned to this sector of the front, had every right to be jealous of my success. For two weeks he had been trying to get through to New York with a broadcast with no success. Then I came along three minutes before broadcast time, for a one-time shot, and got my broadcast through perfectly. It was a score of lucky breaks like this that enabled me to complete my first decade of service with NBC without missing a single scheduled broadcast.

The first time I saw General Dwight Eisenhower was at one of his occasional well-attended press conferences in Paris. His modest manner, lack of ostentation, and open friendliness had made him popular with both the soldiers and the newspapermen of all the Allied nations. His quick mind always caught the implications behind the many penetrating questions that were put to him. I was surprised at the frankness of his answers, and only later discovered that everything he said at that conference was "off the record" until you could persuade the tough military censors to put it on the record. This protection enabled Eisenhower to be at his ease and to answer questions without fearing to reveal any information that might have been of use to the enemy. He discussed the military situation with complete frankness and provided much valuable background information. The hard task was to persuade the censors to release some of the interesting material Eisenhower had revealed. The General himself, I feel sure, would have been less restrictive than his censors.

At this interview in December, 1944, General Eisenhower was frankly pessimistic. He was deliberately conservative in his comment on the progress of the campaign. The reports from Washington had told him about a slackening of effort on the home front due to the unbroken series of successes that followed our rush through France and the advance into Germany.

Eisenhower had a keen sense of public relations with regard to our Allies. At this conference as at many others he gave high praise to the work of the French and the British and took particular pains to mention their success in minor military actions. He knew that French and British reporters were present and always gave them some news that could be featured in their papers.

In the United States we failed to realize the heavy cost of some of the small advances our armies made. I watched the long and careful preparations for an offensive on one part of the front line. It appeared to me to be what I would call a major operation. Several thousand men were engaged. It had been in preparation for two weeks. A vast amount of air and artillery effort was expended. Scores of lives were lost in hard fighting but the objective was achieved. To me it seemed an important and costly engagement. I looked forward to what the official communiqué would say about it and was surprised to see it dismissed with these seven words: "We gained some high ground near Metz." That was all. That was the only comment that will ever be made on these weeks of preparation, on the great expenditure of materials and equipment, and on the many American dead and wounded. "We gained some high ground near Metz."

In Belgium I found life practically back to normal. Brussels was the only Allied capital in which streetcars were running as in peacetime, shops were well filled, the people were well dressed, and where there were few signs of war damage.

The Belgian Premier waxed eloquent telling me of the difficulties he had in working with the Communists in his cabinet. They never respected the secrecy of cabinet meetings. The Communists in the government were not their own masters. They were responsible to the Party Committee which in turn was responsible to Moscow. He said his experience had taught him that no democratic government could ever function efficiently while Communists were in the Cabinet.

The Dutch were not nearly so well off as the Belgians. Much of their country was still being fought over or had been devastated and there were many shortages particularly in food.

My first glimpse of wartime Britain in 1944 indicated less physical damage in London than I had anticipated. I later learned that only one house in every hundred was destroyed although many more were damaged. The British had made great progress in cleaning up the damage as it occurred. I did not see those other British cities such as Coventry that were largely destroyed by concentrated mass raids. The actual bomb damage area in London was limited, but the fire damage was extensive. The dim-out had replaced the blackout and this was a great improvement from my point of view. I still wonder whether the damage from German bombs would have been greater if the dim-out had been used throughout the war.

While in London I experienced the V-2 bombs from which London suffered during the last year of the war. It seemed ironical that this terror weapon should be at its worst when the war had just about been won.

I was at dinner with Lord Beaverbrook, the British newspaper publisher, when I heard what seemed to me a tremendous explosion just outside the window. Although I was a bit alarmed and most curious to know what happened I soon realized that the polite thing to do was to carry on with the conversation as though nothing had happened. Being a good reporter himself Lord Beaverbrook realized that my one desire was to look out of the window so he put out the lights and opened the shades, allowing me to peer out. Although I was sure the bomb must have struck nearby I could see nothing. Lord Beaverbrook called up one of his editors to inquire where this particular bomb had hit. He was informed that it had struck some two miles away from the house where we were dining. Yet the explosion shook the house and rattled the dishes.

The next morning I drove to the block that was hit and saw for myself the great damage caused by that single V-2 bomb. The houses in one square block were pretty well destroyed. Luckily only three people had been killed and six injured. Each bombed-out family was given one hundred dollars for emergency needs. If they needed shelter they were assigned special lodgings. They also got meal tickets to help them until they could get resettled. An efficient team of workmen were pulling down weakened walls and sweeping out the debris. The truck of the Society for the Prevention of Cruelty to Animals was waiting to see whether a buried horse could be dug out alive. It was all just routine and happened every day.

While I was in Britain in 1944 I attended the annual meeting of the Labor party and was greatly impressed by their growing strength. All their leaders seemed to be well informed and competent individuals. They were defending the resistance movements that were playing a large role on the continent without realizing the extent to which these movements were Communist controlled. The British Socialists were calling for a union with the workers of Russia, Germany, and Italy against the Nazis. They opposed the dismemberment of Germany as well as such extreme measures of recrimination as were epitomized by the Morgenthau plan.

The slogan put forward by Clement Attlee was "an international policy of expansion and plenty." Lord Strabolgi denounced the unhappy phrase "unconditional surrender" coined by Roosevelt at Casablanca and blamed this policy for the fanatical resistance of the Germans. Other speakers pressed forward the slogan "workers of the world unite" and urged a union of Communists and Socialists. Several made a careful distinction between the Stalin Government which they did not like and the Russian people whom they did like. They were not so much anti-Communist or anti-Russian as they were anti-Stalin. The Labor party very effectively blamed the Conservatives for the war and the circumstances that made it possible. They kept silent about their own opposition to British rearmament in the 1930's. Again and again they hammered at the old policy of appeasement which they labeled as "Conservative party policy." The Labor party was also criticizing Conservative policy in Greece where British forces were battling against Communist resistance and guerrilla groups. It was not until a group of Laborites returned from a first-hand study of the Greek situation and supported British policy in Greece that the Labor Party changed its official attitude.

I attended a debate on the Greek question in the House of Commons and realized what a wonderful combination debating team the Conservatives had in Winston Churchill and

Anthony Eden. Churchill would hit hard and give no quarter. Then Eden would move in and smooth over ruffled feelings.

Every time I have seen Winston Churchill in action I have become more impressed with the man's greatness. Throughout this entire century he has been one of its dominating and outstanding personalities. Each time I hear him speak I admire his wonderful sense of history, his magnificent command of the English language, his compelling sincerity. No man now living rivals his great accomplishments in government, in personal leadership, or in literature.

Asked to name the most outstanding personality of the past fifty years I would choose Winston Churchill without hesitation. The history of the world might well have been different if he had not lived to rally the British people in the dark days of the Blitz when he could only offer them "blood, sweat, and tears."

26

AT SAN FRANCISCO IN THE SPRING OF 1945 THE WORLD was rudely jolted out of the dream that once Hitler, Mussolini, and Tojo were defeated the peoples of all nations would be able to settle down in peace to work out their individual and common problems. High hopes were expressed when the United Nations conference began in San Francisco. Here at last the basic ideas of the Four Freedoms would be translated into the charter of a practical world parliament. At this conference the United States played that principal role to which we had fallen heir. We had been largely responsible for the preparatory Dumbarton Oaks conference which met during the war on American soil. There was no question this time about United States participation in a world peace organization.

The Charter of the United Nations as worked out in San Francisco contains many well-worded and idealistic declarations of fine purposes. What seemed like practical machinery was established to ease and remove international tensions. But neither the best planned machinery nor the finest declaration of principles can, by themselves, guarantee peace or eliminate wars. For years to come we should not expect the UN to do more than to lessen international tensions and to localize and occasionally mediate minor conflicts. That in itself would be a great deal for a beginning. It would be a sound approach to the ultimate ideal of world peace. The Covenant of the League of Nations and the Charter formulated at San Francisco point the way. They establish an accepted standard of conduct and mobilize world public opinion against those who violate these principles. When fifty-three nations joined overnight to condemn a wanton act of aggression in Korea and pledged their aid to insure its defeat the world took a long step toward organized peace. The success of that intervention will do much to advance the cause of world peace. Failure in Korea would have been for the United Nations what failure in Manchuria was for the League of Nations.

The high hopes with which the UN conference opened did not last long. I was doing my regular broadcasts from San Francisco and regretfully reported the gradual change in mood. From the very start the Russians adopted a truculent and stiff-necked attitude. Despite the personal plea of President Roosevelt, Stalin had initially refused to send Molotov as a delegate to the conference even though every other nation was sending outstanding representatives. Only after the sudden death of President Roosevelt did Stalin agree to send Molotov, as a friendly gesture to newly installed President Truman.

Russian troops were storming and plundering their way across Eastern Europe and it was becoming obvious that the Russians were primarily interested in securing for themselves the spoils of victory. They had suffered devastating losses at the hands of the Nazi armies and were in no mood to negotiate the bases of a fair and equitable peace. They had blocked out their sphere of influence (with our secret concurrence) and would tolerate no interference. The suicide of Adolf Hitler during the first week of the San Francisco meeting signaled the complete collapse of the once mighty German armies. To give the Russians the honor of being the first to enter Berlin we had withdrawn our advance forces thus giving the Red Army a secure hold on half of Europe.

At the beginning of the UN conference news came that the Russian secret police had arbitrarily arrested certain left-wing Polish leaders. These sixteen former underground leaders of non-Communist parties had returned to their country and come out of hiding at Allied request. They were trying to work out with the Russians a compromise on the form of the "liberated" Polish government. Then they were suddenly arrested as "diversionists" which meant that they deviated from the Communist party line. Since they had made no pretense of being Communists the charge was grotesque. Even Edward Stettinius who had been most conciliatory in his relations with the Russians and had worked hard to secure their participation in the United Nations conference admitted to me that he was "highly disturbed." The Atlantic Charter declared that no territorial changes should take place "which do not accord with the freely expressed wishes of the people concerned." Yet Russia's action in Poland was open and outright interference with the "freely expressed wishes" of the Polish people.

The Russians were the last delegation at San Francisco to grant an open press conference. Molotov finally relented and met the press at a conference jammed with representatives from every nation. Molotov spoke glowingly about peace prospects and used all the proper words. But most of his listeners wondered whether he used such words as "justice," "freedom," "equality," and "democracy" as we did.

There were many questions about Poland and the arrest of the Polish leaders. Molotov's blunt but meaningless comment was that the Polish problem should be "settled in accordance with the wishes of the people in Poland."

Molotov did not make a favorable impression at this mass interview. He indicated that the Soviet Union was in no mood to compromise or bargain over issues in which she had a direct concern. Many correspondents who had been sympathetic toward the Soviet Union during the war years were disillusioned before the San Francisco meeting ended. It was soon evident that Molotov was not as much of a free agent at this conference as the heads of other delegations. Again and again the conference was held up while Molotov referred questions back to Moscow. He was free to decide only the most minor issues.

Russia's action in arresting free Poland's political leaders was a clear indication of what we could expect from the Soviet Union. It was a warning that should not have been disregarded. To gain Russia's participation in the United Nations the Western democracies turned their backs on Poland and on men whom we had helped put in Russia's power. Just as Woodrow Wilson accepted a bad peace to get a good League Covenant we set the vicious precedent of selling out a free people to secure Communist Russia's signature to a UN Charter to whose spirit she has not been faithful. A firm stand against Russia on Poland's right to freedom was our moral duty. Even setting moral grounds aside it was to our practical political advantage to be faithful to our commitments and let the Soviet Union stand forth as the pariah among nations for which we soon came to know her.

By the end of the San Francisco meeting the underlying cleavage between Russia and the West had become apparent. The uneasy atmosphere in which the conference adjourned was evident, but it was soon forgotten in the succession of military victories that finally ended the most destructive war in human history and ushered in the atomic age.

The release of atomic energy was one of the greatest triumphs of mind over matter and is probably the greatest single secret that nature is likely to reveal to man in this century. I have seen for myself at Hiroshima the terrible destructive powers of the first atom bomb. In this country I have seen the great constructive potentialities of atomic energy. Man has a new awe-inspiring force at his disposal. Only the future can tell to what ends he will use it.

Since the end of World War II I have spent several months each year in foreign travel. The miracle of air transport has enabled me to travel farther and faster in these past five years than in my preceding sixty-seven years. There are few corners of the globe I have not visited and revisited since the war. Not long after the end of hostilities I traveled through war-devastated Europe and saw for myself the difficulties involved in postwar reconstruction. In Britain I saw the new Labor government take over and initiate a veritable social revolution. In Germany I saw again how difficult it is to reconcile democratic education with military occupation. In 1947 I flew around the world spending time in troubled India, South East Asia, China, and Japan. The next year I was behind the Iron Curtain in Europe. In 1949 I covered the length of Africa from Cairo to Cape Town. During all these travels I have sought the answers to these questions: What chance has democracy to become a world-wide creed? How deep are the inroads of communism and totalitarianism? How is America measuring up to her new responsibility of world leadership?

Until 1948 the world at large was rather skeptical about the ability of the United States to assume its newly won responsibilities as the great world power. Ernest Bevin, Foreign Secretary in the new postwar British Labor Cabinet summed up popular European feeling to me in these words, "Britain grew into her position as a world power through centuries of time. You have had world leadership thrust upon you almost overnight. I hope that your people are conscious of their new responsibilities." From his comments it was apparent he was not sure that our public opinion would back our government in facing up to these problems.

There was reason for Bevin's skepticism. Prominent members of Congress were not enthusiastic about our proposed leadership in world-wide reconstruction. The U.S. along with the other democracies pursued a policy of appeasement toward the Soviet Union in the vain hope of being able to work things out. The Communists took full advantage of our continued concessions. Step by step they expanded their sway over Eastern and Central Europe. By the end of 1945 Russia had completely or practically annexed Estonia, Latvia, and Lithuania; Bessarabia and Ruthenia; parts of Finland, Poland, and East Prussia; Northern Korea, Outer Mongolia, the Kuriles, and southern Sakhalin Island. By February, 1948 Russia controlled Czechoslovakia, Poland, Rumania, Hungary, Albania, Bulgaria, Yugoslavia, East Germany, and North Korea as Communist vassal states. No effective action was taken anywhere to check Russian expansion. Our naïve efforts to "get along with the Russians" only resulted in a constantly expanding Soviet Union. Democracy's stock was low. It looked as though the initiative in setting the pace of world events had passed to the Russians. The democracies seemed unable to generate positive policies in defense of their way of life. The inevitability of Communist victories was accepted. To many the Red wave looked like the wave of the future.

Then in a decisive reversal of policy the United States began to act. Congress voted military and economic aid to Greece and Turkey. The Marshall Plan, a bold program to help reconstruct Europe's economy, got under way. As the success of this plan became evident, Europe for the first time turned confidently toward America as a source of strength and support in resisting Communist aggression from within and without. The postwar collapse of the American economy which had been freely predicted by the Moscow press did not take place. Instead the American standard of living rose to new heights.

The Berlin Airlift was one more proof positive that America was not going to retreat but was ready to assume the responsibilities of leadership. The Airlift was underway when I visited Germany in 1948 and my wife and I had the satisfaction of flying into Berlin with ten tons of coal. Apart from checking Russian efforts to force us out of Berlin the Airlift was an impressive demonstration of British-American airpower. It showed what an important role air transport will play in the years to come. As training for emergency use of airpower to feed, fuel, and maintain a great world capital it was worth every cent it cost. While in Berlin I saw the daily increase in the number of planes flying in and out of Berlin and the steady improvement in efficiency and safety. Considering the numbers of planes flying in all kinds of weather the accident rate was surprisingly low. Ground Control Approach, one of the electronic developments of this century, enabled planes to land under conditions close to ceiling zero. Our Berlin experience advanced the cause of safety in aviation.

On my journey from Frankfurt to Berlin I could see that it was not always easy for our flyers to keep in the narrow twenty-mile corridor to which we were restricted. In bad weather planes flying at a speed of 250 miles an hour could easily swerve out of the narrow assigned lane. Twice in the course of our trip we were "buzzed" by Soviet fighter planes. It was not a pleasant feeling to realize that we were totally unarmed. The British and American pilots who flew food and supplies in to blockaded Berlin gained valuable experience. They showed the same courage and ability that our flyers demonstrated so continuously during the war.

From our first meeting I was impressed with the quiet efficiency of General Lucius Clay, the American Commander in Germany, an able administrator, with a competent staff. We had learned a lot about diplomacy through our bitter experience in three years of trying to "understand" the Russians. Men like General Frank Howley who had daily contacts with them in the course of working out occupation policies in Berlin knew that they were not just "jolly, vodka-loving good fellows." He demanded and received something in return for every concession he made. The atmosphere in American headquarters in 1948 was far more aware than anything I had previously encountered.

General Clay was insistent that the Airlift be continued. "We cannot fail in Berlin," he said. "If we give up here, there will be further pressure on Vienna, and the Russians will gradually push us out of Germany."

There was an editorial from a New York paper on General Clay's desk that recommended a retreat from our firm stand in Berlin. The writer feared that the Berlin Airlift would get us into war with Russia and advised further appeasement. General Clay told me he was greatly disturbed by this editorial. His reaction to this single piece of adverse comment made me realize that a man in his exposed position in a foreign land needs solid backing at home. An American official, working abroad under difficult conditions, is particularly sensitive to home criticism. Without sacrificing the right of objective comment those of us who editorialize on current affairs should try to remember that the man who executes our policy overseas must have home support when he faces foreign opponents.

General Clay explained that as soon as Washington decided to end our policy of conciliation and concession, the Russians decided to do everything they could to drive us out of Berlin. When they could not get their own way they refused all co-operation. They used every possible device to separate the British from the Americans and the Americans from the French. They used every propaganda device to spread disunity among the Western powers. Fortunately their effort only succeeded in further uniting the Allies.

After the Airlift demonstrated our determination to stay in Berlin the Russians abandoned their effort to drive us out by means of the complete railroad and canal blockade. In the spring of 1949 the Russian and American delegates to the United Nations met in New York and worked out a face-saving formula for ending both the blockade and the Airlift. Our success in Berlin showed the Russians that we were finally through with appeasement.

In Austria we have never had the same difficulties with the Russians that we experienced in Berlin. This was due in part to the vigorous attitude General Mark Clark, who headed our occupation forces, took from the beginning. Instead of letting the Russians pound on the table and storm out of conferences he talked back vigorously and effectively. We also set up a much more intelligent system of four-power control in Vienna. There was no Russian veto. Austria was treated as a liberated country. She had the right to make her own laws and these could be vetoed only by the combined vote of the four occupying powers. As a result none of Austria's proposals were vetoed although a few were modified. Vienna is, however, in an exposed and dangerous position. The Austrian capital is surrounded by Russian-occupied territory. The Soviets also control all of Austria's oil resources and the bulk of Austria's food-producing areas.

The Communists have steadily lost support in the free elections held in postwar Austria. Their influence on the course of Austria's development has been limited to expropriation of Austrian supplies, factories, and raw materials. By 1948 Austria was participating in the Marshall Plan and this aid has greatly improved conditions and linked Austria's economy with the West. Austria's leaders assure me that once freed of Russian occupation Austria can develop a self-sustaining economy. That remains to be seen. In a Europe without tariff walls Austria could buy raw materials and find export markets. Perhaps such a Europe will exist someday.

27

THREE COUNTRIES I HAVE RECENTLY VISITED ILLUSTRATE the varying degrees of success with which the West has met the postwar challenge of Russian communism: Czechoslovakia, a total loss; Greece, a partial victory; and Italy, where a resurgence of democratic faith has kept that country outside the Iron Curtain. Although I have watched the steady recovery of France and observed with great interest the socialist revolution in Great Britain, the issues and problems involved in the "cold war" are particularly well exemplified in Czechoslovakia, Greece, and Italy.

Six months after the Communist coup of February, 1948 I managed to visit unhappy Czechoslovakia and observe how the Communists gradually take over a once free country. Before I left New York for Europe that summer I tried repeatedly but vainly to get a visa from the Czechoslovakian Consulate in New York to visit the country. I only received vague noncommittal replies. The Czechoslovakian Communists may well have heard some of my uncomplimentary references to Communist policies. Once in Europe I tried again to secure the necessary permission to visit Czechoslovakia, and in Vienna the local Czech Consulate granted me a tourist visa as a matter of routine. Sometimes it is easier to secure a visa from a foreign consul who does not know the applicant.

In September '48 the Russians were steadily orienting the foreign trade of Czechoslovakia away from the West and toward the East. The usual pressure methods were used. The United States had always been one of Czechoslovakia's best customers but this trade was steadily declining as Russia's share increased. Czech production was also declining, partly as a result of the overly zealous Communist ousting of key personnel. These men were replaced by Communists whose devotion to Moscow exceeded their knowledge of sound business methods or industrial techniques.

The Russians had not yet sent in many of their own agents. They were working through Czech Communist leaders who were sometimes summoned to Moscow for instructions. The chief Communist weapon is terror, and this was being used effectively. When ruthlessly employed, terror reduces the number of Russians needed to govern a country. Midnight arrests, tortures, well-filled concentration camps soon reduce a subject population to inaction or abject servitude. Business was being nationalized on the wholesale level. Only loyal Communists could practice law. All doctors were ordered to subscribe to communism and work for the state. Those who refused were sent to the villages and small towns and placed under surveillance.

A few Czechs still talked hopefully about Czechoslovakia being allowed to participate in the Marshall Plan. Moscow had first agreed and then changed its mind finally refusing to let any satellite state accept Marshall aid. The Russians made one of their great strategic errors when they stayed outside the Plan. Had Poland, Czechoslovakia, Rumania, and Hungary been permitted to apply for Marshall aid, they might well have gained strength for the Communist cause at our expense. These countries could have absorbed large quantities of American goods and transmitted them to Russia. Their participation might have done much to wreck the success of the Plan abroad and to make it exceedingly unpopular here at home.

By expelling millions of Germans from Czechoslovakia that country not only contributed to the sum of postwar human misery but also lost its most competent technicians in the glass and ceramics industry. Many famous Czech products have deteriorated in quality. The conditions under which the Czechs worked had also deteriorated. Their standard of living was steadily declining toward the low Russian standard. The Czech worker had become a slave to the state. All office, store, and factory workers were compelled to "volunteer" for vacation work in the fields. They could not change jobs. Thousands had already fled the country since the Communist coup and tens of thousands were hoping to escape. Their chances were declining because the Communists were tightening frontier restrictions. Some Czechs told me they approved the United States' refusal to send certain materials to Czechoslovakia even though this created hardships. They felt that any diminution of Communist power was desirable.

Only one member of the Czech Government would grant me an interview, and soon after I saw him he was liquidated. This was the Deputy Director of Foreign Trade who though not a Communist party member had toadied to the party. He was most anxious to re-establish trade relations with the United States and tried to give me the impression that business relations could be normalized. He complained about the slowing down of production. "We are finding out," he admitted, "that state control of business and industry causes inefficiency and waste. Some of our newly imposed rules and regulations are causing vexatious delays." The fact that he was not enthusiastic about Communist administration may well account for his early disappearance.

The different newspapers published in Prague all told the same story and followed the Party line. All book shops displayed pictures of Stalin and featured Communist propaganda. A few American books such as Steinbeck's *Grapes of Wrath* and Upton Sinclair's volumes were still for sale, but American papers or magazines could only be had occasionally at one particular newsstand. More and more restrictions were being placed on foreign correspondents. Most of those who were in Prague in '48 have since been obliged to leave.

American Chargé d'Affaires Kekesch arranged for our joint visit to the great Skoda works in Pilsen, one of the world's largest arms factories. Those in charge were still hoping to receive from the United States sorely needed machine tools which may be why they agreed to show us around those parts of the plant engaged in civilian production. Much of the machinery appeared obsolescent. For more than ten years the plant had been unable to secure much new equipment. We were conducted through the plant by the Communist head of the Workers Committee. The actual plant manager appeared to be his subordinate. He was closely watched and was never allowed to speak to us without being overheard. It was carefully explained that the Skoda plant was producing for "all the world." Particular attention was called to some locomotives which, we were told, were to be exported to Turkey. I am convinced that the bulk of this plant's export output goes to building up the Soviet war machine.

Throughout the plant we saw the usual Red propaganda signs spurring the workers to greater production. "No clock watchers wanted!" "Russia gave lives—we give machines!" Nowhere in Czechoslovakia did American troops get the slightest credit for defeating the Nazis.

In the Skoda foundry I saw women pulling cartloads of huge well-filled beer mugs. Free "liquid bread" for the workers is an old Skoda tradition. It was explained to me as a "health measure" which helped men stand the great heat in which they worked. I watched them pause briefly, take a quart mug of beer off the truck and down it in a few seconds. For a brief period the Communists had cut out the serving of beer but when a drastic drop in production followed the beer ration was restored.

The workers earned about fifty cents an hour. They could not quit their jobs without permission of the Communist-controlled Workers Council which ran the plant. On many jobs piecework had been introduced as in Russia. Strikes were outlawed, and some parts of the plant ran two or more shifts. On our way back from Pilsen to Prague we passed a road sign which marked the farthest advance of American troops to Prague. They were stopped to allow the Russians to liberate the Czech capital. The Russians took advantage of our stupidity and immediately installed Communists in all key positions. Thus they paved the way for complete Red control of the country.

Although I dislike the Communists as much as they dislike me I cannot blame them for the automobile accident I was involved in on my return to Prague from the Skoda plant. Our driver was in a hurry and passed a slow, horse-drawn vehicle on the narrow road. Unhappily a truck was coming toward us at that very moment, and a crash was unavoidable. We were all rather shaken and I had to visit a Czech hospital. My desire to complete my European tour and get back home in time to resume my regular broadcast schedule seemed to speed my recovery. It was not until I got back to the United States and was able to relax more comfortably at home that I really felt the delayed effect of the accident.

My general impression of Czechoslovakia was depressing. There was no gaiety. There was a general atmosphere of sadness and drabness. At Munich in 1938 the fighting spirit of the Czechs received a mortal blow. Nazi occupation helped to kill it. When the democracies sold out to Hitler it was as if the Czechs gave up hope in Western democracy and turned reluctantly toward the East. In 1948 they resigned themselves to Russian control without a struggle. Floral offerings under the window from which Jan Masaryk jumped or was pushed to his death showed that some Czechs still had the courage to remember better days.

Several people approached me with offers of many times the legal rate in Czech crowns for dollars. They were collecting *valuta* preparatory to escaping from the country. Many private homes and apartments had already been taken over by the Communists. The whole standard of living was rapidly declining. It was sad to realize that Czechoslovakia, the young Republic born under the American flag, had exchanged freedom for tyranny.

What happened in Czechoslovakia nearly happened in Greece. There the United States faced a difficult problem in foreign policy. After the Nazi occupation the country was in a state of complete disorder. Famine conditions prevailed over large areas. Government was ineffective, reactionary, and corrupt. The Communist and non-Communist resistance groups were warring against one another. Russia and her Balkan satellites were bringing strong pressure to win Greece for communism.

President Truman had announced his program of aid to Greece and Turkey not long before I visited the country. When I asked the Greek Prime Minister why the United States should continue to help Greece he replied, "Greece is Europe's rampart against communism. If we fall, Turkey falls, and the Russians will dominate the Mediterranean. Greece is the place where the battle against Communism must first be won."

Thanks to our aid and thanks also to Marshal Tito's break with Stalin, Greece has been kept outside the Iron Curtain. We should not forget that American economic and military aid was only partially responsible for stemming the advance of communism in Greece. The guerrilla war might have continued indefinitely if Marshal Tito of Yugoslavia had not withdrawn his support. In this instance, Tito unwillingly served our interest even though a short time before he had shot down American planes. Whether he will continue to serve our interests is dubious. He is still a ruthless Communist dictator who does not wish us well. It is fortunate that one of our most capable diplomats, George Allen, is stationed in Belgrade today. On all issues concerning Tito's Yugoslavia we must be coldly realistic. The Yugoslav delegate is the only United Nations Council member who voted against the application of United Nations' sanctions against the North Korean Communists.

Many who visited Italy between 1945 and 1947 came away convinced that Italy would ultimately fall to the Communists. Directly after the war Italy had permitted Communists to participate in the government. Their disruptive activities worsened the already desperate economic conditions. The Communist Minister of Finance in the Italian Cabinet had deliberately tried to sabotage tax collections in the hope that his country would go completely bankrupt and thus pave the way for a Communist coup.

Under such conditions the decisive defeat of the Communists in the April '48 elections came as something of a surprise. The non-Communist parties supported by the Church had united in a vigorous effort to defeat the Reds. United States aid and a flood of letters from the United States relatives of Italian voters also helped tip the scales against the Communists. A few months after the elections the Italian economy had begun to revive. Signs of recovery were apparent everywhere.

I asked Guiseppe di Vittorio, leader of the Communist trade unions, how he explained the election defeat of his party. "It was entirely the result of the Marshall Plan and the efforts of the Church," he said. Large Marshall Plan supplies arrived shortly before the election and the Vatican had participated actively in the campaign. The Catholic Church gave full and open support to the non-Communist candidates.

When I interviewed Pope Pius XII in August '48 I congratulated him on the victory of the Church in the spring elections. To this he replied, "We have not won a final victory. We have only won a battle. The struggle against communism has just begun and must be continued. It would be a grave mistake to relax our vigilance."

In answer to my question as to how the Catholic Church justified its direct entry into the political arena he replied, "The Church did not enter politics in Italy. It entered a struggle for the preservation of the Church and the Faith. It was essential for us to defend the Church against the destructive forces of communism. We know from experience that the Communists do not tolerate religion. Our struggle against communism may be called politics, but it is a defense of the Faith."

I will always remember his gestures as he spoke these words. He raised both his arms and swept them outward to emphasize the world-wide battle against communism. "For us," he said, "what we have done in Italy is no more than the defense of the Church and of the Faith, and that defense is and will remain our sacred duty. . . . In the face of militant communism there can be no weakness, no appeasement. Firmness is essential!"

At this point the Pope doubled his fists and raised them in an almost militant gesture. A moment later he was again the great spiritual leader. With lowered voice he added, "Of course I pray continuously for peace. War would be too terrible. But we must maintain our continued resistance against any Communist advance."

28

FLYING AROUND THE WORLD WAS BOTH A FASCINATING and exhausting experience. The continued heat and the night flying were tiring, but the constant psychological readjustment, the quick succession of the most diverse countries and peoples was what tired us most.

From New York to London to Paris to Rome and then to the Near East took little more than a week. In Egypt conditions had changed little since my first visit some twenty years before. Egypt had achieved political independence but had not gone far along the road of economic betterment. There was the same disparity between the few rich and the many poor. Egypt was still in good part a land of beggars and disease.

The land of the Nile remained a center of Arab resistance to a completely Jewish Palestine. E. A. Ghory, one of the members of the Arab Higher Committee for Palestine, told me that the only solution of the Palestine problem would be an independent Palestine in which the Jews had only minority rights. "Partition is unacceptable to the Arabs," he said.

"The British have always favored the Jews over the Arabs and in that way have encouraged the terror that has prevailed in that unhappy country."

Egypt had welcomed the Grand Mufti of Jerusalem who was the most outspoken leader of the Arab point of view. On meeting him, I was not impressed. He was definitely the fanatic, shrewd and with a striking personality. He is physically small, a complete Oriental, with an innate suspicion of everything Western.

At the beginning of our talk he said bitterly, "The United States has not been fair to the Arabs. Your president is now asking for the admission of one hundred thousand Jews into Palestine without giving any consideration to the cause of the Arabs. Even though you do not have a sizable Arab population in the United States, there is no reason why our cause should not be fairly treated."

The Grand Mufti speaks both English and German, but he conducted this interview in Arabic through an interpreter. This practice of using an unnecessary interpreter is followed by many statesmen when they grant interviews. The time required for translation gives them a chance to consider their replies more carefully. It also is a check against misquotation, which seemed to be of great concern to the Grand Mufti. During the war he had played with both sides and finally aligned himself with the Germans in an effort to promote the Arab cause, but he was still anxious to give the impression of statesmanlike impartiality.

The Palestine problem was before the United Nations while I was in the Near East on this 1947 visit. The British had agreed to terminate their Mandate and violence had broken out between Jews and Arabs. Since then, after much bitter fighting and bloodshed, the new independent state of Israel has been formed with its capital in the ancient city of Jerusalem. This small new nation has made great strides in a short time, but the old problem of relations between the Jews and the Arabs remains to be solved.

My first visit to Palestine took place in 1925, and I was favorably impressed then, as in all my succeeding trips, with the economic achievements of the Zionists and the unselfish devotion with which they were transforming a barren land. Back in 1925 there was little talk about political Zionism. The establishment of an independent Jewish state was not an issue. The statesmanship and wise restraint of the great Zionist leader Chaim Weizmann was most apparent at that time. There were too many other pressing problems to make the creation of a future political state an immediate issue. The Balfour Declaration of 1917 had promised the Jews a homeland in Palestine and that seemed to be all they wanted. However, while the Balfour Declaration promised the Jews a homeland, it also promised the Arabs that "nothing should be done to prejudice the civil and religious rights of existing non-Jewish communities." These two almost incompatible promises have been the cause of much blood-letting and continued antagonism between Jew and Arab.

What the Jews have accomplished in Palestine is truly remarkable. At one of the agricultural colonies, I met a fine, outstanding group of devoted young people. As one of them said to me with pride in his voice, "This is our land and we are making it fertile." They were cultivating the fields successfully. Their leaders were intelligent and self-sacrificing. In a postwar world where so much had been destroyed, it was an inspiring sight to see the constructive efforts that were under way in arid Palestine. Modern agricultural methods were being used. Of course, some of the immigrants had a hard time adjusting themselves to the new life, and a good many left or would have done so if they had old homes to which they could return. Many have skills which are not needed in Palestine and must, therefore, readapt themselves to do what is needed.

Tel Aviv is rightly called the "Wonder City" of Palestine. The modern, well-paved streets, the substantial villas and office buildings, the absence of slums, the attractive public buildings make Tel Aviv the jewel city of the Near East. When you see that pearl of a community and contrast it with the backward Arab towns, you realize that Zionism has brought something constructive and worthwhile to the Near East. To be sure it has done it in great part through the financial help that has come from America. Israel cannot be self-supporting while it must open its arms to so many impoverished refugees from other lands.

Ever since my first visit in 1925, I have realized the complexities of the Palestinian problem. I have always borne testimony to the magnificent contribution of world Jewry and the devoted Jewish immigrants in building up Palestine to make it a better homeland for both Jews and Arabs. I can also understand the resentment of the Arabs at being pushed out and the concern of the British with this strategic corner of the Mediterranean and the rich oil fields by which it is surrounded. Above all, I have been impressed with the fine enthusiasm and the constructive zeal with which Jews from all over the world have devoted themselves to Palestine development. They have made it a home for the oppressed, and they deserve the support of all fair-minded men in the great humanitarian task to which they have devoted so much zeal and sacrifice.

I hope that the future leaders of Palestine will inherit something of the wise and generous statesmanship of Chaim Weizmann. He is one of the few truly great human beings I have ever met. For the older I grow, the more I realize that true greatness lies in character rather than in worldly achievement. Chaim Weizmann has a rare combination of spiritual qualities and sound common sense. He impressed me with his vision and the infinite patience with which he has met the countless problems that have crowded in upon him. There is an interesting parallel between Chaim Weizmann and Mohandas Gandhi. Both were true leaders of a great people. Both believed in going back to the simple things. Both believed that conflicting interests can be reconciled without recourse to violence. Both are men of peace, which explains why Chaim Weizmann has always dissociated himself from the Jewish terrorist groups who later became responsible for the tragic death of Count Folke Bernadotte, the United Nations mediator. Both Gandhi and Weizmann worked with the utmost patience for an understanding with those who were hostile to their struggle for independence. Weizmann said to me on one occasion, "Unless we can find a way of getting along with the Arabs, we are never going to be able to solve our problems."

Both Weizmann and Gandhi carried an air of tranquil self-assurance. Neither permitted himself to become troubled or bitter about the apparent insolubility of the problems they faced. We ordinary humans become exasperated and irritable when a problem resists solution. But somehow Weizmann and Gandhi learned to accept human beings as they are and to deal with them without ever losing patience, tolerance, and understanding.

Mohandas Gandhi was in Calcutta when I visited India in 1947, and I was naturally most anxious to meet one of the world's great men. We arrived in Calcutta in the midst of the celebration of Indian independence. This was a colorful and almost frightening introduction to India. The streets were crowded, as only India's streets can be crowded, with fanatical enthusiasts. There was a mad bedlam of cries throughout the city. Shouts of "Free India" rose from a million throats. Hindus and Mohammedans linked arms as they repeated the cry: *"Jai Hind!"* India arise!

The British Overseas Airline officials were afraid of transporting us through the streets in a distinctively British vehicle. So, to carry us from the airport into the city, they put us into an old truck, less likely to attract attention. However, as our car slowly made its way through the milling crowds, which recognized us as foreigners, we did not encounter a single sign of antagonism. Yet, it was with a sense of relief that we finally arrived at our hotel after a long, slow drive through a frenzied demonstration.

My interview with Gandhi was arranged through the American Consul and the local Indian authorities for the day after Indian Independence Day. It was not easy to drive close to the large private house where he was staying on the outskirts of Calcutta. Thousands of Indians were swarming around the house and grounds hoping to catch a glimpse of their leader. Gandhi, the Hindu, was staying at the home of a wealthy Mohammedan as a gesture of interracial good will.

He was in the city in an effort to establish peace between the Mohammedans and the Hindus and to end the bloody communal riots between the two groups which had been going on for months. They ceased the moment he arrived, such was the moral power of this frail little man.

Inside the house there was as much bedlam and confusion as outside. The room where Gandhi received us lying on his pallet was a bit more quiet, although it was not insulated from the shouts and cries that came from the mobs outside. He apologized for receiving us in a reclining position, explaining that he was still weak from his recent fast. This particular hunger fast was in the interest of Hindu-Moslem reconciliation, and he had ended it a few days before when the riots ceased. He was most gracious and allowed my wife to take pictures while we were talking.

Gandhi was even smaller and more emaciated than I had anticipated. His puny, almost naked body was that of a man who could not have much physical stamina. He was clearly upset by the continued shouting that came from outside, and urged us to come closer to him so that we could hear one another speak. Whenever the cries reached a certain pitch, he put his fingers in his ears and looked appealingly at one of his secretaries who then went to the window and waved at the crowds in an effort to quiet the shouting. This would reduce the volume of sound a bit but as other people began crowding in, the cries reached new peaks of enthusiasm. There was a constant call for Gandhi to come to the window. At least once every hour throughout the day he would rise with difficulty and with slow steps walk to the window. Supported by his granddaughter and secretary, he would stand there briefly with his fingers in his ears and wait for quiet. He scolded them like a father and then urged them to go home and work for Hindu-Moslem peace.

In talking with me, he demonstrated his complete command of all shadings and niceties of the English language. His speech was simple, and the spiritual overtone appeared in every sentence. When I congratulated him on India's freedom, he shook his head sadly and replied, "Our work for the freedom of India has only begun. So far we have only accomplished the negative part of our task. We have won political freedom. But we are far from having won economic freedom and spiritual freedom. Above all, we have not yet established complete peace between Hindu and Moslem. This divided India we have today is not the free United India I hoped to achieve. Our cause will not have triumphed until Pakistan and India are one. That clamor of approval you hear outside is comforting perhaps, but it is only froth and has no deeper meaning. The one happy thing at this moment is that there is no more fighting between Hindu and Moslem."

At this point, the clamor outside had reached a new high point. He motioned to his granddaughter to assist him to rise so that he could once more speak to the crowd. As he reached the window, the shouts reached a terrific climax and I could see that the piercing noise gave him actual physical pain. He put his fingers to his ears while his secretaries vainly called for silence. But at last they succeeded in creating relative quiet. Again Gandhi asked his admirers to do what each and every one of them could to further Hindu-Moslem unity but his words were heard by only a few.

During the interview, I noticed one of his recording secretaries writing with what seemed to be a scratchy, inferior pen. I asked Gandhi if he would accept the American ball-point pen I had in my vest pocket. As I passed the pen to Gandhi, several of his secretaries smilingly stretched out eager hands. Gandhi smiled and motioned them away as he gave the pen to his first secretary. Turning to me he said, with a wan smile, "You see how I am surrounded by selfish sinners!"

A few weeks later an assassin's bullet ended the life of one of the greatest and noblest personalities the world has known. Perhaps Gandhi would have wished it thus for his martyrdom gave an impetus to the cause of Hindu-Moslem unity and has brought at least temporary peace and agreement.

In Pakistan they were also celebrating their newly won independence when we arrived at Karachi. India had just been divided into the two separate independent states, Hindu India and Moslem Pakistan, both new members of the British Commonwealth. The outstanding leader of the

Indian Moslems was the late Mohammed Ali Jinnah. He received us in the British Government House on the first day of his tenancy. Jinnah was at once an Oriental philosopher, a shrewd statesman, and a keen student of the art of politics. I also felt he had in him the makings of an able dictator, albeit one with more than a touch of vanity. He was thin, tall, and intellectual in appearance. When I asked him what was the hardest problem he faced, he smiled and said, "We have so many problems here that it is hard to select one as outstanding. We have nothing but problems." Then he added, "The peaceful transfer of authority that is now taking place here in India reflects great credit upon the British who have finally carried out the promise made by Queen Victoria. And the British have left us a fine inheritance. I need only mention the excellent judicial system they have created. For this and much else we are greatly in their debt."

The future of India looked far from hopeful in the summer of 1947. There was an air of tension and it was feared that civil war between Moslem and Hindu would follow the British departure. While there were bloody clashes with thousands of casualties, no general civil war resulted. Hostility between Hindu and Moslem may continue, but under the wise leadership of Nehru on the one hand and Aliquat Ali Khan on the other, the two groups have achieved unexpected stability. Both sides have realized how much they would lose from mutual antagonism. Only the Communists would profit from more civil strife in India. Because India's leaders know this, they have arrived at a live-and-let-live agreement which could pave the way to enduring peace and perhaps to the creation of the free and united India for which Gandhi lived and died.

On our round-the-world flight we also stopped off briefly in Burma. There the transfer of power from the expert British colonial administration to an inexperienced multi-party Burma government was under way. The chief tourist attraction in Rangoon in 1947 was the great public hall where the coffined bodies of a dozen assassinated cabinet members were kept on display. The coffins were draped with bright red cloth—the Communist color. Unshaded electric bulbs and little white paper parasols added a bizarre touch to this memorial of political murder. Each noon there was a brief ceremony of saluting the dead. The murdered members of Burma's first independent government provided good propaganda for the succeeding administration trying to consolidate its power and suppress a half dozen incipient revolutionary movements. Burma's leaders were also trying to bring some order out of the chaotic conditions in which the economy and finances had been plunged as the result of war.

The American Consulate where my wife and I spent the night was surrounded by guards. Every now and then a shot rang out from some part of the city. Political terror and banditry were rampant. Chinese Communists were already seeping into the country and this pressure has increased with the fall of China to the Communists. The Burmese I talked with were eager to know what the United States proposed to do for Burma. There was a general assumption that it was part of our postwar duty to help Burma develop order and sound political institutions and to lend them the necessary financial support. Years will pass before Burma can become a prosperous well-ordered country. The Communist threat is very real.

The most attractive capital of Southeast Asia is Bangkok in Siam. There are numerous wide avenues and many fine public buildings. The war left this city practically undamaged. The many exotic temples are most intriguing with their infinite variety of Buddhas in gold, silver, and a particularly famous one in translucent jasper, usually called the Jade Buddha.

Siam is relatively prosperous. The considerable quantity of rice, tin, rubber and teakwood she exports each year more than covers her import needs. Because Siam has no tradition of resisting an invader, the Chinese Communists could take over the country if they were so inclined. Successful resistance would require the development of a well-trained and well-equipped army plus considerable help from Britain and the United States. Here is another nation of Southeast Asia where, as in Indo-China, a large amount of outside aid will be needed if the Communist tide pressing down from the North is to be checked or defeated.

When we reached China, it was evident that all American aid had long since been withdrawn. We were doing nothing to help Chiang's armies in the crucial fight for Manchuria which was then under way. Everyone agreed it would not be long before the entire country fell to the Communists. The Reds were winning the crucial battles in Manchuria, thanks to Russian co-operation, and they were steadily pressing southward. It was evident that unless the United States substituted military aid for lip service, the Communists were bound to triumph.

General Albert C. Wedemeyer, with whom I talked at that time, agreed that the Communists could still be stopped. But he pointed out that it could not be done by turning supplies over to corrupt Nationalist generals. We had to control distribution to assure their reaching the front. General Wedemeyer felt that the only thing we could do and should do was to intervene wholeheartedly, even to the point of risking some American lives. There just was no easy way to keep China from falling to the Communists. Yet our State Department talked of Nationalist corruption and Communist good intentions, suppressed Wedemeyer's report, and rejected his suggestions.

Shanghai was a city of confusion, corruption, and disappointment. As I walked about the streets, I saw quantities of American relief goods being sold by street peddlers at high prices. Much was UNRRA relief material which had been stolen to be sold on the black market. Only a small part of our relief material ever reached those for whom it was intended. The few military men we still had in China in 1947 were convinced that without prompt large-scale American aid, Chiang could not defeat the Communists. It was already certain that the Nationalist Army could not stand up against the more efficient Red Army unless we supplied leadership, training, and a large quantity of up-to-date weapons. Morale in the Nationalist Army was virtually nonexistent. After years of fighting against the Japanese, they had little enthusiasm for the fight against the Communists. Desertions were spreading. Evasion of military service was the rule. There was supposed to be compulsory military service in Nationalist China but it could not be enforced. An elaborate recruiting campaign in the city of Shanghai had produced less than three thousand soldiers out of a population of four million. Those with money could buy their way out of service; the others simply went in hiding.

Inflation was running wild. The hotel room we occupied went up in price each day. While we occupied it the price jumped two thirds. Chinese businessmen had lost all respect for their government. Business was in a state of chaos. The government could not collect taxes. Local officials imposed their own rules and regulations on business and transport in an effort to pick up more "squeeze." About the only way to do business was through smuggling.

These conditions of graft and inefficiency must continue in large measure under the Communist government now in power. The Communists will have little more success than the Nationalists in overcoming these basic difficulties. Ruthless terror will help a little but not too much. There does not seem to be any such thing as loyal patriotism in present-day China.

There is strong antiforeign sentiment, and the Communists have known how to exploit this to their advantage. Dislike of foreigners had greatly increased since my previous visit to China twenty years earlier. When we traveled on the Chinese airline from Hong Kong to Shanghai it was: "Stand back until all Chinese are aboard." There was much more than the usual effort to cheat the foreigner, and all relations were tinged with a feeling of hostility. Much of this antagonism had been stirred up by the Japanese, and their slogan, "Asia for the Asiatics." This antiforeign feeling will persist. The Russians will feel it if they ever supplant their Chinese stooges and try to run the country themselves. One thing is certain—the white man will never again regain the advantageous position he once held in the Far East.

The fall of China to the Communists is not the personal

failure of Chiang Kai-shek. He is, I am convinced, a sincere, honest, and able leader. But he was faced with an impossible situation. The blame for the fall of China must be attributed to the devastating effects first of revolution, then of fourteen years of external aggression with foreign intervention, followed by civil war. The fatal blundering of United States foreign policy in the Far East must also bear its large share of the blame.

Tetsu Katayama, Prime Minister of Japan in 1947, revealed some of the psychology of the postwar Japanese when I talked with him in Tokyo. "Japan is pledged to peace. We will never wage another war," he said. "We propose to make Japan a peaceful, democratic nation, though it may take some time. We are earnestly anxious to qualify for membership in the United Nations at the earliest possible moment."

He seemed generally satisfied with the American occupation policies. He hoped that the Japanese trade unions and democratic education in Japan would prevent the rise of another military clique. He was concerned about Communist infiltration into the trade unions for which we paved the way. We ordered that the Communists be released when we occupied the country. They at once began their customary disruptive agitation. Because our occupation continued successfully they have steadily lost mass support. Since I was in Japan, the Communists have been rocked by internal dissension. They were decisively defeated at the polls, and their disruptive tactics were finally curbed by General MacArthur's intervention.

The Japanese have long been accustomed to autocratic rule. For most of them there was little difference between the orders given by their old rulers and those issued by the American authorities. Obedience was instinctive. General MacArthur's wise use of the prestige of the Emperor made it possible for us to take over control in 1945 without the slightest friction. There was none of the sullen resentment at occupation that I had seen in Germany. The same Japanese who had been ready to fight to the death against America accepted the Emperor's command to be completely obedient to the authority of General MacArthur.

The basic problem of Japan is still the same—overpopulation. I could observe it when I first looked down on Japan's highly cultivated mountainsides from the top of Mount Fuji. Japan cannot exist without foreign trade and a merchant fleet. The sooner we help them develop both, the sooner we can cut both our occupation costs and our occupation forces. In time we may also permit Japan to contribute to her own defense against Russian attack. We simply must face the problem of how best to enable the Japanese to protect themselves. We have the same problem as in Germany, and in both cases the ultimate solution will be to help arm our former enemies against our new enemy.

While I was in Japan, I had lunch with General MacArthur. In addition to discussing the problems of occupation, we talked about the Russian threat. He sensed that threat even before the end of the war and never once joined in the fatal appeasement policy. Without placing the slightest restriction on our conversation, he said to me in September, 1947, "Russia's great ambition in the Far East is to take over the home islands of Japan. We can count on the Japanese to resist with all the means in their power. They are anti-Russian and pro-American because of the way their men were treated by the Russians and the way they have been treated here by us. If we have any sense, we will take over the line of Pacific Islands south of Japan, which we now occupy, and keep them under the American flag. With those islands and Formosa in friendly hands and with the United States bases in the Philippines, we can control the Asiatic coastline from Vladivostok down with our available military forces. In the face of Russia's determination to get control of these islands, we can do nothing less. The Russians thought that by letting us run the occupation, we would be sure to fail and then they could easily take over. They were deceived by the critical comments on the occupation which they read in the American Press.

"Now they know better, and we must expect them to stop

at nothing to take over. They may try to assassinate me or they may make an effort to foment revolution. Fortunately communism here is not strong. There are only four Communist members in the Diet. There are some shrewd Communist labor leaders, but I defeated and permanently weakened them when I forbade the general strike. Unfortunately this prohibition has also set back the labor movement as a whole. My task here promises to continue for some time. It will not be finished until a definitive peace treaty has been written and signed."

When I reached Seoul, Korea, from Tokyo in a five-hour flight, I sensed that I had reached one of the most explosive danger spots in the Far East. Our efforts to carry out the Roosevelt agreement to co-operate with the Russians in the occupation had already reached an absolute impasse. Within the country there were many bitterly opposed local factions, and the people were distrustful of their largely self-appointed political leaders.

Korea, first under the Japanese, had been an occupied country for so long that neither the people nor their leaders were ready for democratic government. They are not ready for it today. Under Russian direction the Communists controlled all of North Korea. But they were also strong in South Korea, the section we occupied. Many Korean Communists in South Korea were Russian trained, and they all took their orders from Moscow. Some of their best agents were at work. Living conditions were desperate, and Communist propaganda fell on receptive ears. From the day on which we invited the Russians to occupy that part of Korea north of the 38th parallel, they inaugurated their plan to take over the entire country. At the Cairo Conference and later at Teheran and Yalta, it was decided that Korea should be a united independent country. The ever-present Russian condition for unification was that the country must be Communist controlled. From the first day of Russian occupation, they began to integrate the economy of North Korea with that of Russia-dominated Manchuria and to organize the Communist conquest of the whole of Korea. The more fools we to be taken by surprise when armed invasion began.

Syngman Rhee, who later became President of Korea, told me that he wanted to see an independent Korea established at once. He was sure that if the United States withdrew most of its troops, he could negotiate a satisfactory treaty with Russia. We did withdraw and not long after President Rhee had to flee for his life before the Red Army from the North.

General J. R. Hodge, who was in charge of the American occupation forces in 1947, was convinced that we should either do a thorough and effective job in Korea or else withdraw and abandon it to the Russians. He put it this way, "We are now spending two hundred fifty million dollars a year on Korea. Of that total one hundred fifty million dollars is for troops and one hundred million dollars for preventing disease and disorder. That is a completely negative expenditure of a quarter of a billion dollars every twelve months. If, however, we add one hundred million dollars a year for reconstruction, the rebuilding of factories, road construction, the development of water power, etc. we can build up Southern Korea for democratic government. To do this would present the Koreans with a real contrast between North Korea where the Russians are doing nothing except to build up an Army and South Korea where a real constructive effort would be underway. That would be a sound way of creating trouble for the Russians while we built up Southern Korea for democratic government. If we don't intend to do a constructive job in Korea, we ought to get out. But let us make no mistake. Getting out of Korea means that the Russians take over and we lose Asia."

What General Hodge said to me he must have said to his superiors—which means that when we ordered our troops out of Korea without building up more than a lightly armed constabulary in South Korea, we should have reconciled ourselves to Russian occupation. The inevitable invasion from North Korea came in June, 1950 and with it President Truman's dramatic reversal of our do-nothing Far Eastern policy.

As was inevitable we suffered the early defeats that must

come to any nation that tries to improvise a long-haul defense against a well-prepared neighbor aggressor. Bit by bit the American people learned the harsh truth about the hard fight we face when a far-distant battlefield is selected by the enemy. Russian territory adjoins Korea. America is seven thousand miles away. We have accepted the Communist challenge under difficult conditions. Yet we must now fight and fight hard until we win. It will be our great good fortune if we are allowed to complete the Korean campaign before our troops are needed elsewhere. And once the guns have ceased firing the real battle to save war-torn Korea from chaos and Communism will have only begun. I sincerely hope we will then redeem our pledge to create a united, independent, democratic Korea.

We concluded our round-the-world trip by making the return trip on Northwestern Airlines by way of the Kurile Islands, the Aleutians, and Alaska. From Japan's northernmost home island where we made a fuel landing we were already in 1947 making regular reconnaissance flights to keep watch on any military concentrations by the Russians that might portend aggressive movements toward Japan. Would we had been equally alert in Korea three years later!

The Aleutian base at which we stopped was a bare, windswept island, and I realized why our soldiers were reluctant to accept assignment to that dreary corner of the world, with its constant high winds, cold, fog, and isolation. I saw the strengthening of our military outposts in Anchorage, Alaska and was informed about some of the extensive training in Arctic fighting we were giving our men. These northern outposts will have growing importance in the years to come, and our recent moves to strengthen these defenses are well advised.

This trip around the world gave me a dramatic impression of America's responsible position in the postwar world. There was virtually no country I visited in which we were not exercising an important or dominant influence in politics and economics. Everywhere the leaders looked to us for help, for co-operation, and for leadership. In some places it was just assumed that the United States should, could, and would help them develop their economies and reconstruct their countries. In some colonial areas there was a feeling that we must use our own best efforts to assure their early independence, whether or not we believed them to be ready to maintain their freedom.

Probably the most dangerous illusion we can give the world is that we are both rich enough and generous enough to devote untold billions to raising the living standards of the two billion underprivileged human beings who occupy the globe. Many nations have set their expectations for American aid so high that even the best we could do would still leave them disappointed that we did not give more. Yet, our first rule of help must be that we can only stimulate self-help. Where nothing is now being done to improve conditions outside help alone can accomplish little. That lesson was driven home to me many times when I made my first fairly complete tour of the great African continent.

29

On July 9, 1949, my seventy-first birthday, my wife and I left for Africa. The Dutch Airline, the K.L.M., and later the railroads and air lines of the South African Union carried us from Tunisia on the Mediterranean down to the Cape of Good Hope on the bottom tip of the Dark Continent and back again. This was a distance of some fifteen thousand miles by the route we followed. We had glimpses of Nigeria, French Equatorial Africa, the Belgian Congo, Rhodesia, and South Africa. There is much to be said about each one of these African areas. I will only risk comment on that part of the continent where we had a real chance to study conditions.

We spent a whole month touring the South African Union, entranced with its scenery, its animal life, and its hospitality. The first impression the visitor gets of South Africa is one of wealth. Everything in the big cities of the Union radiates prosperity—the sleek American automobiles, the modern sky-scrapers, the luxury stores, the comfortable hotels. But every-where there is also a certain air of tension which comes from the strained relations among racial segments of the varied populations.

The relations of two and one-half million whites with the eight million black Africans, the three hundred thousand Indians, and the one million people of mixed blood called colored are unsatisfactory to all concerned. They all fear one another, and fear begets hate. Poor soil and the lack of water keep millions of South Africa's natives close to starvation. Issues concerning civic and economic rights stir up bitter controversy. The political pot is always boiling. There are more tensions among racial groups in South Africa than can be found anywhere else in the world.

This is not only true as between black and white. It is also true to a lesser extent as between Boer and Briton. The average Briton in Africa seemed to me to be a liberal, and the average Boer a conservative. The wealthy, powerful British element that opened the mines, created industries, built the cities and railroads, wants the non-Europeans of South Africa to participate in the country's development and to share in its advantages. The average Boer who has lived close to the soil preaches complete separation of the races, *apartheid,* with the black man serving the white man, but not sharing his special privileges. The Briton, while loyal to his adopted country retains a nostalgic love for old England and sees no contradiction between loving Britain as a mother and South Africa as a wife. The Afrikander is still bitter about the bloody Boer War with Britain, fought back in 1899. He remembers his pioneer ancestors, the hardy "Voortrekkers" who peopled the gold-rich Transvaal and the soon-to-be-gold-rich Orange Free State. The Boer has no sense of obligation to Britain or to British interests. Only the popularity of the late Field Marshal Smuts carried South Africa into the last war on the side of the British, and that only by the narrow margin of thirteen votes.

After World War II, General Smuts was displaced by an anti-British Nationalist, Dr. Daniel F. Malan, as Prime Minister. I had an opportunity to talk with Dr. Malan and asked him to summarize for me the Nationalist party creed. Said he, "We Nationalists believe that those who own this land are entitled to develop it and to control it."

Here he was referring to the Afrikaans-speaking whites, the pioneers. Their Dutch ancestors developed Cape Town and the Cape colony. Then just as our own pioneers moved west and opened the country to settlement, the Boer Voortrekkers moved north, conquered the savages, established their homesteads, and thus paved the way for the English settlers who later opened the gold and diamond mines. It is the English who became rich while most Boer farmers remained relatively poor.

The Afrikander insists on South Africa's bilingualism. His own language, Afrikaans, is based on the Dutch language but includes many Boer changes and additions. More than half the white population of South Africa has a Dutch background and is proud of the Afrikaans cultural tradition.

The most unfortunate aspect of today's situation is that the new Nationalist government of the South African Union seeks to turn the clock back with regard to race relations. And so today the great riddle of Africa is for how long so few whites will be permitted to exploit so many Negroes. Everywhere the nonwhites are beginning to press for a higher standard of living and a larger role in the administration.

Cape Town is a city that has cultural charm and a remarkably scenic location. But its progressive colored population is voicing increased demands for better treatment. If these demands are not granted, the nonwhites may well become responsive to radical leadership with all that this implies. The big cities of the Union could readily become a fertile field for Communist propaganda.

In South Africa millions of natives have been "detribalized" to work in the mines, on the farms, or in the cities. They are separated from the traditional discipline of the tribe and the family. Yet they are not permitted to participate in the white man's way of life. Many of them work on contracts that enable them to get home for only a few weeks every year or two. Their life in the overcrowded compounds to which they are confined is hardly conducive to healthy, normal development. They often must walk many miles a day to get to and from work. Compared with most of the one hundred sixty million African natives, even the poorest American Negroes in the wretched slums of our big cities live in relative luxury.

As I watched the burial of a native Zulu chief in the mountains of Natal, north of Durban, I saw that strange mixture of pagan and Christian rites and customs that characterizes so much of present-day life in Africa. A Christian minister pronounced the burial service. His audience included Zulu warriors in full regalia, but carrying sticks for spears. In the background were Zulu women, naked from the waist up. There were formal funeral wreaths and wild native chants. When the Western-style coffin had been lowered into a deep grave in the center of the chief's cattle Kraal, the weaponless warriors spent over an hour killing the chief's steers for the native feast, an important part of Zulu funeral ceremonies. They had to do it without shedding blood, which made the task difficult.

Most of South Africa's wealth comes from gold and diamonds. There are enough of these in South Africa just waiting to be mined to put the entire British Commonwealth of Nations back on a solid gold standard. The only trouble is that all the diamonds available, or even a part of them, could not be sold without breaking the present artificially high price.

The diamond monopoly is probably the world's tightest. Those who manage it know just how many karats of diamonds the world market can absorb each year without breaking the price. The monopoly sees to it that the high price of diamonds continues. The market will never be glutted while the De Beers Syndicate continues to control so large a part of world diamond production. If the present diamond monopoly is ever broken and competing mines produce all they can, diamonds would sell at half or even less than half of what they cost today.

Gold is in another class. Uncle Sam has agreed to buy all the gold the world can produce at thirty-five dollars an ounce. So the African gold mines are running full blast to help us add still more to our twenty-five-billion-dollar gold hoard. Several South Africans suggested to me that we should take a mortgage on a few South African gold mines and not bother to transfer the gold. That would give the Union the credits needed to buy American goods, and we would own the gold without all the trouble of taking it out of one hole in Africa and putting it into another hole in the ground in Kentucky.

While gold and diamonds appeal to the imagination as a quick and easy source of wealth, the real wealth of the African continent lies in the great variety of mineral and vegetable resources. The jungle forests of Equatorial Africa are just beginning to provide the world with a fraction of that African timber growth which rots away each year.

Whenever I go traveling these days, people talk to me about "undeveloped resources," and Africa was no exception. Africa is immensely rich. Nowhere is there more untouched natural wealth, but nowhere is it going to be more difficult to get that wealth out. The British Government, which controls more African territory and has had more African experience than any other, has recently made a miserable failure of growing peanuts in Tanganyika. It selected the wrong areas, brought in the wrong machinery, used the wrong kind of leaders, hired incompetent labor, made impractical plans—wasted millions of dollars in the early stages of the undertaking. A private enterpriser would have pulled out shortly after he realized what he was up against. But then he probably would have investigated all aspects of the project much more carefully *before* investing his hard-won private capital.

The heavily burdened British taxpayer will have to foot an enormous bill for the Labor Government's ill-fated, tragicomical experiment in growing peanuts. This experiment should be studied, not only by those who believe in the greater efficiency of government-run enterprises over private enterprise, but also by those who think the United States Government ought to invest huge sums of the American taxpayer's money in Africa. President Harry Truman's bold Point Four Program on the development of undeveloped areas has created much new interest in Africa. Point Four is an inspiring program and embodies lofty ideals, but it is a program we should embark on only slowly and with great caution. Dollar bearers will always be welcome in Africa. But they should be much more wary than Britain's Labor government was when it decided to remedy the postwar fat shortage in Britain by growing peanuts in a virgin East African area.

I discussed Point Four with General Jan Christiaan Smuts, long the Grand Old Man of Africa. He felt that America had a definite debt toward Africa which can be paid by implementing the Point Four Program. He put it this way, "When you were a young country, you came to Africa for the manpower to till your fields. You took the blacks of Africa, and they helped you make America. Now that you are rich in resources and lusty with power it is only right that you give something back to this continent."

"Suppose you had a billion dollars to spend on Africa," I said to the General, "what would you do?"

"I'd spend every cent of it to promote health," he replied. "I'd make the land healthy with water and fertilizer. I'd make animals healthy by breeding sounder strains. I would promote human health by eliminating the debilitating diseases that now afflict a large part of the population."

I asked General Smuts if he did not feel oppressed by the omnipresent racial tension. He replied as a true philosopher, "This African Continent is too full of fears. You who come here for a brief period are too apt to be oppressed by these fears. Remember what President Roosevelt said, 'We have nothing to fear but fear itself.'

"Here is a land where a man can be at one with himself," he went on. "The true man must learn to be his own best companion. We live too much under the stresses imposed by contact with other human beings. I noticed in your country that people press upon one another. They are too hurried and too harried. A person is only a complete human being when he is by himself. And here in Africa you can be by yourself, and you can be a whole man. So don't take the temporary strains you have found here in Africa too seriously. At the moment we are in a down curve. The bitterness you note is temporary. Ten, twenty years ago there was less of it. Come back a few years from now and I can assure you that things will once more be on the way up—"

"But what," I interjected, "about relations with the natives?"

"That," he replied, "will work itself out slowly. You can't hurry such matters. Under my administration the feeling toward the native was much better. He, too, had a friendlier attitude. He knows that it was our policy to provide every possible opportunity for his development."

My talk with General Smuts came only a few hours before I began the long flight home from Johannesburg to New York. If Africa had more men with General Smuts' humane outlook, with his practical genius, and with his gift for leadership, this continent of fear might soon be transformed into a continent of hope. It is unfortunate that he was not privileged to live long enough to see the reversal of that downcurve in South African affairs to which he referred.

30

THE UNITED STATES AND "SPIDERLEGS KALTY" HAVE come a long way in fifty years. America has proved herself capable of meeting the challenges of the twentieth century. Our country has achieved world leadership in the historically brief period from 1900 to 1950. As for "Spiderlegs," he has lived long enough to be imitated by the President of the United States!

What did I do to deserve this presidential tribute? Nothing very much. I just predicted loudly and emphatically to a vast radio audience on election night that it looked very much as though the delayed country vote would make Thomas E. Dewey our next president. Then, while celebrating his election as thirty-third president of the United States at an Electoral College banquet, Harry S. Truman singled me out, and in a genial, laugh-provoking speech, gave an excellent imitation of my voice, diction, and comment on election eve. Such a rare distinction was hardly deserved. One might think I was the only one who had predicted Mr. Truman's defeat.

Those of us who were born and brought up in this country have much to be grateful for. The Four Freedoms have been for most of us a birthright, a birthright we would like to see extended to every corner of the globe. We have come to realize that we have overseas obligations, that we are part of one world, that we must implement with good deeds, in so far as we are able, the ideals for which we have fought two world wars and for which we are still fighting as this book goes to press. We also know that to be strong abroad is not enough. The cause of democracy can best be advanced by making it strong at home—hence our determination to see that all our citizens obtain the fullest social benefits regardless of color, race, or creed. Our problem is to achieve these for all without sacrificing the freedom and dignity of the individual to the always power-hungry state. For the freedom of individuals to dream and to achieve has made America great.

It is not without significance that even in wartime we refused to restrict our citizens more than was essential. We employed a minimum of censorship, and that only with regard to strictly military matters. To this I can testify personally. Throughout both world wars I was able to comment, editorialize, and criticize our activities at home and abroad. My views were sometimes in accord and sometimes not in accord with the views held by those who directed our government. Sometimes I have expressed majority opinion and sometimes not. Many times I have antagonized large sections of opinion, which have clamored loud and long to have me silenced or controlled. Yet, I have never been put under any political pressure from Washington, even though our radio stations operate under government licenses. Let no one say that we do not have a free radio as we have a free press.

This does not mean that I have escaped trouble in fifty years of editorializing in the press and on the air. For example, in 1933, when I defended the right of the Scottsboro Negro boys to a fair trial, the Attorney General of Alabama made a strong appeal to the Federal Radio Commission to have me banned from the air. Nothing ever came of it. There was another occasion in 1943 when the Columbia Broadcasting System, through Paul White its news director, launched a public campaign against the expression of opinion by radio commentators. Mr. White and CBS never got far in that issue. The public backed up the vigorous protest which it was my privilege to present as the representative of the Association of Radio News Analysts. Dorothy Thompson was among the many who raised her voice in protest against the CBS policy. She summed up the situation in these words:

> One of the Four Freedoms for which we are presumably fighting is Freedom of Speech. CBS last week told its commentators, among them William Shirer, Quincy Howe, Major George Fielding Eliot, Ned Calmer and Edward Murrow, that though they were especially picked as commentators for their "background, knowledge, insight, clarity of thought, and special ability to make themselves understood," they are henceforth never again to express a personal opinion or tell what they think. Reason given is—they might prove to have too much influence and sway public opinion.
>
> There are as many different viewpoints among broadcasters as there are among listeners. Those who listen know that Mr. Howe, Mr. Swing, Mr. Shirer and Mr. Kaltenborn often don't see eye to eye. But two things they have in common: no one could buy them for a million dollars to say what they don't think and all of them have spent a lifetime as intelligent, objective observers of public affairs at home and abroad.
>
> Personally, and speaking as a listener, I want to know what these men think. I want to match my wits against theirs, correct my opinions by the fresh light that they throw on public questions, measure my analysis against theirs.
>
> The question affects all listeners. Do you want to hear fearless viewpoints or don't you? Are all broadcasters to become mushmouths? Are you afraid of being unduly influenced or aren't you? And if men whose background and insight are recognized can't express opinions, who should express them?

Dorothy Thompson expressed in her characteristic forthright way what seemed to be the opinion of most Americans. The CBS proposal to bar comment from the air has long since been forgotten. But it could always be revived.

As for me, some sixty years ago when I was a boy in northern Wisconsin, our house had an old-fashioned water pump in the backyard as well as a more modern water tap in the kitchen. With the first spell of zero weather, the kitchen pipes would freeze up. This meant that I had to go out into the bitter cold each morning to pump water. The private waterworks company, however, kept charging for city water even when I pumped it from the well. I wrote out a fervent protest which was printed over my name by the editor of the weekly *Merrill Advocate*. That was the real beginning of my long career of expressing opinions.

The one thing I remember about this first editorial was the last four lines:

> If the water-works don't stop this
> On my house I'll paste "To Let"—
> And stop paying for the water
> Which all winter I don't get.

And so it was back in the nineties that I began my career as a proponent and exponent of free speech and a free press. In the early twenties, I carried this belief in free speech to the airways with occasional unexpected results. With the tolerant co-operation of both sponsors and broadcasters, I have maintained it ever since.

In the old days whenever a number of outraged listeners or some highly important listener would write CBS that they ought to take me off the air, the first vice-president would call me up to his office for a friendly heart-to-heart talk. He would explain how a smart news analyst could put his personal opinions over to the public without being too blatant about it.

"Just don't be so personal," he would say to me. "Use phrases such as 'it is said'; 'there are those who believe'; 'the opinion is held in well-informed quarters';—and 'some experts say.' Why keep on saying 'I think' and 'I believe' when you can put over the same idea much more persuasively by quoting someone else?"

Whether or not that advice was good I still think that on

certain controversial topics, concerning which I have a deep and passionate conviction, it is both my right and my duty on proper occasions when these subjects dominate the news to tell listeners what is on my mind and in my heart. No news analyst has ever developed a large and loyal following without expressing his personal opinion. No news analyst ever will. No news analyst could be or would be completely neutral or objective. He shows his editorial bias by every act of selection or rejection from the vast mass of news material on his desk. He often expresses his opinion by the mere matter of shading or emphasis. He selects from a speech or interview or public statement the particular sentences or paragraphs that appeal to him. Every exercise of his editorial judgment constitutes an expression of opinion. If he is worth listening to, he will excite some controversy even if the subject he discusses is not usually considered controversial. Controversy is the life line of democratic freedom. Democracy gains when men, when all men, are permitted to "speak what we feel, not what we ought to say."

Before this year 1950 ends, I will have visited Europe again, and particularly Yugoslavia. My passport freshly stamped with the entrance visa to that exciting and controversial country lies on my desk before me. I am most anxious to see for myself the latest developments in Marshal Tito's break with Joseph Stalin. Tito now leans less toward Russia than before, but does that mean that Tito leans more toward the democracies?

As this book goes to press, American troops are fighting, under the banner of the United Nations, against Communist aggression in Korea. President Truman's decision on June 25, 1950, to go all out in defense of Korea under the UN banner will probably remain the most important and the most constructive decision of his administration. By including the defense of Formosa, the Philippines, and Indo-China, he has accepted the Communist challenge to the entire Far East. We lost China to the Communists because we refused to take a necessary risk. We propose to suffer no further losses for that reason. So once again Americans are fighting and dying in distant lands.

While we are watching what happens in Asia, we must not lose sight of Europe, which will remain the area where the decisive battles against Communism will ultimately be won or lost. The attitude and strength of the countries bordering on Russia are of vital importance in any war with Russia—hot or cold. I propose once more to see for myself how matters stand in this vital area as well as in Austria and Germany, living as they do in the shadow of the Iron Curtain.

This fall I hope to undertake a television news program in addition to my regular radio broadcasts. The second half of the twentieth century promises as many marvels as the first half. The further development of television will be one of them. So, God willing, I'll be seeing you. . . .

H. V. K.

INDEX

C

Y

Z